STILL ON FIRE

Field Notes from a Queer Mystic

Still on Fire

Field Notes from a Queer Mystic

Jan Phillips

Unity Village, MO 64065-0001

Still on Fire

Unity Books are available at special discounts for bulk purchases for study groups, book clubs, sales promotions, book signings, or fundraising. To place an order, call the Unity Customer Care Department at 816-251-3571 or email *wholesaleaccts@unityonline.org*.

Some scripture quotations are from the New Revised Standard Version Bible, copyright © 1989 National Council of the Churches of Christ in the United States of America. Used by permission. All rights reserved worldwide.

Cover photo: Jan Phillips
Cover design: Laura Carl
Interior design: Laura Carl

ISBN: 978-0-87159-416-7
Library of Congress Control Number: 2021943693
Canada BN: 13252 0933 RT

*I dedicate this book to all people
who dare to let the old stories go
and create the ones we need
to forge a just and peaceful world.*

Table of Contents

Preface ix

Introduction xiii

1. Finding the Formula for Bliss 1
2. The Long Journey from Religion to Faith 13
3. Putting the Severed Parts Together 23
4. Installing the Software of Catholicism. 31
5. Poems, Not Prayers 41
6. Perpetual Emotion 49
7. Rules of Engagement 59
8. A Night to Remember 69
9. The Darkness That Followed 77
10. Into the Depths 81
11. A Love Affair in Five Parts 95
12. Yvonne's Wedding 115
13. Freedom's Just Another Word—Tales of Coming Out 121
14. The Prodigal Daughters 133
15. The Hundredth Monkey 139
16. Trials in Tokyo 147
17. Nagasaki: Fire in My Eyes 153
18. The Roads Both Taken 159
19. Amazing Grace in the Himalayas. 167
20. India: Mystery, Madness, Magic. 171
21. Sacrament-Makers of Today 179
22. Pilgrimage to the Heart Chakra 185
23. Finding My Balance 195
24. Nothing to Forgive 207
25. The Great Betrayal 213
26. Death in the Valley 221
27. Making It Happen: A Case Study. 227
28. Leaving God for GOD 239
29. Crock of Ages 251
30. Still on Fire. 261

Acknowledgments. 265

Bibliography 267

About the Author. 271

PREFACE

When I started this project, it was meant to be a straightforward spiritual memoir. Gay kid raised Catholic, saved from suicide by a nun, enters the convent at 18, kicked out at 20, spends the next 40 years learning to heal, forgive, find her voice. It was an "if I can, you can" story about disentangling from outdated beliefs, breaking free of fear, creating a life of adventure and purpose. It was a tale of transformation—from indoctrinated Catholic to original thinker, trauma victim to change agent, international photojournalist to spiritual contemplative. A sweeping narrative arc peppered with conflict, loss, turbulence, and triumph.

Then came COVID. Then Ahmaud Arbery, Breonna Taylor, George Floyd, and a litany of others. Then the protests, the rage, the grief, the isolation. And the question for me, a Black Lives Matter ally, a cultural activist, and a maker of change: How does this book matter now? Who will be served by the story of a white girl's spiritual journey?

I stopped writing. I protested, marched, and socially distanced. I prayed and pondered and listened to the wind. Eventually I remembered: *My activism is my spirituality in running shoes.* It is one energy manifesting in two forms: as wave and particle, yin and yang, thought and action. My faith is the sum of my spiritual commitments. My commitments are the foundation for my action in the world. My action in the world is a spiritual force of moral consequence. It culminates in kindness and leans toward justice.

One's spiritual journey, if conscious, is an evolutionary experience. It involves transformation. One often begins with inherited doctrines, established traditions, families, churches, and cultures lay out the rules and regulations. Then one matures, begins to think independently, asks new questions, and arrives at her own conclusions about matters of divinity.

Stories of transformation are necessary today as we attempt to evolve the moral infrastructure of our troubled nation, asking questions we've not asked before. *What can we learn from the earth about change? How do we transform a culture that is rooted in injustice? What are the requirements of this hour for a species on the edge of an abyss?* Every transformed life is a resource here.

Philosopher Jacob Needleman once wrote that *group pondering* will be the art form of the future. Suddenly, faced with demands for isolation and social distancing, millions of people around the world are group pondering on Zoom, tackling issues in every imaginable language. *Evolution is progressing us.* It is causing us to find each other, speak to each other across continents, benefit from the diversity of our experience. For some reason, we were unable to move forward on our own, but the demands of the pandemic led to an outcome we've needed for years: people learning how to be sociable, strategic, collaborative, and collectively creative.

Much of what we know comes from the stories of others. I learn from the storytellers to examine my experience, forgive the trespasses, harvest the wisdom, give thanks for the growth. When people share the events of their lives, it awakens me to this truth: While life happens *to* me, it also happens *for* me and *through* me. I am an agent in the matter. The circumstances I face, I have helped to create.

The stories in this book begin in the convent where I prepared to make vows of poverty, chastity, and obedience. I wore a veil. I confessed my sins. I prayed to be different, to not be gay, to not love whom I loved. But that did not happen. I was sent home before vows, an unbearable rejection I barely survived.

Unnavigable roads exist between who I was then and who I am now. The terrain stretches from a Catholic school in upstate New York to a Buddhist retreat in the Japanese Alps, a mountain path in the Himalayas, a Hindu ashram in Gujarat, India. The path weaves through Selma, Alabama; Little Rock, Arkansas; the Navajo Nation; Nagasaki. I remember the peaks, the feeling of awe, the wet smell of monsoon, the cliff's edge where I stood frozen, afraid to move. It's a mystery, this evolution from frightened to fearless, this resurrection of a life from death to rebirth. The veil is thin between silence and song.

To blend contemplative practice and social action is a spiritual discipline, an exercise rooted in the word *disciple*. I am a disciple of the teachers who preached kindness, justice, care for the forsaken. "What you do for them, you do for me … and what you see me do, you can do and more." Those words of Jesus inform what I do, influence what I believe. *You belong to each other. Be food for each other.*

Prayer in motion is illumined action, and illumined action rises from a sea of deep peace.

The Buddha, it is told, said to his students, "Engage with joy in the sorrows of the world." This is the story of my attempt to do that.

Introduction

I'm a photographer. I've been looking through the lens of a camera for 50 years, and through its tiny aperture, I find myself wherever I look. Images are my currency. They tell me everything I need to know. They tell others what I want to say: This is who I am, this is what I cherish, this is what happened.

Every story is made of pictures: "She knelt by the bedside." "She entered the dark cave alone." "She watered the flowers with her tears." Always a beginning, a conflict, a resolution, an ending. The story may be short, but an arduous journey separates beginning from end. It is fraught with danger. Questions crash like waves against the shore of our minds. *What are you made of? What are you after? How will you survive this?*

Tribulation is the medium of self-definition. I know who I am through my dealings with trouble. Conflict is a mirror, reflecting my grit—every struggle an opportunity to see what I will live for, suffer for, die for.

When I was a child, I prayed to be a martyr. I memorized the Baltimore Catechism. I hated myself for being queer. I read the lives of the saints and went to daily Mass. The Catholic Church owned my imagination. It colonized my brain before I was 10. I thanked God I was born Catholic, though it was my religion that made me wish I were dead—such an evil, sinful person I thought I was.

My quest to disentangle from the Church has been a struggle for self-preservation. I am who I am because of the Church, and yet I was forbidden absolution, denied the sacraments for being a practicing homosexual. These contradictions are grist for a genius if Baudelaire was right and I keep my sanity.

I am one of millions in a modern-day Exodus movement, abandoning religious institutions, rejecting traditions that are sexist, homophobic, patriarchal, and hurtful. I am the author of my own Apostle's Creed. I write my owns psalms and lamentations. I do not study the mystics and prophets of the past. I am in conversation with the mystics and prophets of today, and together we are cocreating what the future is calling forth.

The story you're about to enter into is a tadpole to frog story, told in human terms. We witness transformation everywhere we look—caterpillars to butterflies, embryos to toddlers, winter to spring. It's all we know. Life, death, rebirth.

Biologically, evolution happens to us. But to evolve spiritually, we must engage in the process consciously. It requires our complete participation—body, mind, soul. To evolve our own lives is an act of unremitting will, a commitment to rise above the binary. It is the supreme performance art, the act of melding into Creation Itself and recalling ourselves as Nature, perfecting our human talk as trees do their tree talk and rivers their river talk.

The gateway to our spiritual path swings on the hinges of conflict. We meet up with trouble and we make choices in the face of it. We pivot one way or another, letting hindsight, for the most part, determine the efficacy of our decision. But there is another way to do it. There are ways to minimize the danger and maximize the outcomes, practices that tone the spiritual muscles, silence the voices that demean us, dissolve beliefs that belittle our magnitude. Everywhere around us are lifelines that can keep us afloat.

There are turning points galore in all our lives. Turning points when we change direction, change opinions, change careers or lifestyles or lovers or our bodies. Nothing alive escapes the winds of change. We set our course Monday morning and by Friday find ourselves heading east instead of west.

Some of the changes we create. Some of them are creations of others that we become enmeshed with. Tragedies and tribulations occur. Since we *are* Nature, our lives follow Nature's course. Redwoods do not rail against the forest fire. The shore does not run from the tsunami. But we are the meaning-makers, and every one of us makes a different kind of sense from sorrow. Even now, in a global crisis, some grieve the losses while others make art of its gift to us. It's a mystery, all of it. As the physicist Niels Bohr wrote, "Opposite a true statement is a false statement, but opposite a profound truth is another profound truth."

Once we know our turning points, we can compile the story of our life, find its meaning—a sacramental undertaking to a story-driven species. Whether you recall your pivotal events chronologically, plot them graphically on a spiral, or open a world atlas and draw a circle around every location where your life fell apart or opened up, it doesn't matter. All roads lead back to your center. You survived. The minefield of your life is safe now. You can revisit the past and pick up the pieces.

In order to make sense of the story of my life, I looked back at the points where I ran into the demons, lost my way, got rescued by a beautiful princess, narrowly escaped being thrown in the moat, found my power just in time, and lived happily ever after. Turning points—the ones many have known (the sad stories, the divorces, the early deaths, the suicidal son, the ex-con, the transgender family member in transition)—this is where the juice is. These are our bodies; this is *our* blood.

Every day is a new canvas, and the past offers us perennial reference points for guidance. Sometimes we look backward to remember mistakes we want to avoid in the future; sometimes we just sit there in the mud puddle of it all until the water settles and we can see our way clear. The past holds us to it until we process it—assess what it took from us, what it gave to us; understand who we are now because of it. After that ritual dance, we can bow to it and bid it *adieu*. For a while.

I have gathered my stories to share because I am a storyteller before I am anything else. I am the product of the events of my life. I am derived from them, as I am derived from the sugar maples and red cedars and white pines of my youth. I am who I am because of them. I am the standing rock in the canyon shaved by the winds, shaped by the floods, sanded by the droughts, naturally exposed, a daughter of the Mother, an activity of Nature.

My life is a mosaic of broken glass, a work of art composed of fragments, gathered from the past, and handed to the future. These are simple stories, *finally*. The tempests have subsided. The blood has dried, the tears evaporated. Angst has given way; awful has turned to awe.

Life hides its wisdom in dark corners. Tragedy begets insight if one reaps it, works for it, braves the dark until a pale blue light rises in the East. These times may be prophetic times, may be our opportunity to rise up and become the people our sacred texts call us to be. The upheaval of what we knew may be giving way to a new dispensation. This may be our chance to right our wrongs, or not; clear our waters and skies, or not; create a just and equitable society, or not.

Only time will tell. Only the future will reveal whether we as a people accepted our power, shone our light, and took this whole world into *our* healing hands.

My Gratitude to Catholicism

Thank you for the Mysteries—
joyful, sorrowful, glorious—
and for teaching me early
that the Divine is too ineffable
to ever comprehend.

Thank you for the communion lines
I watched every Sunday—
for the holy water font
with something wet and real
to dip my fingers in and feel
the difference between before and after.

For the Bishop's slap on my cheek
confirming me as a warrior for peace;

for the flame in the sanctuary
that let me know God was
in the house;

for the Stations of the Cross
that gave me a path to walk
with the love of my life;

for the ciborium full of hosts,
the ever-changing rainbow of vestments,
the gold monstrance of Benediction,
the frankincense, the Novenas,
Perpetual Adoration.

For the ashes on Wednesday,
the washing of feet on Thursday,
the tears on Friday,
the tabernacle—empty—on Saturday,
the Hallelujah Chorus on Sunday.

For the statues of the saints
lined up on my dresser, giving me heroes
a cut above what my culture offered.

For the scapular tangled up
in my undershirt, the miraculous medal,
my white Missalette,
St. Christopher on the dashboard.

For the fish on Friday
that made something sacred
of an average day;
for two years in the convent to learn
the necessity of solitude and prayer,
community and service.

I loved you then
and thank you always—

but I will not return
until you open your doors to me
as a woman, a lesbian, a prophet and priest.

My altar now
is the world at large.

The candle announcing
the presence of God
burns day and night
wherever *I* am.

I am a servant of unity.

The language of this church
is my mother tongue,
but I would rather be fluent
in the language of Love.

Chapter 1
Finding the Formula for Bliss

I tell you this because the story you are about to enter amazes me still.

Knowing who I am today—an original thinker, a cultural creator, a social activist—it is astonishing to me that my first steps as an adult were into a religious community where I wore a veil, pledged obedience to my superiors, prepared for a life of chastity.

It's taken me 50 years to unravel this mystery. Fifty years to understand how and why I created these circumstances, which (as you're about to discover) took me to unimaginable heights and depths.

Who was this girl who chose a life where a veil was required? What would cause a creative young woman to decide on a career that forbade sexual expression, insisted on obedience? How did she acquire a belief system that devalued her worth, and why did she let it guide her?

This happens to women.

This is how it happened to me.

★★★★

—St. Joseph's Provincial House, Latham, New York, 1967

It was a balmy fall day in September 1967 when my family dropped me off at St. Joseph's Provincial House, never knowing when they would see me again. I'd waited six years to trade the hazards of my life as a queer outcast for the safe shelter of a quiet convent. The world was in turmoil, I was in a tailspin, and a house full of prayerful women seemed like paradise.

I decided at age 12 to be a nun. This was because Sister Helen Charles, my sixth-grade teacher, kept me from killing myself. I couldn't change who I was, and from everything I'd learned from the Catholic Church, I was on a path going straight to hell. At least that's what I thought until Sister Helen Charles came along. She turned me around like no one I'd ever known.

Nuns had to have some kind of superpower if they could save a kid like me, and that's what I was going for—a superpower that saved lives. Whatever happened to nuns when they put on that habit, I wanted that to happen to *me*. I wanted to save lives too.

It was being homosexual that made me want to kill myself. As far as I knew, there was nothing worse than being queer. They were perverts, sinners, hated by God, hated by just about everyone. Lezzies, bull dykes, fags, queers, lesbos—all damned—and there I was, one of them.

The Motherhouse, as it was called, was only four years old when I got there, built to accommodate the growing numbers of women who were checking the Bride of Christ box as their career choice. In those days, classified ads were still broken down into "Male" and "Female," and careers for women were limited. Teacher, nurse, nun, housewife, secretary, clerk typist, maybe gym teacher if you were lucky. In my graduating class at St. Anthony's, girls never talked about being anything other than one of the above.

Four hundred sisters lived in the expansive structure: teaching sisters, nurses, college professors, and retired, sick, and hospitalized nuns. An entire wing of the building was dedicated to the novitiate, and there were more than 130 women in different stages of novice training. I was about to become part of a "sisterhood" unlike any I could have ever imagined.

Closing the door on our red Chevy Bel Air that day felt like closing the door on trouble. The Vietnam War was raging. Race riots had erupted in 150 cities. Police from New York to San Francisco were attacking homosexuals, and soon our nation would be weeping over the My Lai Massacre and the assassinations of Robert Kennedy and Rev. Dr. Martin Luther King, Jr. As fast as I was running toward a life of prayer, I was running away from a life of turbulence, both inside and out.

Twenty-nine others joined me that day to begin life as a Catholic sister. We were a homogenous group, mostly 18-year-olds and recent Catholic school graduates. We arrived from every part of New York State, all white, lower to upper middle-class, and all similarly indoctrinated into Catholicism. Once all the parents had left, a few novices showed up to give us a tour of the novitiate and show us to our bedrooms. We were told to change into our convent clothes and promptly return to the postulate, our main meeting room. It was there we met our Superior for the year, Sister Mary Matilda, a short, pudgy, soft-spoken postulant director who had me questioning my vocation the minute she spoke.

Sitting at her desk in the front of the room, she gave us a visual once-over then launched into her first lecture. Barely moving her lips, she uttered words I hadn't heard in my entire lifetime. "Sisters, you are in training for the vows of poverty, chastity, and obedience. We take the rules seriously here and disobedience will not be abided. You will carry out your assignments in silence, maintain silence in the hallways, and once you have made your final visit to the chapel at night, you will be under Grand Silence," a phrase that fell from her lips like a boulder.

I looked around the room to see how this registered with the others. Eileen Gregg sat across from me and I caught her rolling her eyes. She was a few years older than the rest of us and from somewhere close to New York City. Way more sophisticated than I was, I could tell. Her dismay set me at ease.

"Once you leave the chapel and begin Grand Silence, you will keep custody of the eyes." Again, a new phrase. It sounded like something from a divorce trial.

"This means that you keep your eyes lowered. Once you are under Grand Silence, there is no communication. You go to your room, brush your teeth, and turn off your light by 9 p.m."

Our days began at 5:30 a.m., when a clanging bell obliterated everyone's dreams. Sisters on three floors scurried to the bathrooms, slipped into their habits, and glided down the dim hallways to get to chapel in time for Lauds. It was a stunning sight, the sanctuary full of sisters chanting prayers that monks and nuns had been singing for centuries. Lauds was followed by Mass, which was followed by a breakfast of oatmeal, eggs, white toast, canned fruit, prune juice, and coffee.

The dining room, referred to as the refectory, was large enough to accommodate everyone in the house.

The refectory where everyone sat for meals three times a day.

Sister Marion Ripski was the provincial director and the "Queen of Everything." She sat at the head table with her very important assistants. Handpicked novices waited on them like royalty. I knew the minute I saw those novices I never wanted that job. Too much pressure. When Sister Marion was done with her meal, she rang a little bell and everyone in the room stopped talking, stood up, said their grace after meals, and piled their dirty dishes onto the stainless-steel carts.

After breakfast, we were off, each to our assigned charges. Some worked preparing meals for the house, some of us washed dishes in a steamy room, piling plates and bowls into a machine the size of a rhinoceros. Another team worked in laundry, washing linens and underwear for everyone in the house, with a few sweating at the mangle, pressing sheets from breakfast till lunch.

Corridors on every wing were dotted with novices on their knees attacking scuff marks with pink erasers. A few put their lives at risk polishing linoleum floors with buffers weighing more than they did. I once saw 4'11" Carleen Scarsi swinging off the handles of a rogue buffer. As for me, I was stuck at the hot end of the dishwasher.

After finishing our morning chores, we stopped in chapel for prayers, then headed to our classrooms on the ground floor. After class, more prayers, meditation, service to the elder sisters or other charges (the convent term for work assignments), lunch, work in the refectory, postulant training, recreation, more prayers. Every minute of the day was planned for us and by the time each day was over, we fell into our beds exhausted. This was a boot camp I hadn't anticipated.

I had no idea what would be expected of me when I entered—what vows were and why we made them, what I'd have to forfeit of myself, or deny or suppress. Didn't know and didn't care. It seemed that the rules were deployed mainly for discipline, so I decided for myself which ones to abide by. I'd learned growing up to follow my own guidance system, since I didn't trust anyone else to keep me safe.

People betrayed queers all the time. You think you have a girlfriend until she latches onto a boy and there you are, left alone. You write a love letter to a high school friend you have a crush on and the next thing you know she's sent to a boarding school out of town and you can't go out for a month. Confide in one person about your secret and before long you're the laughingstock of the class.

Peoples' decisions to be "good"—good Catholics, good citizens, good anythings—often lead to some weird backlash on the other end. The more fervent some Christians are, the more hateful and intolerant they become of others who don't measure up, like "good Catholics" carrying "God Hates Fags" signs at a Pride parade. Who'd ever think of that except religious zealots pretending they know what God likes or doesn't?

I rarely measured up to people's social expectations, as in *well-behaved, follows orders well, eager to please.* I was a renegade on a path of her own making and that's why it was a conundrum to people who knew me, why in the world I was joining the convent. Why would a spirited, freedom-loving, adventure-seeking girl choose a profession that required a veil, a habit, and vows of poverty, chastity, obedience?

What they didn't know was that it all went right back to sixth grade and the nun who resuscitated my love for life. It was a miracle how she entered right into me, and fired up an ember that was barely burning. How she knew I was suicidal, I'll never know. How she knew exactly what to do, well, that story comes later. For now, let's just say the only thing that made sense about my being in the convent was that I was there to learn how to keep kids from hating themselves, same as she did for me. That's what I signed up for. Like so many of the young men who went into the military after Pearl Harbor or September 11. They didn't give the rigors of boot camp a single thought. They didn't worry about freezing cold bivouacs, long runs carrying heavy equipment, the loneliness of being halfway around the world and separated from their loved ones. They had a mission in mind and they kept their eyes on that. My eyes were not focused on the short term, the training, the discipline. My eyes were focused on the final outcome, and whatever it took to get there, I was prepared to do. At least that's what I thought when I entered.

The only Friends Visiting Day we ever had. I'm in the middle here, with best friend Bonnie's hand on my shoulder.

Bad Postulant

Skipped
confession; broke a plate; wanted
everything; smoked in the woods;
fell for a novice; rabble-rouser; burned
with desire; cried out for help;

Remember
O Most Gracious Virgin Mary
that never was it known
that anyone who fled
to thy protection, implored
thy help or sought thy intercession
was left unaided.

stole
priest's food; hungered for justice;
stole kisses; complained about rules;
stole wine; laughed out loud; refused
to obey; lay down with the novice;

Inspired by this confidence,
I fly unto thee,
O Virgin of virgins, my mother;
to thee I come, before thee I stand,
sinful and sorrowful

loved
too much; whistled in the hallways;
spoke when forbidden; on fire with
longing; stood out; black sheep; failed
sewing; kissed in the night;

O Mother of the Word Incarnate,
despise not my petitions,
but in thy mercy hear and answer me

clowned
around; owned her ideas; spoke out;
spoke back; stood tall; stood
too tall.

Amen.

And so it was. I did everything in my power to stay true to myself while getting through this training so I could get on with the work of saving lives. Despite my hubris and shortsightedness, lessons from the Far Beyond orbited my way, disguised as usual in chaos and conflict.

I struggled to preserve my autonomy and resist self-effacement, but was summoned to the Superior's office repeatedly for "sitting too high on your horse." An unruly soldier, I readied for battle because that's all I knew. *Resist all forces that belittle you.* Their mission was to reshape us, but I never welcomed their attempts at reconstruction. They felt like an assault, as if the goal was to replace the person I was with the person they wanted me to be. In the Superior's office I'd hear the same lines:

"How you feel about this, Sister, is of no concern to me."

"What makes you think your opinion carries any weight?"

"If you didn't have so much pride, this wouldn't be a struggle."

The girl who entered that convent in 1967 would be hollowed out, stripped of the old, readied for the new. Oddly enough, while a part of me resisted it, another part prayed for it. I embodied paradox. I wrote songs that signaled my surrender even as I held my ground, and the whole community sang right along with me:

> *Come Lord Jesus into my heart*
> *make it your home, Lord,*
> *make it your dwelling place*
> *and reign forever in peace.*
>
> *I want, O Lord, to be with you always,*
> *to leave you never alone;*
> *may I be there wholly, awakened in faith,*
> *offering, loving, adoring.*
>
> *My whole being aches to be emptied*
> *and filled with your precious love;*
> *this grace I desire that my life shall be*
> *not mine, but a radiance of Yours.*
>
> *With joy and gladness I sing alleluia*
> *in praise to you my God;*

in thanksgiving for the love You have shared
I offer my life to You.

While I reared up like a stallion against the rules of the novitiate, in chapel I knelt in adoration. In this house of many women, I met my demons, went to battle, and took a few early steps on my hero's journey. As I stood at the gate between adolescence and womanhood, the community mirrored back to me the woman I was becoming. Faithful, strong-willed, resilient, vital. It was a house of belonging and more often than not, I felt I was home.

The activist/journalist Anna Louise Strong wrote in *I Change Worlds: The Remaking of an American*:

> We humans are herd animals of the monkey tribe, not natural individuals as lions are. Our individuality is partial and restless; the stream of consciousness that we call "I" is made of shifting elements that flow from our group and back to our group again. Always we seek to be ourselves and the herd together, not One against the herd.

I did my best to be *myself and the herd together* and failed as often as I succeeded. To be both required a willingness to dissolve boundaries, to detach from self and its wily whims; it called for a humility I did not possess—to surrender, to trust, to free-fall into the fray of community life itself. In the postulate alone were 30 women still under 20, biologically ready for mating rituals, studying how to live chaste lives. From one angle, it was impressive; from another, a crime against nature. I was one of them sitting in the front seat of an emotional roller-coaster ride.

Both our inner lives and our outer lives were under scrutiny every waking hour. Community living demanded attention. Living together, dealing with each other's idiosyncrasies, rising above concerns of the self, and giving more care to the needs of the whole—this did not come naturally.

Then there was the prayer life, the hours of meditation, private prayer, common prayer, Lauds and Vespers, the Stations of the Cross, daily Mass, weekly confession, which was fraught with the stress of inventing sins when none had been committed. With so much prayer and meditation built into our days, internal combustions were commonplace. *I thought this and now there is that. I was one way and now I am another. I used to grumble about meditation, now I can't get enough.* My interior landscape shape-shifted like desert dunes in a windstorm.

Our lack of exposure to the outside world—we watched no news whatsoever—kept us in a state of grace that counterbalanced the turbulence unfolding around us. The cultural zeitgeist of the late 1960s did not penetrate the walls of the novitiate in any visible way. I couldn't have told you a sexual revolution was going on, that Marvin Gaye just released "I Heard It Through the Grapevine," that the Big Mac just went on sale at McDonald's and cost 47 cents, or that CBS aired *60 Minutes* for the first time.

I lived in an alternate reality, shrouded in silence and prayer. While all hell broke loose in the streets of America, all heaven was breaking loose in the safety of our Motherhouse. I couldn't see the cities on fire, sparked by racism and outraged citizens who'd reached their boiling point. I couldn't see the escalating peace movement or the rise of a new wave of feminism—but the spirit of those movements, the hopes, the struggles, the changing of the guard: that was in the air I breathed.

While I was praying for peace in the world, 475,000 troops were serving in Vietnam and peace rallies multiplied as protesters against the war increased in number; Muhammad Ali was stripped of his boxing world championship for refusing to be drafted into the U.S. Army; in Detroit, 7,000 National Guard were brought in to restore law and order as race riots consumed the city; Rev. Dr. Martin Luther King Jr. was assassinated; Robert Kennedy was assassinated; the first Black Power salute was seen worldwide on television during an Olympics medal ceremony; President Lyndon Johnson signed the Civil Rights Act of 1968; the Beatles released *The White Album*, featuring songs written when the band was in India attending a meditation camp; Pope Paul VI banned Catholics from using the contraceptive pill for birth control; 50,000 people participated in the Poor People's March on June 19 in Washington, D.C.; students occupied Columbia University to protest its affiliation with the Institute for Defense Analyses; NASA launched Apollo 7, the first manned Apollo mission; and down the road from me, Joseph Campbell was teaching mythology at Sarah Lawrence College and encouraging people to "follow their bliss."

I never laid eyes on a *Follow Your Bliss* bumper sticker, but I shared the sentiment. The whole idea of it would have been admonished by our superiors—*your happiness has nothing to do with what we're doing here, sister.* It would have been rebuked as self-seeking, self-centered, the antithesis of what we were there for: the sake of the whole, not the one.

Ironically, while they would have pooh-poohed the pursuit of happiness, the community delivered the recipe for it on a golden platter. *We do not care if you are happy or not, but oh, by the way, here's the formula for bliss.* The superiors divided our days into four parts—for prayer, solitude, community, and service. Time to be alone. Time to be with others. Time to pray. Time to serve. While I agitated for change about every other petty thing, our days unfolded in bliss-bestowing balance. I wasn't conscious of how this worked. I didn't reflect on the relationship of a balanced life to deep joy. I just knew I loved my life there, until I got called out for my failure to obey.

I hadn't entered the convent to learn obedience. I had entered to become a nun who would save lives. I pushed back against the rules, hell-bent to complete the training on my own terms, but *that*, as it turns out, was impossible. Nothing was going to happen on my own terms. Within months I'd fallen in love, and my superiors, suspecting the worst, shifted into gear and reined me in, starting a conflict I barely survived.

I was a toddler then, about to take my first step on a path to the Promised Land. I wobbled all the way.

Chapter 2
The Long Journey from Religion to Faith

I tell you this because in the course of our lives, we are often called to let go of the old and make room for the new. It is a critical part of our evolution, this shedding. It's what Nature does, and we, as Nature, participate in its cycles.

As we mature, we let go of simplistic ideas handed down to us when we were toddlers. We take ownership of our thoughts, deciding which ones to release and which ones to keep. This letting go starts early, as we recall from our own experience with Santa Claus, the Easter Bunny, the Tooth Fairy. But we are young then, and so resilient.

Later, it becomes more difficult. The myths and fables have sunk their roots into our bones and marrow by the time we reach puberty. Our identity is grafted onto them. We pledge allegiance and give our lives, at times, to defend them. They are salt in the sea of us.

Catholicism was this to me. It was installed into my cells at an early age. It was mystical, sensual, all-pervasive. I drank it in and loved its taste, its smell, and sound. The Eucharist, the wafting frankincense, the music flooded into my pores like water from a sacred well. I was awash in a wave of holy wonder.

All my life, Church was something wondrous that happened to me. I was its recipient. Then a day came when I was asked to embody this religion.

To say what it meant to believe. To consider how I moved in this way, and not that way, because of it. I was asked to create a living faith. Leaves began to fall from the tree of me.

This is what happened.

★★★★

— St. Joseph's Provincial House, Latham, New York, 1967

A priest named Father Grabys, a tall, burly Lithuanian, came in three times a week to teach us theology. The morning he entered the room, we were seated at our desks with our hands folded. The seats were in perfect rows, all facing forward. A crucifix, as always, hung on the front wall. On this morning, he unloaded an armful of books on his desk, then swirled around to face us.

"All right, let's hear it," he said in a thick accent. "Here you are, ready to marry God. Tell me something about this God you love. Someone, stand up and tell me about this relationship of yours."

Right away I didn't like him. How were we supposed to say something about our relationship to God? People didn't talk about that. We knew what we knew from the catechism. We had all the facts, but he was asking about feelings. That was uncharted territory. And I liked it that way.

No one raised a hand.

"Someone?" he barked. "Can't someone say something? You're dedicating yourself to God and you can't say why or what this God means to you?"

One postulant raised her hand, stood up, and uttered the familiar words: "God made me to show his goodness and to share his everlasting life with me in heaven."

I nodded my head in agreement, having memorized this bit years ago just like everyone else in the room. Right out of the Baltimore Catechism.

The priest looked dismayed. He frowned and half-shouted, "That's it? That's all you got?"

"Yes, Father."

"Sit down," he said, looking around for another hand. "Someone else!"

Another brave soul stood up saying, "In God there are three Divine Persons, really distinct, and equal in all things—the Father, the Son, and the Holy Spirit."

I nodded again in the affirmative, and again Father Grabys grimaced. "Is that the best you can do?"

"Yes, Father."

"Next!" he yelled, as she took her seat, looking around in wonder.

By now, we were all confused, but one more raised her hand.

"God can do all things, and nothing is hard or impossible to Him."

"Sit down," he barked again.

Rolling his eyes, he crossed his arms and surveyed the whole group of us with a look of disdain. By now, blood was rushing up my neck. Beads of sweat broke out on my forehead. I had my first anxiety attack. A fat tear dripped down my cheek.

Why was he so mean? I wondered. He asked for our ideas about God and when we shared them, he took a sledgehammer and smashed them into smithereens.

Finally he spoke. "You should be ashamed for having nothing more than catechism answers to this question. Are you just a bunch of parrots, repeating everything you've been taught? Hasn't anyone here gone beyond the Baltimore Catechism in your thinking?"

The air was thick with silence. Hands were folded, eyes cast down. A few more tears cascaded down my face. I prayed he wouldn't call on me.

"You must come to know what is true about God from your own experience," said the priest. "If you are to be a religious worth your salt, you have to arrive at a faith that is deeper than your learning—one that rises up from the nature of who you are. Your faith must be rooted in your ultimate concerns."

I had no idea what he was talking about. I'd never heard anything about ultimate concerns before, but Father Grabys insisted we get at the root of ours. He waved his arms in the air shouting about creating a faith for ourselves. I looked up at him, watching spit fly off his Lithuanian lips, wondering how in the world anyone builds a faith for themselves.

Wasn't faith something I was born into? Something I inherited, from the outside? I was a Catholic by default. They told me everything I was supposed to believe. That was the point, wasn't it? As far as I was concerned, I was just lucky to be born into the one true faith. I didn't have anything to *say* about it. That's what infallible popes were for.

Father Grabys was trying to grow us up. Here he was with a class of mostly 18-year-olds who believed everything they had ever been taught. We had never *pondered* our religion. We didn't have feelings or opinions about it. We prayed to the One God, the Holy Trinity, whose only pronouns were he, him, his. Now suddenly we're being asked to share the nature of our relationship—a total invasion of privacy it seemed to me. I raised my hand.

"Father, we've been studying our faith since second grade. We've memorized everything. We know every answer to every question. What you're talking about we never learned," I said. "I don't even know what you mean when you talk."

He towered above us, his brow furrowed. "What you believe, that is religion," he said. "Who you are, what you live for—that is faith. They are two different things, and *faith* is what we're here to explore. Your faith is what you must create and declare—your faith which is and will be the very *essence* of your spirituality." His voice was thunderous, cracking and booming on words like *faith* and *essence*. His thick Baltic accent added to the drama.

"You can let go of religion right now," he added. "Let go of all your beliefs for a while. Put them up on a shelf for this semester. I will teach you how to create a faith that will see you through everything."

I didn't *want* to let go of any beliefs. They were all I had. And they were enough. I didn't need anything more. As we continued on in the class, the biblical paradox that says we must lose our lives in order to find them began to make sense. We could no longer fall back on ready-made answers. Now that all our memorized dogma and doctrine was on the back shelf, it was unavailable to us. Our religion had been shelved, and our faith was about to make an entrance.

Like an Olympic coach, Father Grabys pushed us beyond our comfort zones. "Think of faith as a plan for action, not a set of beliefs," he shouted, writing it on the board in big white letters:

Faith = action (based on commitments)   ✓
Religion = beliefs (based on doctrine)

When we squirmed in our seats, rubbed our heads, stared blankly into our notebooks, he reminded us that *what* any of us believe is not the essential thing.

"Don't look for beliefs! What you believe doesn't matter here. What matters is what you feel strongly about, what you are committed to, what is your ultimate concern."

My stomach churned. My brain ached. What in the hell was he talking about? I was an A-plus student, bright as a sunny day, but I couldn't get what he was asking for. I was mired in the software I'd been programmed with. It was a story that I loved, thoroughly believed, would go to my death defending. I was Peter Pan in some kind of Neverland. God was out there in the heavens taking care of everything. That's all I knew and all I repeated.

Commitments require a sense of self, a sense of purpose, and even more, a sense of agency. One needs a feeling of self-authority to act, to say, *Yes, I stand for this and not that.* This was contrary to what I'd learned. All my life I'd been taught what to think, not how to think—shaped by *Father Knows Best*, shaped by God the Father, shaped by women earn less, men are the bosses, only boys can be presidents. I didn't have agency. I was no agent of change. I had no sense of authority, and what sense I did have they were trying to beat out of me, it seemed, the whole rest of the time.

At night, Father Grabys' words circled in my head like goldfish in a bowl.

"Forget what you have learned."

"Think of what you stand for."

"What is it you care about?"

"To what are you committed?"

He wanted us to create something real from the grist of our lives—to claim what moved us, to be willful, to take our power. His pursuit was to wake us up. His assignment: to involve us in our own spirituality. While our superiors drummed at us about obedience and humility, puncturing whatever sense we had of self-importance, this priest did the opposite: He demanded that we examine our conscience, discern our own values, proclaim out loud our self-created faith.

I don't know how the others were dealing with all this. Even in the few minutes of recreation we did have in our busy schedules, no one ever brought up this situation when we had time to talk. Ask anyone else now who was in that class what happened and they'll never remember it as I do. It was my watershed moment.

I didn't know what I believed outside of what I'd been taught. I knew the Church couldn't be right about everything. There was friction, and plenty of it—my being queer and having to hide it, my dad being a non-Catholic and not suitable for heaven, relatives who left the Church because they had too many kids and the Church said no birth control.

I remember hearing Lenny Bruce once say that people were "leaving the churches in droves to find God." An exodus movement away from the churches did gain momentum in the '70s after Vatican II, after the sexual revolution, after "Question Authority" and "Follow Your Bliss" and "Don't Trust Anyone Over 30" bumper stickers covered fenders across America, broadcasting a new era of autonomy and liberation from the old. Then as now, research on religions in the U.S. showed a steady growth in the exodus community, leading to a serious decline in church attendance among all mainstream churches. While I was preparing to marry God, people by the thousands were getting divorced from him.

And here I was, in a convent, trying to get my arms around what I was committed to. According to Paulo Freire, we are conditioned, but not determined, and the more people accept the passive role impressed on them, the more they adapt to the fragmented view of reality deposited in them. That was exactly where I was, right along with all the other postulants in the room. We had been conditioned, but now we were about to determine something for ourselves.

Throughout the semester, we avoided the catechism, recited nothing from memory. It was a generative time. A time to create. A time of loss, anxiety, fear. Week after week, I stretched and struggled to let go of ideas that no longer served me. I didn't *want* to let go. I liked how it was—the comfortable certainties, the security of proclamations handed down by popes from generation to generation. I worried about being original in matters of faith, but Father Grabys insisted.

"This is your spiritual life," he'd remind us. "Who better to create it?"

We asked him repeatedly what he meant by ultimate concerns. When we did, he got up from his desk, moved closer to our seats, and surveyed the whole room before he spoke, incredulous that this was taking so long.

"What are you *living* for?" he'd shout out, trying to blast inroads in our neural networks. "What means so much to you that you would give your life for it? What *matters* to you? What are you committed to? What will never happen in your presence?"

He hammered at us from every angle—he, Michelangelo; we, his David. He chiseled away at our memorized ideas, our childish concepts, until he carved right into the core of our beings.

Father Grabys' questions were Himalayan and I was barely at the foothills. I tried to remember what Jesus said, thinking I couldn't go wrong with him. I hadn't studied the New Testament, but I'd heard his words in hundreds of Masses:

> *The kingdom of heaven is all around you; it is inside and above you; it is like yeast, like a pearl of great price, like a king preparing a wedding banquet, like a man beaten and lying on the street; it is who you are; it is your neighbors and your enemies; it opens its doors to you when you forgive, when you are generous, when you help others; it welcomes you when you give praise and thanks; it is visible and invisible; it is like a seed germinating; it is a house built on rock; it is forever; it is yours, you belong; I am in you and you are in me; we are One with the Father; it is like the lost sheep, the lost coin, the lost son, coming home.*

I could practically hear his voice. I knew what he was talking about. For peace and justice to take root around me, I myself have to be peaceful and just. For light to shine in this world, it has to pour forth from where I am standing. If kindness and mercy are to prevail, it must prevail in *my* life, in *my* thoughts. Everything I desire emanates from within. I am the chalice holding the Holy Light.

I was finally ready to proclaim my self-created faith. I hadn't lost anything at all, but I had gained a life, a spiritual life, which until then I'd never been able to claim. Now that I comprehended the meaning of ultimate concerns, this is what I shared:

> *I am committed to being a peacemaker and to insisting on justice wherever I am.*

I am committed to caring for others as I care for myself.
I am committed to being a light in the world, wherever I am.

Faith and religion took up separate residences in my body: religion in my brain and heart, faith in my gut, my hands, and legs. Faith would be my lived-out religion, born from my body and inseparable from my soul, an act of self-revelation.

I had faced a threshold that terrified me. I resisted, but I did not turn and run. I found muscles I had never used, a voice I had never heard, and now that I had borne witness, I was prepared to live by this faith I had just given birth to.

And after all this, I was still intrigued by the priest's original questions: Who was this God I was dedicating my life to and what was my relationship with him all about? Was what I had learned about God inhibiting my ability to *experience* God? What part of myself had I denied to conform to the teachings of the Church? What about the underlying secret of my sexuality? What might become of me if people found out?

Exploring these questions opened my eyes to a past I had hidden and led me down pathways I had tried to avoid. I couldn't keep pretending. I had to love who I loved. I had to stop hating myself for how I was made. The monastic life revealed something to me I could never have known had I not entered into it, and what I was about to discover about God and myself would change me forever.

In Praise of Doubt

When I was certain,
I had no time for nonbelievers.

I carried the one true thing
in my suitcase
from place to place,
half-wishing more people
could share it,
half glad they weren't all called.

With nothing else
to make me special,
this being chosen
was my claim to fame.

A priest once said:
It takes the same training
to make a Francis of Assisi
as it takes to make a terrorist.

This seemed a lie
when I was certain.

Now that I dwell in
the mansions of Mystery,
I see its truth,
I feel its blade.

Chapter 3
Putting the Severed Parts Together

I tell you this because our stories are rarely as neat as we want them to be. I wanted to tell you the story of why I entered the convent—for a life of service, prayer, community—but it was "not the whole story," said the past, tugging at my writer's arm.

Yes, I was running toward a good life, but I was actually running away at the same time—from a culture that shamed me, a family that might not accept me, a world that didn't seem to have a place for me. I wanted to be safe.

There, I said it.

The whole story includes the shadow, offers up a more honest narrative. Until I see where the shadow is, I can't be sure where the light is coming from.

I was like the Marine recruit, on my way to boot camp because I didn't know how to make a life. It's not that I wasn't patriotic. It's just that there are all kinds of ways to look at a story.

What others thought of me used to mean a lot. Today it barely registers. A lot happened between then and now to make that difference.

Here's where it started.

—Syracuse, New York, 1958

We moved to Syracuse when I was 7 years old, in 1956. My father's back was getting worse, and he needed work that was less labor intensive than the grocery business. With some help from my uncle, he landed a job as teller at the First Trust and Deposit Bank on Warren Street. Every day, he put on a suit and tie, overcoat and hat, and walked half a block to the bus stop where a Syracuse Transit bus delivered him to the bank. He left at eight, returned at five, every day for years. Shirts starched as hard as cardboard from Brighton Dry Cleaners, clip-on ties, a fedora hat. A far cry from the rubber boots and bib overalls of his dairy farming days, but, as far as I could tell, he loved the city right from the start. Settled right into it like a kitty in a basket.

As for me, I was terrified. *I just wanted to be safe* and this city didn't feel safe. It was my first encounter with the *other*—with Black people, people in wheelchairs, poor people, drunk people, people crowding busy streets, shopping in stores with elevator operators transporting them to basements, mezzanines, and second floors. I found city life chaotic, and I had no idea how to go about making friends.

Marcia Sprague lived right next to me, and Judy Weld up the street was her best friend, so they were my first attempt. I could get two for one if I was lucky. They seemed to like me and I'd been invited over to both their houses, so things started out well.

One Friday afternoon the three of us made a plan to ride our bikes to Elmwood Park the next day. I was thrilled. I finally belonged.

"I'll make us sandwiches and we can meet here at 10 o'clock," I said.

"Okay, I'll bring potato chips and Judy can ask her mom to make some cookies for us. Her mom makes great cookies," said Marcia.

"I know," I said, remembering the smell of peanut butter cookies wafting through the house the last time I was over. Mrs. Weld was the closest thing to a TV mom I had ever encountered. She didn't have to work because her husband was a pharmacist, and Judy and her brother Mike each had their own rooms filled with toys and posters on the wall. I'd never seen anything like it.

Judy piped in saying we should all bring a quarter so we could buy drinks at the Elmwood Market. We agreed, then I raced home to tell my mom about our exciting plans. My mother liked picnics more than anything else, so I knew she'd be happy.

I woke up early Saturday morning, reeling with excitement. I made three peanut butter sandwiches, threw in some Oreo cookies just to be safe, and packed them up in a brown bag. Ten o'clock came and went. No Judy. No Marcia. Finally, after waiting a half hour, I walked up to Judy Weld's house and rang the doorbell. Mrs. Weld opened the door, pretty as always in her blond pageboy and crisp, cottony apron. The smell of chocolate chip cookies drifted out from the kitchen.

"Why, hello, Miss Jan. What can I do for you?"

"Hi, Mrs. Weld. I'm trying to find Marcia and Judy. We're supposed to be going to Elmwood Park today. I have our picnic all ready to go. Do you know where they are?"

"Oh my," she said. "They didn't mention that. They both went up to the Riviera Theater about a half hour ago. With the cartoons and two movies, they'll be quite a while."

I tried not to cry in front of Mrs. Weld, who was so pretty I wanted her for my own, but my lip started trembling right there on the gray planked porch. No matter how cavalier I tried to act, my face crumpled up right in front of her. She started to say, "Come in and have some 7-Up," but I was already turning away to keep my pride.

"No thanks! That's fine. Tell them I'll catch up with them later. It's okay!" I said all in one breath as I raced off the porch.

I ran home to my mom who was at her Singer sewing machine altering dresses for Avis Needham. My mom took in sewing once we'd moved to Syracuse since my dad's job at First Trust and Deposit didn't pay enough for all our bills. She was always at the sewing machine.

"I hate girls!" I said to my mom as she scrunched the hem of Avis' green wool dress under the sewing machine needle. "They lie! They hate me and I hate them! I'm never playing with them again! I'm sticking with boys from now on."

After my declaration, I went out to find Mikey Ganley and Mike Weld, Judy's older brother. They stuck together like glue and loved the same games I did—football, kickball, playing Army in the sandlots, shooting snowballs in the winter. It was great playing with them, but more often than not, at the end of a game, the two of them, without even

25

talking about it, would jump on me and pummel me till I was close to tears. Their big thrill was making me cry. My big challenge was getting out alive without crying.

I just wanted to be safe.

This went on for years, this Jeckyll and Hyde routine, where they'd be best friends one minute, then transform into monsters. They shoved snow down my jacket, piled on top of me, slabbed mud all over my face, tied my hands behind my back as a big joke. They never drew blood but they let me know for sure that boys ruled the world. At least the world I lived in.

I put up with it because they were the only friends I could find, and I had stopped trusting girls. But it came at a steep price. Every year, more and more of who I was disappeared. By age 11, I was a shadow of myself.

I loved being a pirate on Halloween. Nobody had to know I was a girl or a tomboy or a misfit. I didn't have to act some way that didn't feel right. I was just me. And for once, I was safe. Nobody was going to come around and beat me up.

26

On the first day of sixth grade, I entered the classroom of Sister Helen Charles defeated and depressed. By now, I'd read enough religious pamphlets on homosexuals to figure out I *was* one and there was nowhere to go for help. I'd taken to leaving suicide notes in the bathroom wastebasket, explaining that I just didn't fit in and couldn't make friends and that was that. "Dear Everyone," they would start, then an apology. "I'm sorry I had to do this. It wasn't your fault ..."

I'd crumple my notes up a little and place them on top of the trash, as I pondered my ways and means. I don't know whether anyone ever saw them or no one took them seriously, but I do know that those particular calls for help went unheard. I appealed to the saints on my dresser— St. Teresa, St. Philomena, the Blessed Virgin Mary. I asked them all repeatedly to send me clues about ending my life because I couldn't keep on with it feeling like I did.

As it turns out, it was a nun who had the magic wand. Sister Helen Charles saw something worth saving in me and called in my mom for a visit in the convent parlor. According to my mother, who told me the story years later, the conversation went something like this:

"Your daughter is smart as a whip but she walks around with her head down. She doesn't talk to anyone and doesn't let anyone in. What's the problem?" asked the nun.

"It started when we moved to the city a few years ago. It's been hard for her to make friends. I think she feels bad about being a tomboy. Kids make fun of her; they beat her up. She's always coming home with a bloody lip and bruises, but I don't know what to do," said my mom.

My mom had grown up on a farm with 10 brothers, and bloody lips and bruises were commonplace. When I complained once that the boys had shoved my face into the dirt, she responded by saying we all had to eat a peck of dirt before we died—though I don't think she admitted this to Sister Helen Charles, who had read up on child psychology and had a few ideas for my mother.

"I have a plan," said the nun. "There's a new thing out called positive reinforcement. I'd like to try that on her, but I need your help."

"How does it work?"

"Every time she does something well, praise her. Go out of your way to notice all the good things. Praise her in public. Praise her when you're alone. Let's see if we can turn her around so she believes in herself again."

My mom said she wasn't all that enthusiastic about extravagant praise-giving, especially since she had two other kids at home who weren't going to get that, but she agreed to give it a whirl and see what happened.

I didn't notice any changes at home, but in school, it was like night and day.

"Jan Phillips, you're such a good speller. You win every spelling bee we have!"

"Jan Phillips, what a great athlete! You're always the best at Capture the Flag on the playground!"

"Jan Phillips, you're so artistic! Will you stay after school and help me with the bulletin boards?"

At first, I thought something was wrong, or the Sister was losing her mind. No one ever praised me like that. I didn't know what to think. It couldn't be real, could it? She couldn't really mean *me*, could she? But it went on. I stayed after school to help with the bulletin boards, and she kept it up, praising my intelligence, my creativity, my athletic abilities. She watched every move I made, looking for good things to point out.

The popular kids started asking me to do things with them. And the underdogs, the group I had always been part of, they still looked up to me. I was a bridge between the two. I defended Billy Hogle when they made fun of him for being poor, or for having dirt under his fingernails. Or when they mocked Dorothy Money for being fat, or Bonnie McHale for being so tall—I'd call them on it, in front of everyone.

Then, one day it happened, like a caterpillar turning into a butterfly. Right then and there, at age 12, I woke up and knew I was a leader. I knew I could help people. I had a mission. I'd found my superpower. My life had *meaning*.

It was also the day I decided to become a nun. Because if that's what nuns did—change people who wanted to die into people who were excited about being alive—then that's what I wanted to do. I was going to enter the convent and save lives like Sister Helen Charles saved mine.

At least, that's how I thought of it at age 12. Reflecting on it now, I see more subtle forces were at work. Something deeper pushed me in that direction, and it wasn't my faith. It had nothing to do with religion. It was my survival instincts.

I just wanted to be safe.

The extrovert in me took the lead, presenting with confidence, good instincts, ideas brimming with purpose. The introvert inside remained hidden, without a voice, but relieved that decisions were being made to protect her.

It's uncanny how it works, that all these years I believed in the story I made up when I had barely reached puberty—and there *was* truth to that—*that Sister Helen Charles kept me from wanting to die and I might be able to do this for others as well*—but there was much more to that choice to enter the convent, and it's still unfolding after 50 years.

I knew it would be a *safe* place. I wouldn't have to deal with college applications. I wouldn't have to talk with anyone about getting married. I wouldn't have to deal with men at all. Check. Check. Check. I loved prayer. I loved solitude. I loved community. More checks.

But I would love women, too, and there was the danger, though I could not have known it when I chose religious life. I had not yet kissed a girl's tender lips. I had not yet been entangled heart to heart, limb to limb. I had not yet burned with desire, had not known temptation, had not kept secrets, had not faced a Superior who lay in wait for this spark to combust into an unmanageable fire.

What I was on my way to becoming at that point was a mystery to me. What passion would feel like in the palm of my hands, what it would taste like as fear on the tip of my tongue, smell like as honeysuckle climbing the gate of my heart, these I couldn't know. What shocks I would endure, what price I would pay to stay honest—a cost I could have never calculated.

Every one of us is undergoing our own personal odyssey on planet Earth. Everything happens for our benefit—*to* us, *through* us, and *for* us—that we learn about being human, being family, being global citizens. We are here to gather experience, feel feelings, exhibit kindness and compassion.

When we get old enough, we can look at our life story as if looking at a globe, spinning it around, saying, "Oh yes, I see why this happened ..." or "I now understand why that happened ..." When we review it in the light, look at its many dimensions, characters, lessons, we begin to see our own agency in the matter. We see where we were the agent of change, where we caused something to occur because of what we said or did.

People often want to tell their sad stories. As soon as they have my attention, they launch right in with the grim details. They speak as if they were victims of their own lives, targets in a country and western tune where somebody had it out for them. But with a little coaching, their power in the matter comes to the surface. They're able to see how it all turned out for the best. They start to think of themselves as creative agents, cocreators in cahoots with the invisible forces of the Universe.

When we have properly processed the events of our lives, the most apt response is, "Thank you." And until then, we just keep working our stories as they work us—wrestling, wrangling, complaining, milking them for sympathy—whatever we need to do until we grow up and remember that *this* is what we are alive for. To have these shocks, to feel these emotions, and to get on with the business of putting the severed parts together.

Chapter 4

Installing the Software of Catholicism

I tell you this because it happens to all of us. They want to shape us into their image. They want to spare us injury. They want us to color inside the lines, blend in, stay alive.

They do not think of it as programming. They would not use the words social conditioning. But every child knows the feeling of constraint.

We came here to explore, to invent and create, to fly, in whatever ways we can.

But those who are responsible for us, who brought us in, they have forgotten mostly everything about flying. They say they are too busy to create.

They fail us, without meaning to. They will defend every choice. "For your own good," they will say again and again.

And no one is wrong. It's just how it goes round and round.

★★★★

We had religion classes every day and memorized the Baltimore Catechism, which gave us all the answers we needed to know about God, Catholicism, and how to act. There was a program to be installed and we were the hardware. Thinking on our own was discouraged. Every Catholic family in my neighborhood had a Bible the size of a breadbox displayed in the living room, but no one was encouraged to read it. Unwritten law: We couldn't be trusted on our own. You needed a priest to help you sort things out if religion was involved.

One thing I wanted to know was why my father, who was not a Catholic, was not going to be allowed into heaven. How could the God I was supposed to love come up with an idea like that? And another question had to do with my mom's best friend Pat Kubler. This one came up every year because every Lent we went to daily Mass at 7 a.m. and took Pat Kubler with us. What happened there befuddled me.

Mass on weekdays was short and sweet during Lent. No sermon or incense or singing. Communion time arrived early, and when it did, Pat never got up to receive. She stayed in the pew, hunched over, half-kneeling, half-sitting. I'd look back at her from the line to see if she might change her mind, but her head was always down. *Why was she so deep in prayer?* I wondered. *Why didn't she receive communion?*

One day when I was alone with my mother, I asked her why Pat didn't get communion.

"Pat had to divorce her first husband, so she can't receive the sacraments."

"Why'd she have to divorce him?"

"He was violent. He wasn't a good husband."

"You mean he hit her?"

"Yes."

"Then it wasn't her fault."

"No, she had to leave him to protect herself and her children."

"Then why is she getting punished?"

"It's just the way the Church is. She remarried and now she can't receive communion. That's how it works."

So now my question is why can't Pat get communion when all she did was protect herself? Rules all over the place kept getting handed down no matter how contradictory they were. My dad couldn't go to heaven, Pat couldn't go to communion, and all those Protestants were just doomed as far as I was concerned. It was tricky figuring the whole thing out. Since none of my dad's family were Catholic, what was going to happen to all of them? It made me a nervous wreck just thinking about it.

My parents were both close to their families, and every other weekend we drove two hours north to visit both our grandmothers. This was way up north in New York State, almost to Canada, and occasionally, in mid-winter, we'd find ourselves in a blinding snowstorm on the way home. One Saturday night, after inching our way for miles during a blizzard, we stopped to spend the night at my Aunt Beulah's house. This was my father's sister who was also not Catholic, and I was terrified we'd wake up on Sunday and have to go to their Protestant church, which is exactly what happened.

Regardless of my pleas against it, my mother rounded us all up and we headed for the Congregational Community Church in Mexico, New York, along with my Protestant cousins. As soon as I entered the bland sanctuary, I was suspect—no saints on the walls, no kneeling benches, no holy water font, no candle burning on the altar. How would you even know God was there?

That's how my brain worked. Catholicism seeped into my cells, coursed through my veins, blazed through my neural networks. The teachings were installed like a software program, downloaded for memorization, reinforced with the richness of ritual and sacrament. The religion took root emotionally and psychologically. The sacraments were sensual, transporting, almost mystical with the accoutrement of celestial music coming from the choir loft, the fragrance and sight of incense furling heavenward, the hosts lifted up, priests kneeling, people bowing, fingers crisscrossing every chest.

The priests' regal vestments with their exotic names—amice, alb, maniple, chasuble, stole—their colors fluctuating with the liturgical seasons: white for rejoicing, worn at Christmas and Easter; purple for penitence, worn during Advent and Lent, then rose in the middle when we are halfway through; and red for fire and the presence of God, worn on Pentecost.

Every Sunday, altar boys glided across the sanctuary lighting candles. They rang bells at the consecration, delivered water and wine, held patens under our throats when we received communion, lest a crumb of the Body of Christ tumble earthward. Priests swung incense burners full of frankincense in every direction, transubstantiated bread into the body and blood of Jesus, performed sacraments to grace our lives: Baptism, Penance, Holy Eucharist, Confirmation, Matrimony, Holy Orders, Extreme Unction (Anointing of the Sick).

Every human sense absorbed that magic, soaked in those mysteries. We owned holiness. We smelled it, heard it, tasted it, touched it. I stood in the pews Sunday after Sunday, holy day after holy day, belting out hymns like a Salvation Army soldier. I believed what they said to believe. I was transported by the fire, the music, the gold monstrance, holy water flying this way and that during benediction, the church filled to overflowing with families kneeling in unison, standing in unison, sitting in unison.

As for my cultural messaging, we watched *Leave It to Beaver*, *Ozzie and Harriet*, and *Father Knows Best* every week as a family, getting our clues about womanhood, family-making, and child-rearing from June Cleaver, Harriet Nelson, and Margaret Anderson. My mother never rolled her eyes or said out loud that "mother" might know best every once in a while. Were we all under some kind of programming spell?

We sat there entranced, all five of us, my dad in his green chair smoking Lark cigarettes, my mom in another chair crocheting, three kids sprawled out on the floor or couch. I was probably not the only one secretly wishing life would work out for us like it did for Beaver and Wally.

There were a lot of things I didn't understand but had to accept because my father made the rules or the culture at the time dictated it. I couldn't be president of the 6th grade class, even though I got most of the votes, because only boys could be president. Sister Helen Charles counted the votes as we watched, placing one after the other in a tall pile on her desk. Two little clumps of handwritten ballots sat beside the towering stack of votes for me.

"Well, class, it looks like Jan Phillips has received nearly all the votes. Forty for her, six for James Hoffman, and four for Samuel Tremont."

I was elated. I'd gone from a nobody to a somebody in such a short time since she'd launched her positive reinforcement campaign on me.

Now that I liked myself it seemed that other people started liking me too.

"Since only boys can be president and vice president," she said, looking right at me, "you get to decide, Miss Phillips, if you want to be class secretary or treasurer."

"I'll take secretary," I said, walking up to her desk to get my red badge.

No one jumped up and yelled, "Not fair!" Everybody saw that I got most of the votes, but we all knew how things went—boys lead, girls follow. Values like that were handed down silently, mother to daughter, father to son. I can only imagine what the boys hear: "Now son, there's one thing you've got to know growing up in this country: Men have the final say. You'll always be the boss. Never let a girl take your power."

In my home, the rule of the house, which I hated, was no talking about politics, sex, or religion.

"How come we can't talk about anything important?" I'd ask my mother while she cut out a pattern on the kitchen table, her pinking shears zigzagging through the material.

"Because your father said so."

Never any conversation. No debate. Your father said so.

My father inhabited a culture he never challenged. He was middle-class, but he was male, white. He had all the power he needed. What was there to challenge? As far as I knew, he never knew how it felt not to be in power. He never talked about who he had power over, except to blame others for being poor, lazy, taking handouts. No reflection on our privilege. No talk around the dinner table of social issues, turning tides. No talk at all from him. He shunned involvement in the community, never took part in any group bigger than a foursome around a pinochle table.

My father didn't have a sense of his role in the creation of things. Just like his parents and those who went before—they kept on handing down the same program, like mine only not Catholic. He became what they said to become. He was a product of his culture. Head of household. Bring home the bacon.

The culture I inhabited was entirely different. I knew from the start I was in for it. I wasn't just a girl, I was worse than that: a girl who liked girls. And being this way, I resisted nearly everything, I churned with questions, hated "how things were," never believed for a minute that my father knew best. One day he proved to me he knew practically nothing.

I was in the living room listening to Roy Orbison with my new friend Althea Gibson when my father walked in from work. He threw his hat down on the chair and stormed into the kitchen where my mom was at the sewing machine. I heard him yell, which was a rare thing since he hardly ever raised his voice. My mother said something like, "Now, Lee, you know she has a hard time making friends," at which point I decided it was time for Althea and me to go to her house instead.

I loved her house. Its smells were different from mine. Ham hocks or chitlins cooking on the stove. Collard greens in the sink, ready to wash. Sweet potato pie or biscuits on the counter. Curtains more often closed than flying in the breeze like my mom liked. It was a more private house than ours. Doors locked during the day. Windows all closed, but the rooms always neat and shiny with the smell of Pine-Sol coming from the bathroom.

When I got home from Althea's for supper, my father was furious.

"Don't you ever do that again!" he shouted.

"Do what?" I asked.

"Bring that colored girl into our house. I don't want you hanging around with her."

"But Dad, she's my new friend. We play tennis at Kirk Park all the time. We like each other."

"I don't care who you like. I make the rules here. What will the neighbors think?"

"Dad, she *is* our neighbor. She lives next door to the Pelkeys. They live on this street!" That's when I knew how little he knew.

"Don't you get smart with me. Just stay away from her."

I cried myself to sleep that night, not knowing what to say to Althea. Could I just sneak around and not get caught? The next morning I asked my mom why he thought Black people were so bad.

"He won't even let me play with her. What's the matter with him?"

"Oh honey, your father's just that way. He thinks that way because that's what his mother and father thought."

"Why doesn't he have his own thoughts? He's a grown-up, isn't he? Aren't you supposed to know the right things to think when you grow up?"

36

"There's nothing you're going to do to change his mind. And your father has the final say. So just do what he says. That's how we do it in this house." *Pow!* Might as well have been bullets packed in those sentences.

If you ask me, this is how the whole mess gets passed down from generation to generation. These words flew out of my mother's mouth as natural as can be. She wasn't even mad about it. Just told it like it was. Only that wasn't acceptable to me, and I was not going to go along.

Racism was installed in my father just like Catholicism was installed in me. He never thought to question it, same as me, which is the privilege of being white in a white majority, or Catholic in an institution that thinks of itself as the one, true faith. If you rule, you're happy with it. No questions asked. But I had a lot of questions about race, particularly since it just got personal and I had to lose a friend because of it.

It wasn't long before race issues came to a boiling point and Syracuse, New York, had its share of rioting. As usual, there was no one there to explain it, to help any of us understand where it came from, or what we could do about it. When fights erupted between kids from our school and the public school down the street, adults did everything to separate us and keep us quiet. No community leaders stepping up. No addressing it from the pulpit. No mention of it in the classrooms. Just silence. Don't talk about it. You don't have any power anyway.

Our entire Catholic education was a training ground for powerlessness, at least from where I sat. I didn't question much about my faith, though I did have those burning questions looming in the back of my mind: *Why was my mom's friend Pat punished for doing the right thing? What about my dad and heaven?* And the big one that never disappeared: *How come homosexuals were considered sinful even though there was nothing we could do about it?* I went to church all the time, had statues of the saints lined up on my dresser, and read about their lives instead of reading Nancy Drew or the Hardy Boys. Didn't that count for anything?

These questions ate away at me. And as I read more and more about the saints and martyrs, I started thinking about dying for my faith. I'd lie on my bed at night thinking up scenarios for martyrdom.

It would make my life so much easier if I just died young and didn't grow up being a woman who loved women. I knew I was headed for that, and death seemed the only way out. I'd already fallen in love with a babysitter, my sister's fourth grade teacher Miss Mahon, and Sister Grace. I swooned for them. Wrote them secret love notes. I was never going to not be this way.

With my babysitter Joannie Murphy. She was the first woman I fell in love with.

In our religion classes, we read lots of gory stories about martyrs. The girls were usually young virgins who were killed in the act of saving their virginity. I had statues of some of them on my dresser, which was so wobbly they fell over constantly. I glued Philomena's head on more than once, and Joan of Arc's arm and flag had been separated from her body since the first week I got her. Elmer's glue was helpful, but it never lasted long after the first reattachment.

I felt happy and holy about my longing to give my life for God, though it looked more doubtful every day that I might have a chance to do that. I fantasized about it occasionally. Some bad man would attack me for being Catholic. He'd torture me and demand I deny God. I'd cry out, "Never!" and he would beat me more. He would ultimately kill me and the headlines would call me a modern-day martyr who gave her life for God. Delusions of grandeur, I think it's called.

It never occurred to me how sick that was until I was in my 30s and heard a Jesuit priest, Father Anthony De Mello, say during a retreat:

"The same training it takes to make a Francis of Assisi, it takes to make a suicide bomber." It takes the same kind of programming: Tell them what the truth is, tell them that only you have it, tell them it is worth dying for. You end up with a populace who idolizes martyrs, who believes in holy wars, who can't think critically, who will die for a cause they are told to die for.

If I had been raised in the Middle East, I could have been praying the same prayer to be a martyr for my faith, and I might have been in a family that applauded the idea. When I realized that—how conditioned I had been without even knowing it—I started my campaign of original thinking. I paid attention to as many thoughts as I could, trying to discern which were original to me and which were being filtered through my religious lens. This happens to most of us in one way or another.

Children are vulnerable and susceptible to religious messaging because we are looking for approval when we're young, looking for ways to stand out and be noticed. All I wanted was to be noticed for something they thought was good. The Church offered me a stage where I was comfortable and not a misfit. If you don't count the whole homosexual thing, it was a perfect fit. I was in training to be a Francis of Assisi and I was right on track, metabolizing every message I received.

This was the greatest thing that ever happened to me—being born into this church, this one, true church. How lucky was I, how proud, and how confused that I was still a sinner in its eyes—a sinner because of something deep inside that I couldn't do anything about changing.

Chapter 5
Poems, Not Prayers

I tell you this because, if you are lucky, someone came into your life with a torch at a time when all you felt was the dark. Or perhaps, it was the other way around. You were the one who lit the way for someone who was lost or despairing. We take turns at these things.

What helps is to hear the stories of these encounters. What helps is to have our memories jolted so we can be grateful again, say thank you again, remember we are not and never have been completely alone.

All nature works this way. It supports life. It is the proper order of things that we are not abandoned; that in our darkest hour, someone knocks on the door, unfolds a blanket, fills a cup with soup for us.

This story is part one of an ongoing narrative. I am who I am because of this woman. This book is in your hands because of this woman. She is about to enter your life and you will learn from her as I did. Not the same thing, but she has something for you. It may change your life. That's what stories do.

****

From the first day of class in 1964, Sister Robert Joseph let us know we were in for something different. When she sauntered across the threshold of homeroom 10B, 35 of us stood, made the sign of the cross, and began the usual prayer, "O Jesus, through the Immaculate Heart of Mary ..."

She stopped in her tracks and raised her hand.

"None of that," she said. "Pass these down," handing out freshly minted mimeo sheets to every kid in the front row. The familiar smell of fresh ink wafted through the classroom as we distributed the papers.

On the sheet, in perfect Palmer Method handwriting, were written the days of the week with a poem under each. The first was "Consolation" by Elizabeth Barrett Browning. The next was "Leisure" by William Henry Davies, then "Because I Could Not Stop for Death" by Emily Dickinson, "When I Am Dead, My Dearest" by Christina Rossetti, and "God's Grandeur" by Gerard Manley Hopkins.

Our job, she informed us, was to stand up every day at the beginning of class and recite the poem of the day. No prayers for us.

Within a month or two, we had memorized them all. We quoted snippets in our out-of-school conversations with burgeoning pride. The boys on Craner's Corner recited lines from Dickinson just to show off when the girls walked by. Poetic plumage.

On a March day in 1965, we all stood when the bell rang and started a poem from e.e. cummings. Halfway through, Sister Columbine, the school principal, entered the room and announced that Sister Robert Joseph would be gone for a few days. "She's flown to Alabama to march with Dr. Martin Luther King from Selma to Montgomery."

We gasped in unison. Sister Columbine showed no emotion, neither pride nor fear. "Now class," she said, holding up her right hand to silence us. "Everything will be just fine. You get back to your studies." We opened our books, fumbled around with the handouts on our desks, but I'm sure mine was not the only stomach turning over. She was our favorite teacher. Why would she have gone to such a scary place? We'd already seen photographs of terrible violence down there. Fear for her tasted like gun metal in my mouth.

Our own city of Syracuse had erupted in race riots that year, and violence between the students at St. Anthony's and Roosevelt High was so severe police patrolled the streets keeping whites on one side and Blacks on the other. The school district staggered the times when our schools were let out and forbade any lingering along the way. We were told to avoid certain streets. Meanwhile, Sister Robert Joseph had joined the Congress of Racial Equality, a nonviolent, interracial organization, and was developing relationships with Black leaders and activists.

Race was the cultural issue that was up for us, and yet the subject was not addressed in any of our classes. The nuns had been told not to speak about it. None of my friends had parents who talked about it at home, at least with them. There was no counsel toward unity, no conversations about diversity. My father continued to blame Blacks for the violence, as if there were no roots to the uprising. He never connected the dots between poverty and resistance, privilege and oppression. There was no analysis, no effort to discern what was wrong and how to right it.

Years before an interstate highway had been built right through the city, displacing hundreds of homes and families in Black neighborhoods, leaving in its wake an array of ugly brick buildings, the projects, that became a breeding ground for trouble. Instead of reaching out to create a community of cohesion, to work together for safer neighborhoods, white people, including my father, put their homes up for sale.

We were teenagers, forming our social consciences, trying to understand cultural dynamics, experiencing an outburst of violence that we couldn't comprehend. What we needed were adults who could help us think, train us in imagining a future and taking steps to create it, and now the only one we could count on to ask us what we thought was risking her life on a highway in Alabama.

Newspapers had carried photographs of cops from the South letting dogs loose on marchers, then spraying them with fire hoses in Birmingham, Alabama. The week before she left, *Life* magazine published a photo-essay on Selma called, "The Savage Season Begins" with pictures of police beating marchers with billy clubs, Blacks wounded and bandaged, white helmeted cops chewing on cigars as they waited for trouble. The crowd of activists had a mixed complexion, with students, clergy, and community members of all ages and races, many whom had traveled from the Northern states.

The march Sister Robert Joseph participated in was divided into three segments along the 54-mile highway from Selma to the capital, Montgomery. The issue was voting rights. Discriminatory practices, like literacy tests, kept millions of African Americans in the South from being able to register and vote, and this march was a protest against that injustice. Dr. King had informed President Johnson well in advance that it was going to take place.

The Selma March kicked off on March 7, 1965, in response to the death of activist and deacon Jimmie Lee Jackson, who was fatally shot by a state trooper 17 days earlier during a peaceful march in nearby Marion, Alabama. The key organizers were James Bevel of the Southern Christian Leadership Conference and Amelia Boynton, a former suffragette, Tuskegee graduate, and leader of the American civil rights movement in Selma. They were joined by 600 people.

Once the unarmed marchers passed over the county line, state troopers attacked them with clubs, whips, and tear gas, an event that became known as Bloody Sunday. Amelia Boynton, in her mid-50s, was beaten unconscious and a photo of her lying wounded on the Edmund Pettus Bridge was publicized worldwide.

The second march took place March 9. Troopers, police, and marchers confronted each other on the bridge, but when the troopers stepped aside to let them pass, King led the 2,000 marchers back to the church. He was obeying a federal injunction while seeking protection from a federal court for the march. That night, a group of white men beat and murdered civil rights activist James Reeb, a white Unitarian Universalist minister from Boston.

The third march started March 21. This was the march Sister Robert Joseph joined, along with 2,000 others. Alabama Gov. George Wallace was opposed to desegregation and refused to protect the marchers, so President Johnson stepped in. He sent in 1,900 members of the Alabama National Guard, the Army, Military Police, and Federal Marshals. After walking 12 hours a day and sleeping in fields along the way, the marchers reached Montgomery on March 25. Thousands more had joined the campaign, and 25,000 people made it to the Capitol building that day to support voting rights.

Sister Robert Joseph returned to school the day after she flew back from Alabama. The hem of her habit was tinged with dirt, her shoes caked with the red dust of Alabama. She had been told not to talk about her days on the march, so the class went on as if nothing had happened. But silence about an incident never weakens its pulse. It was a pivotal moment in the lives of her students—a moment where we learned what it means to take a stand for justice, to turn the other cheek, and to be a peacemaker in a violent world.

I idolized this nun. There was nothing provincial or petty about her. She didn't care what anyone thought. She laughed when the whole class went on strike one day and marched out of school in protest at someone being suspended. While all the other teachers looked out at us from their classroom windows, horrified at our bold independence, she cheered us on from her homeroom window, her tight fist high in the air.

As an avid reader of *Harper's Magazine*, she'd often stride into the classroom announcing strange tidbits from Harper's Index, a collection of eclectic facts, to get our attention. Though she did this countless times, there is one I have remembered verbatim after all these years:

SISTER ROBERT JOSEPH
Religion, English
Social Studies

"One out of six farm boys has had sex with an animal before the age of 16," she announced as she entered the room and sauntered to her desk, her arms full of books.

We were shocked into silence. It was too much even for the boys who at that age were having sexual thoughts every three seconds and verbalizing most of them. If a photo existed of our faces that day, you'd see 40 students poised at their desks with mouths hanging open, staring straight ahead in disbelief. I think it was her strategy for gaining control of the room. She who shocks the most, controls the most. It certainly contributed to the authority she had. Over her own life, she had none, to be exact, bound as she was by her perpetual vow of obedience to her superiors. But with us, she owned authority. We idolized her en masse. She was like a nun doll come to life—a superhero. She would not let us down and she would always come to our defense.

Sister Robert Joseph was the only nun who ever made us feel as if what we thought and felt about things mattered, and that gift was priceless.

One afternoon during my junior year, I lingered after school until there were just the two of us in the classroom. I was about to tell her my plans to enter the convent and ask if she'd be my sponsor, a nun mentor who offers support to a young postulant as she starts her religious life.

I was already in love with her, in the way that every gay teen falls in love with an inspiring teacher. I didn't fantasize about her, or long to be in a relationship with her, but I coveted time with her. I wanted to be like her. I wanted her lust for life. Mistakenly, I thought she'd be thrilled when I told her what I had in mind for my life.

She was shocked. Almost angry.

"You don't want to do that. It would be a terrible mistake," she said. "They'll kill your spirit."

I didn't even know what she was talking about.

"No, they won't," I said defiantly. "I've wanted it since sixth grade. It's the perfect life for me."

"I'm telling you, you won't survive it."

"I will too. I'm cut out for it."

I continued to appeal, and she continued to resist, finding new ways to say it would be a complete disaster.

"You're too alive for them, Jan. They'll make it impossible for you."

What she couldn't share with me then was that she was in counseling herself about leaving the convent, having been persecuted for being too alive, too earthly. There were 20-some nuns living in the convent with her and not one said a word to her when she returned from Selma. Her Superior forbade her to speak about it. Here she was in her early 30s, in the midst of a social upheaval, undergoing her own seismic shifts, and no one in her life was showing up like a friend, or a sister. That she bonded so deeply with her students was no surprise, there being no one else to bond with.

Sister Robert Joseph, I learned years later, was in the midst of a crisis of faith during those years, questioning God and all the dogma of the Catholic Church. None of it meant anything to her anymore. Hence, the poems over prayers. She wanted to protect us from religion.

She cheered rebellious originality, self-authority, intrepid speaking,

46

the end of hesitancy, and the honoring of static traditions. She tried to steer me toward a life that would fit my bold contours. She begged me not to enter the convent but she lost that battle. I told her I'd find someone else to sponsor me if she wouldn't.

Reluctantly she agreed, and the two of us marched forward toward a future that only she predicted correctly.

Chapter 6
Perpetual Emotion

*I tell you this because I faced a moment of reckoning here, and stories like .
these can be helpful when we are down to our embers and have forgotten
fire.*

*"Not to decide is to decide," is the first quotation I encountered in the
convent. What we do not do carries as much weight as what we do, on
some occasions. What I did not do here matters greatly. It is where the
lesson is.*

*This is a story of passion that raged like a wildfire in the forest of my
heart; a story of longing, burning desire, and tenderness, above all.*

What do you do for love?

"I don't know," you might think. "It's been so long."

*But has it? Are there not people around you who love you, who need
your love? What do you do for them? Do they know it? Do they feel you?*

Are they more alive because of you?

★★★★

The metaphors that Sister Mary Matilda used to cut us down to size annoyed me. I hated being minimized. What pride I had I earned the hard way. I thought of it as a badge of honor. *Finally, she has some pride in herself.* So when they tried to shake that, early on in my career as a postulant, I resisted.

The focus on humility wasn't enough to make me want to leave the convent though. I'd never do that. I'd been called to this life since sixth grade and I took my vocation seriously. It was my destiny. And I was proud of that too.

. So when Sister Mary Matilda drilled away at our pride, trying to get rid of our city girl ideas and attitudes, I held fast. She'd say things like: "Each one of you used to be a big frog in a small pond, but now you're nothing but a small frog in a big pond." That was her way of saying, "Welcome to religious community. You're a nobody now."

I never knew which vow that notion was attached to, but I guessed it was obedience. We couldn't make our own decisions anymore. We had no independence. Everything we did was in obedience to a rule that was handed down by one Superior or another, in this case Sister Mary Matilda who was in charge of the postulants.

One day in postulant training class, she said, "You all think of yourselves as a candle—an important, unique candle—but not anymore. We're going to melt you all down, get rid of that 'uniqueness' that fills you with pride, and make one big candle from all that wax. You won't think so much of yourselves then."

She delivered that one with a wry little smirk and I didn't appreciate it one bit. The whole idea rankled me. I decided early on that I'd go along with things like this, as long as I could be true to myself in real life. In one ear and out the other.

I didn't pay much attention to rules if they didn't match up with what I wanted. It didn't take long to figure out how to get the Pepsi machine to work when it wasn't visiting day. That was easy. Plug it in. And I started collecting quarters from my parents whenever they came to visit so I could get Pepsis for a few of us at a time. It also didn't take long to notice that our chaplain Father Battaglia's freezer was filled with a ton of goodies we never had access to, so I'd pilfer whatever I wanted from his treasure chest and just wait for them to thaw out in my room. I had shrimp, coconut cream pie, Eskimo pies, and Sara Lee desserts on special holy days.

One rule I didn't mess with was Grand Silence. We'd hear legends about people being sent home for uttering one word during that time, so I followed that one religiously. Until they made it impossible for me to obey.

It all started during lunchtime recreation. After our kitchen charges were done, we had about 40 minutes to "recreate" before postulant training. That meant we could talk out loud, walk around St. Ann's Circle, play tennis if we wanted, walk through the woods. It was our outdoor time. And on Mondays, Wednesdays, and Fridays, we were allowed to mingle with the novices. This was a big deal because the novices all had their own meeting rooms, their own superiors, and we hardly ever got to be with them.

During the first few weeks there, after some of our joint recreations, I became friends with a second-year novice, Sister Marie Catherine. She was tall, freckled, funny. She sat right behind me in chapel and I could tell she was there just by the smell of her Jean Naté. We were both reading Teilhard de Chardin and kept our copies of *The Divine Milieu* in our pews. Often, when I'd stop in chapel to read after I'd finished class or charges, she'd be in her pew doing the same. That's why I wanted to talk with her, to see what she was thinking about his huge ideas.

As a paleontologist and mystic, his writings and concepts were all new to me. He invented words and entered into the universe like a miner with a headlamp on, burrowing deeper and deeper into the heart of matter until he saw God looking right back. I'd underline the phrases I needed help with—cosmogenesis, noosphere, the divinization of matter—and hoped Sister Marie Catherine could help me out with them.

Everything he wrote made my insides quake. He'd fallen in love with matter at an early age when he became fascinated with rust on a piece of iron. Because he felt the Divine in every particle of matter, he believed that "we live steeped in [the] burning layers" of the very God we seek, who is molding and shaping us every moment of the day. He called this process "hominization," the spiritualization of nature and all living things.

Just as Father Grabys was doing in the classroom—taking all my old ideas and turning them inside out—so was Teilhard doing in the chapel. Before either of these two men came along, I was perfectly content with my beliefs. I had them all organized, all memorized, all lined up in neat little rows. Then the priests showed up and turned my cart of certainties upside down.

After a semester of struggling through Theology with Father Grabys, I was now facing one of the greatest mystical thinkers of all time, whose ideas turned on the lights in new areas of my brain. I read every sentence over and over. I devoured and digested his mysterious paragraphs, struggling to make sense of his words and sentences, then attempting to translate them back to myself in a language I could understand.

After an hour of meditating on his words, I would write down in my journal what I thought he was trying to say: Genesis did not happen once. Creation is not over. The cosmos expands continuously, and that itself is the very act of God being. God is the unfolding. The Creative Force, the God people seek, is pounding on our door day and night, penetrating us, saturating us with love. There is nothing for us to seek.

Day after day I would work on a page, trying to metabolize his meaning, simplify his complexities. Occasionally I'd come to a passage I had to mine line by line, like this one from *The Divine Milieu*:

> In action I adhere to the creative power of God; I coincide with it; I become not only its instrument but its living extension. And as there is nothing more personal in a being than his will, I merge myself, in a sense, through my heart, with the very heart of God. This commerce is continuous because I am always acting; and at the same time, since I can never set a boundary to the perfection of my fidelity nor to the fervour of my intention, this commerce enables me to liken myself, ever more strictly and indefinitely, to God.

When I tried to translate it to myself it came out like this:

> When I act, I am the extension of creation, which is another name for God Unfolding. I act from my will, which is my most personal possession, and my actions bind me to the heart of God.

I couldn't wait to talk this over with Sister Marie Catherine. I wanted to see what she thought about the "will" part and its being the pathway to union. It was the opposite of what we were learning about will in our formation classes. There, the will was suspect, something to be subjugated. We were supposed to give up our personal will in deference to our superiors' wills. That was the basis of obedience, as I understood it, and though I wasn't enthusiastic about obedience as far as vows went, I had a deep interest in obedience to—or the honoring of—one's personal will when it came to merging with the Divine. That idea excited me.

The next day was Monday and I couldn't wait for recreation. I had my book with me and was on the lookout for Sister Marie Catherine. What I didn't know was that I was the subject of someone else's lookout. Sister Marie Catherine and I were being watched by our Superiors on those days of joint recreation. Both Postulant and Novitiate Directors had offices with picture windows overlooking St. Ann's Circle. They could see who was with whom on those Mondays, Wednesdays, and Fridays, and what they discovered was that I was always with Sister Marie Catherine, my Teilhard talking partner.

It was a thrill to spend time with her. I didn't have an intellectual relationship with anyone in the Motherhouse in which we talked about ideas, tried to figure out what an author was saying, and applied it to our spiritual practice. Many things were new to me that fall, including the whole discipline of prayer and meditation, spiritual reading, Divine Office. There was a whirlwind of spiritual activity, much of it formulaic when it came to prayers, but for meditation and spiritual reading, we were free to explore.

That I ended up ensconced in Teilhard's *The Divine Milieu* is a mystery and a blessing. My class with Father Grabys was challenging enough, but Teilhard's words electrified me. He brought God so close I couldn't tell where I began and God left off. My spiritual life was breaking open and I was happy to have Marie Catherine as a companion through the *unknown* I was exploring.

As the weeks passed and we shared more time together, my affection for her grew. I looked forward to those days we could talk. I woke up excited about it and went to bed thinking about it. I was falling in love with her. I was in love with who I was becoming in her presence, because of her, because of the ways she heard me, saw me, reflected me.

I couldn't wait for my 40 minutes with her on those three days a week. When I caught a whiff of her Jean Naté in the hallway, my whole body shivered.

Then one day in late November, only a few months into my friendship with her, I was summoned to the office.

"Sister, I'm afraid you are spending too much time with Sister Marie Catherine. This might be leading to a particular friendship, and we can't have that."

I was unclear about what that phrase meant exactly. Sister Mary Matilda had brought it up briefly in class one day but never actually defined what it meant. It was delivered along with a dozen red flashing lights. I think the words *carnal* and *unnatural* were also mentioned. I wasn't paying much attention because it all felt ridiculous to me and I'd tuned it out. But now I was wishing I'd listened more carefully.

Sister Marie Catherine and I hadn't done anything wrong. We only met when we were allowed to. And we talked about Teilhard for the most part. We didn't talk about ourselves or any desires. We didn't flirt or write love notes, though I knew I was in love.

"We're not doing anything wrong," I said. "We're just friends."

"Just friends don't meet at every opportunity to the exclusion of everyone else," she said snidely. "Just friends don't go off by themselves, huddling and whispering, and letting no one else in."

"People can join us if they want."

"I watch you down there, heading off on your own, the two of you. I'm telling you, you're heading into dangerous territory."

"But Sister, I swear, we're just good friends," I repeated, pleading for some understanding. "She helps me understand Teilhard de Chardin." Nothing helped.

"You are forbidden, as of today, to go anywhere near Sister Marie Catherine. You are forbidden to speak with her anywhere at any time. And if you pass her in the hall, you must keep custody of the eyes."

I couldn't even look at her, according to their rules. I was officially split from my one and only best friend, from my budding beloved, from the first woman I had ever thought of as a soul mate.

This was a rule I could not abide. It felt, in a way, like a crime against nature. They were taking something so beautiful, so life-giving, and turning it into something perverted. What this triggered in me was so deep its cellular traces are still carved in my bones.

I knew what was happening in me was momentous. I knew I was falling in love, but I could not think of that as wrong. She was my particular friend and I was lucky to have one, is the way I saw it. People need that. So I was at odds with the whole shutdown right there. I wasn't the problem. Their pettiness was the problem. Their minds in the gutter were the problem. Their refusal to help us develop sturdy relationships with healthy emotions was the problem. And I was not going to collude in the continuation of this appalling approach to human behavior.

All my life people had tried to make me feel bad about who I was and what I liked, and they were doing the very same thing—trying to convince me I was wrong. Forbidding me to be me. I was smart enough to pass their battery of MMPI tests with all their homosexual-baiting questions: *Are you attracted to masculine women? Are you attracted to feminine women?* Did they think I wouldn't see through that and know to answer *no* to every question, despite what was true?

So much got triggered in that office—all those bullies from my childhood, all that blood and tears and agony, all my prayers for it to be different and despair that it wasn't. My self-hatred, my suicide notes, my whole reason for being there: to save kids as Sister Helen Charles saved me. On that day, in that straight-backed chair in front of that postulant director, I vowed, for once, to be true to myself, and I didn't turn back.

I went to the chapel, entered the pew where Sister Marie Catherine sat during prayers, and picked up her copy of *The Divine Milieu*. I took it to my room, wrote a note, placed it next to her bookmark, and returned it to her seat in chapel. It read, "Told I can't see you anymore. Not going to do it. Will come to your room at 10 p.m. We can make a plan."

As it turns out, she had been given the same directions by her novice director. No more communication with me. Custody of the eyes if she sees me. Unsettling accusations of particular friends and carnal relationships. Stuff of nightmares.

The hallway was dark and quiet save for the soft sounds of sleeping postulants. I walked the length of the hall, opened the door to the exit stairway, and climbed the flight of stairs to the second floor where I found and entered the room of Sister Marie Catherine. She was sitting on the edge of her bed waiting for me, shrouded in silver moonlight. We were both wearing our nightclothes, black cotton robes covering our full-length white cotton nightgowns.

It was the first time I had seen her without her veil. I touched her cheeks and her short auburn hair. She wrapped her arms around my waist and pressed her face against my robe, warming my flesh with the heat of her breath. Neither of us knew what to do next. We just held on—me standing there, her sitting on the side of the bed. We held on and cried, trembling and weeping as quietly as we could.

It was our first act of resistance and the first of many nights we would betray Grand Silence. All our creative genius went toward subterfuge as we planned meeting after meeting in secret places. We met in the trunk room in the basement, in the reference stacks in the library, in a tiny crawl space outside the choir loft.

In public, I never looked up when I saw her coming. Never spoke a word or took one step toward her on those days the others recreated with whomever they wanted. If anyone *was* watching—as they had been earlier—all they would see was evidence of obedience, a novice and a postulant happily mingling with other sisters as if nothing ever happened, as if a revolution within were not being waged.

Who's to say, if we'd never been split, whether our relationship would have evolved to kissing and hugging? There's no way of knowing whether, without that pressure, that inhumane ruling, we would have just remained friends and not ended up cuddling night after night in a forbidden room, on a forbidden bed, at a forbidden hour.

Our intimacy was an oasis in a barren desert. We hardly talked, hardly touched, save for the long length of our bodies, fully clothed, pressed together in solace and sweetness. Every novice and postulant was exhausted at the end of each day, and we were no different—awake long enough to find each other and give thanks for that treasure, but collapsed into sleep only moments later and usually awakened by the clanging bell.

Whatever they feared about carnal relationships never transpired between the two of us. I left notes in her books all the time, but questions mostly, or statements of amazement at the mind of this mystic who wrote hymns to the earth, who affirmed between all his lines lives that were courageous, on fire, of God—our lives, it seemed, our courage, our fire.

We survived the year and were never discovered. Our conversations continued to deepen, though the decibels shrank, as we were always hidden, always whispering, whether the silence was Grand or mediocre. I wrote her poems, made her holy cards, wrote a love song for her. The risks we took for that relationship never even measured on the Richter scale of risk. We never even paused to weigh the pros and cons.

We never asked, *Should* we? We only asked when and where, knowing that connections like ours were gifts from the heavens, full of grace. While I was in training for a vow of obedience, I decided day to day which rules to obey, a practice that foreshadowed trouble ahead.

What was happening to me was happening in the culture writ large, though I knew no details since we were spared the news. People my age were questioning authority, seizing their power, walking in rhythm to their own inner beats. Rules everywhere were up for grabs—in churches, on campuses, in boot camps, and on battlefields.

The zeitgeist favored authenticity, resistance to authority, speaking truth to power. I lived as true as I could to those values, though I learned early on the consequences of speaking too much truth to the one in power.

Along with mystics like Teilhard, Thomas Merton captured my attention as did the activist pastor Dietrich Bonhoeffer. Reading their words shaped my consciousness and guided my actions when my own independence was on temporary hold. They pulled me forward, kept me buoyant and spiritually balanced when the community I belonged to failed to think big.

I vacillated between heaven and hell, freedom of mind and constraint of body. The environment was a paradise—the grounds, the chapel, the building itself—and the intentions of every nun there so noble, to be a force for good, a light in the world. I could barely breathe for the joy I felt when the chapel was filled with the young and the old, the frail and the hardy. The holidays and holy days were feasts for the soul—the music, the rituals and liturgies, the endless procession of sisters to the communion rail and back.

It was all I ever wanted, yet I couldn't scale down to the size they required. I couldn't do it in my heart, in my body, or in my mind. Obedience was a remote idea, a far-off destination in the landscape of my mind. It never won out in the war against my passion. I needed my fire, the heat of my feelings. I needed them to navigate, to intuit my moves, to sense the truth. My passion *was* me, and without it, I didn't know who I was.

Just as the soul cries in the presence of truth, so does the heart move in the direction of ardor. It cannot be forced to do otherwise. My emotions, in order for me to be whole and to grow, had to be free to explore what awakened them. They had to flow like a river through the canyons of my being. My feelings could not live in an environment of suppression. They were alive, they were of God, and they would not be silenced.

In time, Sister Marie Catherine professed her temporary vows and moved to a different wing in the house. It was a relief, in a way, to have her gone and get out from under the attention of our Superiors' watchful eyes. As friends and intimates often do, we lost touch in time, separated now by new rules in the Motherhouse that kept professed sisters away from those of us in formation.

But trouble never left, for its source was in me and the conflicts only escalated as I became more and more myself.

A Sonnet of Gratitude

Let me now, before another sun does set
on words which from my heart do seek release
Confess to you these thoughts yet unexpressed
of love you have unearthed and joy unleashed.

When in my hour of dark your lamp did shine
across my path to light another way
Then did I feel the hand of the Divine
come touch my night and shape it into day.

We walked through canyons deep and valleys wide
alone in body, yet in spirit one,
While miracles were wrought before our eyes
bestowing Light more radiant than the sun.

A truer sister none could ever find
Nor any thanks to God compare to mine.

Chapter 7
Rules of Engagement

I tell you this because it's about weathering storms.

Because each one of us has to work out what we need to shelter in place, to survive the turbulence, keep our ground.

Stories are the best tools we have to awaken the imagination, which is the requirement of this hour. How do we inoculate ourselves against despair? How do we climb back into the Mother's lap, revive our reverence, return to awe, our original state?

We're wired to think "If someone else can do it, so can I." It's part of our buoyant nature. When I hear the story of how you survived, how you managed through a crisis, I believe again I can make it through my own.

This story is about resilience. It's about a time when I had to choose between self-love and self-betrayal. It's about hard decisions, hardheadedness, and hardships that serve as a springboard for change.

★★★★

—St. Joseph's Provincial House, Latham, New York, 1969

On the morning of my 20th birthday I woke up at 5:20 a.m. when the bell rang, calling us to Lauds and daily Mass. Dozens of handmade holy cards fanned out in disarray under my door. I gathered them up and stuffed them in my prayer book as I hurried out to chapel. The sacristan glided across the sanctuary lighting candles while younger sisters wheeled the elders into their spots near the altar rail. I opened my Office Book to look at my cards. The first was an image of a burning candle with the words of Thomas Merton printed in calligraphy: "*I am steeped in the presence of God until it makes me numb.*" No words could have better described how I felt about my life.

After a year in the postulate, we became first-year novices. It was referred to as our Canonical year, and the focus was on prayer, spiritual reading, meditation, and household chores. The only classes we attended were art, music, and theology. We had no interaction with the outside—no magazines, no television, no movies, no pop music. It was 1968 and as the bottom dropped out of the world as I knew it, I tumbled willingly toward the Great Unknown, guided by the words of Thomas Merton who said, "Our real journey in life is interior." That was enough for me, or so I thought.

We kept silent during all our charges, moving wordlessly from morning duties to chapel prayers, meditation, choir practice, art class, Stations of the Cross, afternoon chores, prayers, theology and novitiate training classes. I was still immersed in the writings of Teilhard de Chardin and Thomas Merton, the mystic and the monk, and Dietrich Bonhoeffer was awakening me to the gospel of social justice.

I had raised myself on biographies of the saints but never encountered faith as fierce, as alive, and as personal as the faith of these three men. Teilhard introduced me to a God I had not imagined—a creative force that penetrates and saturates the entire cosmos, that is so alluring every iota of matter is drawn to it, returns to it, becomes one with it. Every sentence he wrote was a hymn that resounded in the caverns of my being. Through his words I began to understand creation as an expression of supreme intelligence.

God was not a *being*, but a *becoming*. Not a mysterious figurehead in the heavens who said, "Let there be Light." God was Energy Itself, Light Itself, that *became* matter—is *becoming* matter, is "mattering" through us—and evolving into galaxies and planets, sea dragons, and chrysanthemums, mosquitoes, and manatees. "Matter is spirit moving slowly enough to be seen," wrote Teilhard. Einstein expressed the same when he came up with his theory of relativity. They are the same energy moving at different speeds. Matter is slowed-down light, gravitationally trapped energy: $E=MC^2$—energy equals mass times the speed of light squared. We are the Divine in slow motion. Same essence, different forms, different speeds.

"The divine assails us, penetrates and moulds us," wrote Teilhard. "We imagined it as distant and inaccessible, whereas in fact we live steeped in its burning layers." His love affair with creation carried me to the heart of the earth and the edges of heaven, while Merton took my hand and headed east.

A convert to Catholicism and a Trappist monk, Thomas Merton was intrigued by the otherness of Buddhism. He wanted to experience the wholeness of an East-West fusion. Born into the yang of Christianity (*Go and teach all nations*), he sought out the yin of Buddhism (*Be still and see that all is perfect*), believing that a synthesis of the two would lead to a higher awakening.

In 1968, as I devoured his autobiography, *The Seven Storey Mountain*, Merton received permission from his abbot to visit Asia. During his time in India, he was escorted by Harold Talbott, who became his guide to Tibetan lamas in India's Himalayan region. Talbott introduced Merton to the Dalai Lama and they met three times, sharing information on the practicalities of monasticism as Merton's order practiced it in Kentucky and the Dalai Lama practiced it in Dharamsala, India.

Merton told the Dalai Lama that he was returning to Asia to study *dzogchen* and the Dalai Lama walked him through the first steps, but the process ended abruptly when Merton was somehow electrocuted in Thailand. He died on December 10, 1968, only months after I had claimed him as a teacher. After his death, I read everything he wrote, studying his photographs, dissolving into his poetry, absorbing whatever I could from this mystic and weaver of worlds.

Merton grafted the branches of Zen and Tibetan Buddhism to the tree of Christianity and shared the results wherever he went. He made a case for mystery over certainty and spontaneity over conformity—concepts I cherished in the privacy of my mind but struggled to achieve as a first-year novice.

The freedom and movement I experienced in my spiritual life contrasted with the constraints of religious life. In my private hours of prayer, I flew like a Pegasus through the sky of ideas, free to evolve and have my own thoughts. I imagined a future of autonomy and self-agency, a future of action and compassion. And yet, in the communal world of the novitiate, I felt bridled to the past, memorizing *Maxims of Perfection* from the Middle Ages and following rules I had no say in creating.

Rather than probe the depths of our changing selves, we recited rules of conduct for "souls who aspire to great virtue," teachings handed down from our community's founder, Jean Pierre Medaille, in 1640. I recited them along with every other novice, a sign of obedience and self-abnegation, but deep inside, that winged horse reared up in resistance to the very ideas embedded in these strange and hurtful maxims:

- *Advance good works till near their completion and then, if it can be done easily, let others finish them and gain all the credit. (3:15)*

- *Rejoice that others are highly esteemed and in all things preferred to you. (3:10)*
- *Make so perfect a sacrifice of your will that you completely destroy self-love, and deliberately desire nothing but the accomplishment of the will of God. (10:7)*
- *Conceal, if possible, the graces God bestows on you and, when you can do so with prudence, make known what will lower you in the esteem of others. (3:13)*
- *Do not imagine that you have attained to the perfect love of God until the action of grace has destroyed in you the last remnant of self-love and transformed you into Christ. (9:11)*

We prayed prayers of renunciation, also from our founder, as part of our practice for acquiring detachment and union with Christ:

Lord Jesus ... I desire to die to myself ... to renounce myself entirely ... to strip myself of all creatures and even of all affection for them ... I divest myself of all my desires, of all self-love, and I disown all feelings, from whatever source they come ...

It tortured me to say these prayers. I *wanted* my feelings. I *wanted* my desires, my longings. I *wanted* to love myself, for in *me* dwelt the Creative Force and for that I rejoiced. These were conflicts I could not resolve. To be obedient, I had to follow these rules, pray these prayers, but to be true to the self I was becoming I had to fulfill *my* desires and express *my* feelings.

Our novice director, Sister Elizabeth Thomas, warned us anew about the dangers of "particular friends" and relationships that could become "carnal" if we were not cautious. In case previous threats hadn't sunk in, she cautioned us against intimacy and close friendships, encouraging us to suppress our feelings, turn our backs on whatever fires blazed in our young and curious hearts. I'm sure she covered a variety of spiritual topics, but after a heart-wrenching year of secrecy with Sister Marie Catherine, my antenna twitched at every mention of the word "particular friend" and "carnal." It seemed as if she were talking directly to me, knowing I would be the one to fall in love with someone, *be* carnal, actually engage in intimacy with a real person. And, of course, she was right.

I hungered for it. I would suffer for it. Go without food and sleep for it. Intimacy was my sustenance. The whole cycle of love I experienced in the postulate with Sister Marie Catherine repeated itself in my canonical year. I fell in love again with a novice who received me as I received her—emotionally, spiritually, psychologically. Sister Rose and I were not lovers. We were beloveds. Supports for each other. Sustainers. And when my Superior called me into her office to inquire into the nature of our relationship, I responded in complete honesty.

"Yes, I entered her bedroom."

"Yes, I spoke to her during Grand Silence."

"Yes, I have kissed her. I have held her in my arms."

These were major offenses, not only because we were forbidden to enter another's bedroom, but because I had already been warned not to talk to her and ordered to keep custody of the eyes if we met in the hallway. And I responded just as I had a year ago—by disobeying those orders. Eventually Sister Rose and I started communicating by letters and holy cards, by notes written in prayer book margins, by secret meetings in secret places. Every cell in my body was ignited by those encounters. Every molecule came alive in those forbidden moments of tenderness.

I didn't know what was going on, other than I was in love and the energy love unleashes was flowing through me like a river. I didn't have words or labels for it. I didn't think of myself as a homosexual. I just knew I wanted to be with the person I longed for. I was not interested in "conquering" any desires or overcoming any temptations. What my superiors thought of as carnal and looked upon with disdain, I saw as beautiful and looked upon with wonder. I loved being in love. I loved having someone special to share the deeper things with. I *wanted* the forbidden "particular friend." I wanted that intimacy, that human touch, that hand in my hand. Intimacy, for me, was intertwined with my spirituality, and yet, for my superiors, it set off alarms. Isolating me from the others was all they knew to do.

My stomach churned at the conflict I faced between obedience and desire. Why did my community have to think so small? Why did they have to focus on such petty things as particular friendships when the universe around us was exploding into God? I prayed every day to be released from their judgments. I prayed they would see that my personal relationships and my spiritual life were fueled and fed by each other—

and that to tear them apart caused irreparable harm to both.

The words of Merton, Teilhard, and Bonhoeffer inspired me to take ownership of my life—to be what I was meant to be, to define the perimeter of my own spirituality, and to discern what that was through my own prayerful process. Their writings pushed and prodded me. They were the future pulling me toward it. As the afternoon light cast rainbows on the marble floor, I sat in chapel, breathing in their words, reveling in their ideas as they rippled through my veins.

All three men stressed love and unity as the true destiny. Through their writings and lives, I came to think of intimacy as a matter of the soul more than the body, a state of presence, complete attention, unfettered affinity. Intimacy was a good thing. It was not precluded by the vow of chastity. Not something to focus on, worry over. But that thinking did not comply with the rules of the novitiate.

Being told I couldn't be with someone I felt close to—couldn't speak to them, make eye contact, had to avoid at all costs—made it all the worse. It exaggerated my loss and magnified my longings. I was too emotionally immature to be thinking of sex, but I craved connection, relationship, partnership. I loved community and thrived in that collective environment, but something in me longed for an other. All the dramatic change and growth in my inner world sought a correlate in my outer life.

In the novitiate, my expedition into the sacred went deep, not far. I was no longer searching for an unattainable being. I was dowsing for the Divine inside me. I sat in prayer and meditation not because it was required by my Superior, but because it was required by my soul. Why, then, was I being denied the very thing I needed for my own evolution—a witness to my journey, another soul to share with? Never had I been so lonely in the company of so many women.

As I was coming to understand it—through the works of these masters whom I devoured late into every night with a blanket under my door to hide the light—it is through the outpourings of our most *personal* selves that the Light of Light takes shape in the world. Incarnation was not a one-time event. It is an ongoing phenomenon. God did not just visit the earth once in the body of Christ. That creative force is unfolding every minute of the day in every direction and we are *of* it and *in* it. Or as Teilhard described it: "Man discovers that *he is nothing else than evolution become conscious of itself* ... The consciousness of each of us is evolution looking at itself and reflecting upon itself."

I came to believe—through immersing myself in the writings of my teachers—that the Divine is more unavoidable than inaccessible, and becoming "one with" requires no travel, just a shift in awareness. There is nothing to seek and nowhere to go. Everything I desired was right inside me. Spiritually speaking, I was being constructed from the inside out, and the words of these mystics fired up my neurons and blazed new pathways in the contours of my brain.

The contradictions I wrestled with as a first-year novice were huge. The rules of the novitiate provided the recipe for perfect joy: equal time devoted to solitude, community, prayer, and service. I thrived on that balance. I loved every part of it, from meditation to chores, from singing in the choir loft to the chasm of solitude. The external structure was perfect.

We sang all the time in the novitiate—at Mass, at all special occasions, during recreation time, after novitiate training. I wrote songs that we sang as a community in chapel. We performed one for the bishop when he visited. Singing took me somewhere safe and beautiful.

As joyful as I was being a part of this community, a seismic wave surged within me. My identity, my spirituality, my consciousness, my feelings about authority and vows shifted like tectonic plates in my fiery core. I strove to think for myself. I followed the rule of my own conscience. I stood with the others and recited prayers I was fast outgrowing, but I would not obey orders that insulted my soul.

As I reckoned with the dualities between spiritual freedom and spiritual formation in the novitiate, I vacillated like a pendulum between desire and denial. Intellectually, I evolved by reading and reflecting on the works of my teachers. Merton introduced me to Buddhism and a streamlined Zen approach to awakening through contemplation. Bonhoeffer was Merton in work boots, Teilhard in coveralls. His beliefs were traditional and ordinary but embodied in every action he took. He may not have been fearless, but his faith led him to heroic action, led him to martyrdom, not for inherited beliefs but for his inherent knowing that it is right to lay down one's body for a noble cause—for him, in resistance to Hitler's regime.

Teilhard's ideas took me far beyond the confines of my Catholic upbringing and offered me a God that was accessible in me and in the ground on which I walked. He spoke of a God whose fullness I was a part of, a body whose being I *belonged* to. Through his visions I saw a new world and felt a new hope. His ideas took root in the soil of my mind and like a seed, I germinated, shedding a shell I no longer needed.

Then a tiny green shoot sprouted and aimed upward facing the light.

Chapter 8
A Night to Remember

I tell you this because it is good to hear each other's grief. Good to cry with another, to unfurl our own unattended sorrows and admit the ordeals we have borne and survived.

I spent 20 years with this wound, with no triumph in sight. What I knew was unspoken shame, undiluted grief, unmitigated rage. They owned me. I was their possession. To master my ordeal was simply impossible, until it wasn't.

It is possible that one person's story can alter the course of another person's trajectory. It could happen that you are bound up in a grief story now, that rage is a fire in your mouth, that you worry you might die of loneliness or loss or lack of love. It could happen that this story wakes up a sleeping part of you. It is possible that it could help you get out of bed and begin building the life you came here to live.

I am telling you this because it might break open your world, your heart, as mine was broken open. We are so much the same. That's what I'm trying to say.

★★★★

It was a warm, humid evening in early June. Birds chirped in the chestnut trees as the sky turned mauve and the sun moved west. The dining room was crowded for the day's last meal, as Chapter was in session and change was in the air. Chapter was the decision-making body for our community, composed of the provincial director, the vice provincial, and about a dozen of their counselors.

They made all the policy decisions about important matters, including where the professed sisters would be missioned and which sisters in formation would advance to the next step. One by one they reviewed every case. Novice directors made recommendations and Chapter had the final say. That's what they called themselves. Chapter. Novices who were prone to worry started getting nervous days before the session started. I did my best to calm them down.

"Come on," I'd say. "Why in the world would they send you home? They *need* us. They're always looking for more vocations and here we are. Relax!"

I never worried about Chapter. I knew I was meant to be there. I'd known it since sixth grade and never imagined anything else. As far as I was concerned, we were all in our proper places and God would see to it that we stayed there.

The sound of Sister Marion's tiny bell broke our silence as she signaled to the room she was done with her meal. Hundreds of sisters rose from their seats, made the "Sign of the Cross," offered thanks, and delivered their dirty dishes and silverware to the stainless-steel carts. The novices in charge of evening chores headed straight for the kitchen, wrapped aprons around their waists and necks, and took their positions. My job was to transport the dishes from the carts to the loading end of the dishwasher where two novices fed them into the mouth of the steam-billowing machine.

At the other end two sweat-drenched sisters, nearly invisible in the cloud of mist, unloaded the scalding dishes. They stacked them onto wheeled carts, which another novice rolled out into the kitchen as soon as they were filled. The dishwasher had a room of its own and it took six of us to keep the operation running smoothly.

I was just wiping the sweat off my brow when I saw Sister Elizabeth

Thomas, our novice director, walking toward me. Her face was typically stern and hard to read. In fact, her whole body was hard to read. Some days I wondered if she had any emotions at all under that flesh, given how committed she was to squelching mine. With one finger, she beckoned me over. "Follow me, sister" was all she said, and I followed her down the back stairway, past the laundry, down the long, dim corridors until we came to the hall of parlors, which were used for visiting days.

Each parlor had two or three chairs in it, an occasional piano, a crucifix on the wall, a painting of St. Joseph or the Holy Family, and an end table or two. We entered one and Sister Elizabeth closed the door behind us.

"Have a seat," she said, taking one herself.

We sat face to face in two hard-backed straight chairs. Our knees almost touched, we were so close to each other.

"Do you know why we're here?" she asked.

"No, Sister," I replied.

On the long trek to the parlors the only thought I had was that she probably wanted me to move some furniture. I was one of the stronger novices, a good athlete. It made sense she would have asked me. Had I known what was coming, I would have fainted on the spot.

Sister Elizabeth, perfectly composed, her hands in her lap, looked me in the eye and said, "Chapter has decided you're not to continue your novitiate."

She didn't blink. I didn't move. This had to be a mistake. I stared blankly at her face while my entire body started to burn. Tectonic plates shifted below. The ground of my being rumbled. A tsunami of sorrow towered offshore.

"You know why, don't you?" she asked, her voice faint and far off, as if miles away.

I had already left my body. Cyclones took shape over every ocean. Black holes formed in the Milky Way. The rings of Saturn wobbled.

"Sister!" she said, to retrieve my attention. "You *do* know why, don't you?"

I returned to my body and continued to stare, my mouth hanging open, my brain spinning out. How could she do this? What is *wrong* with her? Doesn't she know who I am? Somewhere in my brain a thought registered that this must be hard for her as well, but I was the one whose life was ending. She was the one with the orders. Who cared how hard it was for her?

For all the trouble I was, I thought she valued my faithfulness to life. We were two goddesses sitting on different clouds in the heavens. We each had our domains as far as I was concerned. She was my Superior, to be sure, but she was not the boss of me. I didn't understand at that time the Himalayan nature of my ego. I only knew that I'd be true to my passions any day before I'd be true to commands that silenced me. I might not have known who I was, but I was beginning to learn who I was not.

The reality of what was unfolding in that parlor was too much of a shock to absorb. This was my dream turning into a nightmare. How could I stay conscious for it? I kept floating off.

"Sister!" she repeated, trying to get me back into the room. "You *do* know why?"

"Yes, I guess so," I lied, closing the door to words that might kill me. And from the moment I said it, I wished I hadn't.

I knew I'd disobeyed a lot of rules. I knew I'd fallen in love though they ordered me not to. I knew I was a renegade with a mind of my own. But I knew also that I was called to be there, that I had a vocation. This was my home, my *life*. I had no plan B.

Why specifically did Chapter decide to send me home? I would leave not knowing, not hearing the litany of wrongs I'd committed.

"All right then, wait here and I'll be right back. Your parents will be here in half an hour," she said, exiting the room.

When she left, I collapsed onto the floor, pressing my face into the tapestry seat of the chair I'd just occupied. I knelt on the cold linoleum floor, clinging to the sides of the mahogany as if it were a life raft. A fire raged through me—burning my eyes, scorching my throat. A volcano erupted in my gut. I wanted to wake up, to have this nightmare *be* that; not something real, not this horror, not this destruction of my entire life. I couldn't face it. I would not survive it.

It was my fear alone that stopped this descent into hell. What if I couldn't stop crying? What if I couldn't stand up? What if I died there, a body unable to bear the unbearable? My own dreaded thoughts jerked me back into action. I *had* to get up. Sit back in that chair. Get myself together. My parents would be there in half an hour. My life was about to transform into something I had never prepared for. I had failed. I was being ejected, rejected by God himself, for it was to him that I had offered my life. The chances that I had taken cost me the world. The acts of disobedience, the hubris, the pride of thinking I was above the fray. I realized many years later that I had gambled everything for love and I had lost it all.

My sense of presence came and went. The trauma sustained was all interior, but nothing survived the incineration of my dream. Voices in my head called me back from the place I'd escaped to, urging me to become present and stay there. *Act as if nothing is happening. Nothing is happening here. Nothing is happening. Just act normal.* My brain changed gears to navigate the battlefield, closing every border that danger could cross. While a part of me went numb in sheer disbelief, another part bore the brunt of the unfolding assault. Adrenaline flowed through my veins like an anesthetic. As a part of me went numb, afraid of feeling, the rest of me sat up, hands folded, eyes closed.

When Sister Elizabeth Thomas came back into the room she carried the dress I had worn when I entered, that balmy September 15, 1967. "You can change into this," she said. "There's a restroom down the hall. And we'll be wanting your veil."

"Yes, Sister." I took the dress, opened the parlor door, and walked down the hall. When I looked into the restroom mirror, I barely recognized the face I encountered. All that vitality, gone. All that lust for life, disappeared. No one home.

I removed my veil, regarding the shortness of my hair without emotion, without regret. Two days before I had cut it haphazardly with a razor blade, never imagining the horror of this evening. Certain that I would not be strong enough to survive this shock, I remember thinking, *I will not live for this to matter.*

Slowly I unzipped and stepped out of my novitiate clothing, then pulled the foreign dress over my head. I returned to the parlor and took my seat, keeping my head down. My shoulders curved inward, my back hunched downward as my body cocooned itself for protection. My thought drifted to the others, sitting one flight above us, about to be told I was no longer with them. They were my tribe. In many ways, I was their leader. For two years we had gone through everything together— worked together, prayed together, played and cried and sang together.

This would shake their world too.

"Can I say goodbye to them?" I asked.

"No, that wouldn't be a good idea. We prefer that you don't communicate with anyone here in the future. It'll be best if you don't return to the Motherhouse."

An arrow struck the bull's-eye of my heart.

. "How will they know what happened to me?"

"I'll see to it. They will keep you in their prayers."

Footsteps in the hallway intruded into our conversation. We heard muffled voices, the sound of the door closing in the parlor next to ours.

A wave of panic washed over me as I imagined this nightmare ensnaring us all.

"What am I supposed to tell my parents?"

"Just tell them you don't have a religious disposition."

I nodded my head, as if to acknowledge that was the case, after I had discovered a God that I was *immersed* in—a God that I was part of, a cosmic body that I was a cell in, that was constantly unfolding in me, through me, *as* me. After I had traded religion for a faith of my own, committed to a spirituality of justice, peace, tenderness, and mercy, I nodded my head to accept the verdict: guilty for lack of a religious disposition.

We stood up, and Sister Elizabeth knocked on the parlor door, then opened it.

I stood in the doorway, a shadow of myself. My mother and father lunged toward me, as if defending a helpless cub. "What happened?" my mother cried out, reaching for my stiff body. "You were so happy here."

My father, never happy that I had entered, never demonstrative in any emotional way, wrapped his arms around my mother and me. We huddled in silence until I repeated the words that felt like a lie.

"I just don't have a religious disposition," I said flatly, my voice distant and detached. "We can go now."

Sister Elizabeth ushered us up through a private staircase so no one would see us. It led directly to the front door of the provincial house where my parents' car was waiting. By now the humidity had turned to rain and the mauve sky turned to midnight black. We got in the car, heading for the thruway, and the long, lonely drive back to Syracuse.

My father drove in silence, but occasionally a question drifted back from my mother.

There was no one there to answer it. I sat in the back seat with my forehead pressed to the glass, silent for the two-hour journey to what they called home.

Chapter 9
The Darkness That Followed

I tell you this because if I confess my sins there is a better chance that you will confess your own, then leave them like a bag of trash at the landfill, not to be seen or heard from again.

There comes a time when we stop telling our tales of woe. When we stop milking our sad stories for sympathy or whatever else we hunger for. I only know this because I became exhausted with the telling, though it ate at my heart for decades, and still makes me weep as I tell it and type it one last time.

I splashed my sorrow over all these pages to let you know how it's done, that it's all right, that, at the end, there is a wisdom, a forgiving, the pit is filled up and a garden grows on top.

We are the Earth's children, creatures who suffer along with the rest. We are beset by plagues, by war, by hunger and fear—and we have a lifetime of unknown length to right what wrongs we can.

We are no strangers to the dark these days. We are awakened by the hand of the Great Unknown and fall asleep to the sound of our soul's lament. What we thought of as normal is afloat in the sea, caught in a bottle, never to return. We are waving goodbye to the world we have known, and as we turn to face our empty canvas—artists at life—let us make together a future that is fitting and right for the children to come.

—Syracuse, New York, June 1969

My parents had moved while I was in the convent, so the house we returned to was not familiar to me. Nothing was familiar. Miniskirts and marijuana had blossomed on the cultural scene, the sexual revolution was in full bloom, and Woodstock was about to explode in full, tie-dyed color. The world I left in 1967 was not the same world I returned to in 1969. Nor was I.

I had grown accustomed to silence, prayer, daily meditation. I was not used to television, music, alcohol, pot, and cigarettes, which permeated the environment I'd reentered. I was traumatized, as if returning home from a war, though the reverse was also true. Friends and family didn't know what to make of me. I was not the party animal everyone remembered.

In my parents' new home, I had my own bedroom and bought a supply of candles and incense for my prayers and meditation. I tried to explain to my mother what I needed.

"Mom, every day I will take two to three hours to be alone in my room. I'll be praying and meditating. If my door is closed, please don't knock or disturb me."

"Sure!" she said, giving me confidence that she was on my wavelength, aware that I transformed my bedroom into a chapel twice a day, the only thing I knew to do to keep my sanity.

But as it turned out, that was not the case. I know this had nothing to do with her love for me, that it was symptomatic of the problem of most churchgoers who think it's only in that building they experience or practice their faith, but anytime she wanted me, or someone called, she'd burst through the door as if I weren't there, or call out loudly, "Jan! Phone's for you."

No matter how hard I tried to fit back into the secular world, it never worked. I didn't care about what other people cared about. I didn't want to go out dancing or get drunk on cheap beer. I didn't want to watch *The Brady Bunch* or *Bewitched*. My ears hurt at the sound of Led Zeppelin and Iron Butterfly.

I just wanted my silence back. I wanted my community. I longed for

Lauds and Vespers, for the "Hallelujah Chorus," for the river of black habits flowing to the cemetery after each funeral Mass, the orange juice machine I was in charge of, the bowed heads of the elders praying, the smell of incense. Every sense called out for the familiar.

I walked to the mailbox every day hoping the letter would be there: "We made a mistake. We want you back. Come home soon." That hope was the only thing that kept me moving through time. I lived between two worlds, finding fault with the one I was in, harboring illusions about the one I'd left.

I went to church with my mother but found it deadly. Half-empty pews, half-hearted responses, fewer than half even attempting to sing. Where was the spirit, the love, the full-throated faith signs I'd grown used to? Would I ever find it again, out here in this foreign world? Would I ever find a community of people who were in love with the Beloved and sang about this at every opportunity?

I returned to my job as a waitress at a country club in Syracuse. I had worked there the summer before I entered and had grown close to several of the families I waited on. None of them had the slightest idea why I entered the convent in the first place. They were thrilled I was back so I could lead a "normal life." They wanted the best for me, I knew that, but their comments stirred up emotions that brought me to tears. How does one apologize for crying into a Reuben sandwich?

"We knew you wouldn't like it."

"I'm so glad you left that crazy convent. It's no place for a bright girl like you."

"Thank God you're home. We always knew it wasn't right for you."

I couldn't communicate how happy I had been there—that even though I rose up in resistance against being silenced, even though I willfully disobeyed my Superior's orders if they separated me from someone I loved—it was my place of balance, my cocoon of transformation, the only home I ever wanted.

I tried to come up with cheery responses when they commented on why I was back again. I tried acting as if the ground where I stood was not shaking below me. I was breathing on my own, but it wasn't apparent how I *lived* and *moved* and *had my being*. I failed, again and again, to master my ordeal. Disavowing reality took all my energy. Waiting at the mailbox, hoping for things to change, only prolonged my grief. Until I accepted what *was*, I could not, would not, heal.

By September, three months from my dismissal, I knew I had to leave the Northeast. I had to get away from everyone I knew and begin a life as far away as possible. As the maple leaves prepared for their green to disappear, I disappeared on the highways heading West.

I had another loss to face that was nearly as weighty, but luckily for me, I never saw it coming.

Chapter 10
Into the Depths

I tell you this in case you ever spiral downward, ever lose yourself so completely that you don't remember who you are.

It's a frightening thing to lose your way. One day you're waltzing down your street of dreams, on top of the world, and the next you're in an alleyway, half-clothed and delirious. It can happen to anyone. I only know this because it happened to me. The narrative changes but the arc stays the same—she had a mission, entered the forest, met the demons, fought for her life, found her voice. At least we hope for that ending. And sometimes hope is all we have—a thin thread of it, connecting us to a future only half of our making.

In the Night of Unknowing, one is never sure if the light will return. One chooses, and chooses again, and again, pivoting sometimes, plummeting others. It is a perilous journey, but our initials are carved in that place on the map. It is meant for us.

My journey through this time was arduous. It demanded all my attention. I was a child in adult clothing. No one came to take my hand, to acquaint me with the perils, remind me they were passing. I blundered my way through till the sun finally rose over the mountains to the East. There are many ways to grow ourselves up, to evolve ourselves consciously. This one here, I would not advise.

★★★★

—Newport Beach, California, March 1970

Shortly after I arrived in California, I remembered the upcoming birthday of one of my good friends in the novitiate. I'd been told not to communicate with any of the sisters and had followed that order, but now I was about to do what I wanted. I was going to make a present for Sister Lois and send it to her. It would be a handmade book of photographs and quotes that would let her know, in a kind of secret language, what had become of me.

The night I was dismissed, the novice director did what she always did when a sister left. She wrote the news on the blackboard. "Sister So-and-So is no longer with us. Please keep her in your prayers." That was it. No conversation with her or among ourselves about the one who had left. It was brutal.

All those novices I left behind after two years of living together had no idea what happened that night. And they had to figure out on their own how to deal with their grief, just as I did. But it had been nine months now, and I was about to break my silence. I knew the book would be seen by Lois' Superior, as mail was censored before we got it, so I kept it as impersonal as possible. No card. No letter. No notes on the page other than quotes from authors we'd loved, songs we'd sung together, prayers and poems we'd passed back and forth. The photographs themselves carried the freight of my emotions. They were my voice, speaking in images. They said what I couldn't say, reflected my tangled feelings, my attempts and failures to get past the loss.

With a Kodak Instamatic camera in hand, I searched for subjects that would expose my interior, portray my battle to reassemble a life. I rummaged for images that would *be* the words I wanted to speak. I went to the mountains, the desert, the ocean, and the forest hunting for pictures that said I missed her terribly, was struggling to find myself, still had hope even though my faith was waning. I found myself reflected in parched desert floors, redwood saplings, homeless park dwellers. I photographed footsteps dissolving in the tide, my body against a 12-foot cross, my shadow on the steps before a locked church door.

Images of crashing waves and toppled sandcastles, friends huddled on a moonlit beach, a woman alone strumming a guitar, birds soaring into golden sunsets—each reflected what I felt but could not say. They were metaphors to carry Lois from her world to mine.

As the photos were printed, I entered the story that each one told, wanting to be sure they conveyed what lived in the muscles of my heart. It was not just the chaos, but my conviction to thrive that I wanted her to see; not just the loss, but the uplift that came in unexpected ways. For the first time, as a young adult—I was trying to become a person, an individual, with thoughts of my own. Trying to connect my parts: the sacred and the secular, the holy and the human. Despite the emotional upheaval, the loss of separation, I had an independence now I'd never had before. I was on my own, free to be and do whatever I wanted— the upside to the collapse. Total freedom was twinned to my grief, but the question loomed on my path to selfhood: What would I make of this newfound freedom? Would I be the fool, the Prodigal Daughter, or would I choose wisely? Would I follow the rules set in stone by the society I was a part of?

The quest for images for Lois' book took me to the underworld of my own life. If I was going to depict my feelings, I had to know them, embody them. I had to put each one on like a robe, feel its weight on my shoulders. What does despair look like? Or longing? Or hope? My vault of vulnerabilities creaked open and one by one I felt them, named them, and made a photograph that represented them.

Each image bore a sacred truth and told a story of the wreckage and the resurrection. *Dear Lois. This is how I'm doing. This is how I miss you. This page here is my loss. And here is the joy I am trying to hold to. Here is the fragment of my faith that remains. Here is my long, lonely howl in the night.*

Making that book gave me a way to let the grief out—to speak it and release it, a little at a time. My sorrow became less a malignancy to

destroy and more a companion to befriend. It would be with me as long as I agreed to drag it along, as long as I held to it like a child with a teddy bear. Until I needed it no more, which would take some time and assistance from others.

As I glued each photo onto the page, I was grateful for its power, praised its lumbering ways, like a beast of burden laden with bags. The patent leather shoes at the seashore carried emotions so many years old—not like the fresh paint of my convent grief, but yellowed and cracked like an ancestor's photograph—so much said in shades of gray; nothing missing but the DNA.

When I started the book for Lois, I didn't know where it would take me, to what depths it would lead. I'd never tried to speak without words before. I'd never undertaken a creative journey that didn't have a prescribed ending or a semi-clear pathway. This endeavor, though it spoke of grief in secret code, also helped me transcend that grief. Revealing myself was a way of healing myself.

It didn't matter that I used a Kodak Instamatic, that the photos were small, grainy, out of focus, that there were typos in my quotes. What mattered was the truth-telling, the connection, the intimacy that was afoot. That was the magic.

II.

Shortly after I moved to Newport Beach, I looked for a parish where I could volunteer. I had not given up on the Catholic Church. In fact, I looked for one to harbor me. There was a church near me, right on the beach, and I approached the pastor about offering folk masses.

"I'm afraid we don't have the resources to do that," said the priest.

"You don't need resources," I said. "I'll take care of the music. What I can't find, I'll write, and it won't cost you a thing. It'll be great for the kids too."

I offered to teach guitar to the teens who were interested, and the group of us would provide the music for one Mass on Sunday.

Reluctantly, he gave me a chance and within a few weeks I had a group of three students who were learning all the songs we needed for a Mass. We sang songs from Ray Repp, Peter Scholtes, Sebastian Temple. The four of us, with our four guitars, harmonized to tunes like "Here We Are," "Allelu," "Take Our Bread," "They'll Know We Are Christians By Our Love."

We were on fire. Nobody questioned the language, the wording, the theology we were presenting. It was all about the Lord, all He, all Him, all His, and it never occurred to me anything was wrong with that. I was just happy to be back in a church singing my heart out.

Now that I had found a church, I would participate in the sacraments and let grace help turn my sorrow into solace. I went to confession one day and acknowledged to the priest that I was homosexual. It wasn't that I was asking for forgiveness. I was born that way. I hadn't done anything wrong.

But the priest did not see it this way. He ordered me to renounce my homosexuality. He wanted a promise I would never act on it, when I was already sharing a house with the woman I loved. Already sleeping with her. Already making love.

Rosie, formerly Sister Rose, left the novitiate shortly after I did and moved to California to be with me. I vacillated between bliss and self-contempt, as did she. It was heaven to be with her and hell to think it might be wrong. Both of us were still Catholic, still abdicating our authority to the Church. Neither of us ever said the word *lesbian*. Or *homosexual*. Or *gay*. We didn't label ourselves or talk about what we were doing. We didn't know anything except there was a magnet between us, a force that had both of us spinning.

She was afraid of what people would think. Four women lived in our house on the beach and our relationship was never brought up. As if it weren't real. We slept together every night. We kissed, held hands, cuddled, made love—and pretended all the while that that was not the case.

There was no language to speak of it. No circle to share it with. No others in our lives who were like us: women of faith, good-hearted women, full-of-light women, women who tried to dedicate themselves to God. The contradiction was fierce. It felt so right to be loving her, to be so happy, to be finally reunited with the woman I was told not to talk to or look at again.

I *wanted* to hold hands in public. I *wanted* to be able to talk about it, but Rosie was afraid. She loved me, but she wasn't a lesbian. It was just me that she loved. Our relationship was an aberration. It wouldn't last. It couldn't. She wasn't cut out for it.

I told Rosie about my experience in the confessional. "He denied me absolution, unless I promised to stop being homosexual."

She stared at me with wide eyes. "What are you going to do?"

"I don't know, what do you think?"

"Well, we can try it," Rosie said, and we did.

The two of us tried for weeks to be straight. We stopped touching each other. I shot pool at the local pub and tried to act as if men mattered. I feigned interest in sports, trucks, tools, but the whole thing failed. I dated a few men, but each date was deadlier than the other. They bored me and annoyed me with their constant advances.

I couldn't *not* be homosexual, any more than I could *not* be blue-eyed. It was a condition of my being. Cellular. Baked in. Since I was a child, I had longed to be in the arms of a woman. I loved being in love but hated the darkness that trailed behind it. I just wanted to cherish whom I cherished, but there was always danger, always risk. Furtive behavior was not forced upon me. It sprung up from inside, where, instead of self-love, hatred and anger had taken root. I was a walking weather system—a hurricane of rage, a blizzard of despair, a cyclone of inner chaos.

The struggle to be inauthentic exhausted me. All the work involved in pretending not to be who I was wore me down. I was caught in a conundrum. All my life, as a Catholic, I turned my power over to the priests, the bishops, the pope. I put my faith in them, believed in them. I believed in the teachings of the Church, and yet, here I was, a woman of faith, a woman who wanted to serve and be of use, guilty for no reason except an accident of birth.

I was created as I am, I told myself. I did not choose anything about my sexuality. I came in this way and I am a child of God. Let the Church say what it wants, let the priest refuse to absolve me. It's out of my hands.

I returned to the confessional and told the priest I had tried being heterosexual, dating men, lying about my feelings. I tried pretending but that seemed a greater sin.

"You will have to do what you will do, but I cannot change myself," I whispered through the brown cotton screen.

"In that case, I refuse you absolution. I refuse you the sacraments. And I refuse to have you sing in my church and teach my students."

He knew who I was. I was horrified. I didn't think they could see who was on the other side, but he recognized me and that was the end of our folk masses, the end of my service at that church, and the end of

Catholicism for me for a long, long time.

Weary of the emotional turbulence, Rosie eventually left California and returned to Syracuse. She met a man and married him. On a visit back to the East Coast, I dropped by to see her at her new house in the suburbs.

Her husband was sitting in a comfortable chair watching TV. It was Saturday afternoon, probably sports, but I didn't notice. He looked Italian—handsome, hair just beginning to thin, trim and dressed well for a lazy afternoon. The house smelled of meatballs and sauce. Long velvet drapes shrouded the windows. The wallpaper was flowery and darker than I like. When Rosie introduced me to the man who had replaced me as her intimate partner, he looked my way for a second, smiled, and called out a friendly "Hello! Nice to meet you!" I couldn't help but like his smile.

If he only knew, I thought, my brain on fire with vivid memories.

"Oh, come upstairs," Rosie said, as if she wanted to scurry me off before I said anything embarrassing. "I have to show you my new window treatments."

We headed up the plush, taupe stairs. "Window treatments" was an expression I'd never heard before.

As we stood in their master bedroom, all the love I had ever felt for her rushed through me. Memories from the novitiate when we kissed so innocently in those forbidden spaces. Memories of being separated from her when my desire for her felt so urgent and deep. Memories of lying next to her in the middle of the night, thinking I finally knew what they meant by *ecstasy*. Overcome with surprise to be so desired by another human being. Memories of the night they dismissed me. No way to see her. No way to reach her.

Then her finding her way to me, living with me, sharing the chaos that was too cavernous for words. We suffered terribly together. We experienced heaven and hell together. And now I stood in her master bedroom, a maelstrom of desire, remorse, regret.

"I hired someone to help me with the colors," she said.

"Do you ever think of us?"

"Don't you love it, how the mauve bedspread brings out that color in the curtains?"

"Do you ever think of us?"

"I can't let myself. It was another life. I'm not that woman."

"Do you miss me?"

"I'm too busy. I can't. It wasn't me."

Her denial stung like a wasp. It *was* her. We *did* do that. She *did* love me. But it was in her past now.

"Do you have to dismiss it? Can't you say any of it was beautiful? That it was what you wanted?"

"It wasn't me. It wasn't right. I'm sorry."

"Okay, I get it," I said, turning to go. I left the room, walked down the stairs, passed by her husband, and walked out the door, never to see her again.

It happens that way sometimes. Like *Brigadoon*. All heaven breaks loose for a spell, then the curtain comes down, the set changes, and some people forget it ever happened. At least, that's what they say.

III.

I had found work as a waitress as soon as I arrived in California. It's all I knew to do. I had waitressed all through high school, and as soon as I was home from the convent I returned to a waitressing job at the Lafayette Country Club in Syracuse. When I arrived in Southern California, it was my go-to plan.

No one took education too seriously in my family. Neither of my parents had gone to college, and my sister did the traditional community-college-until-you-find-your-husband thing. I was on fire for learning in the convent but had no idea how to pursue an education once I was out. I'd never applied to college before.

So waitressing it was, until they discovered I was only 20. I couldn't serve drinks since the legal age in California was 21, so they fired me on the spot, after three short weeks of employment.

I pored over classified ads daily but had no skills to match the offerings. Finally, I called an employment agency and worked with a woman named Addie. She had me create a résumé and send it to her by mail. It was pathetic. Counter waitress at W.T. Grant, doughnut-maker / waitress at Mr. Donut, waitress at the country club, postulant, novice. Skills: serving, cleaning, praying, singing.

Addie called me and said the outlook was grim.

"Can you type?" she asked.

"No, not well," I confessed, having cheated my way through Sister Mary Beatrice's Typing 101 class.

"Come to my house. I'm going to give you a typing lesson and a test."

I did. She tried. I was terrible. Thirty words a minute with a ton of mistakes. She did her best to find me work, calling every day to say how difficult it was because I had no skills.

"Nobody needs someone who can pray. And we're not in the business to get people waitressing jobs."

One day she called, excited with an opportunity she thought might work for me. It was for a clerk-typist for the Bank of America.

"Don't worry. There's really not much typing involved. Mostly sending invoices and bills of lading. It's in Orange, at the administration office," she said. "And they pay $320 a month."

Turns out, Orange was a 35-minute drive from my house by freeway. Rosie had dented my car in a parking lot and it was in the shop. All I had was my Honda 125-cc motorcycle.

"Dress up nice, put on some make-up, and show up early. You have a 2 p.m. appointment with the president, Mr. Benninger, on Thursday."

I foraged through my closet, found one dress, some pantyhose, and a

Me (left) and my cousin Cheryl on our motorcycles.

pair of low heels. I had no makeup and no intention of getting any. Thursday came and I checked my map, put on my dress, heels, and helmet and jumped on my Honda. I got to Orange in plenty of time but got terribly lost trying to find the administrative building. I was in tears by the time I arrived and had already decided I didn't want the job. It was too far. I had to get too dressed up. And I couldn't type anyway.

They sent me right in to Mr. Benninger's office where he sat behind a mahogany desk the size of my kitchen. A trail of smoke curled toward the ceiling from a Winston cigarette burning in his ashtray. Everyone in the administrative building had ashtrays and cigarettes on their desks. He offered me one. On any other day I would have taken it, but I quickly declined.

Mr. Benninger wore a blue pinstripe suit with a gray shirt and pink tie, which made him feel somewhat accessible for some reason.

"So," he said, stretching out his long, lanky legs while peering over his horn-rimmed glasses at my résumé. "What do you think you have to offer the Bank of America?"

I hadn't changed my mind about not wanting the job, so we had an awkward moment.

"I'm sorry, Mr. Benninger, for wasting your time. I really can't even type. Addie said I could probably do the job anyway, but I don't think I want it because it's just too far, and I am just so sad ..." I trailed off into my whole litany of sorrows, crying my way through the list of reasons why I was not the right person for the job. Sent home from the convent, no college degree, no marketable skills, fired from waitress job, riding a motorcycle to work because of a crashed car. By the end, I started making up reasons, one of which was that I couldn't afford to live on what they were paying.

You'd have thought I was talking to a confessor instead of a potential employer. He took casual drags off his Winston as I lamented and when I was finished, I sat limply in the chair, staring into the threads of his Oriental carpet. Silence and smoke filled the air.

When I looked up, he was looking at me with a smile on his face. I didn't know what to make of it.

"I'm sorry," I said, standing up and heading for the door. "So sorry to have wasted your time."

He called out in a slightly louder voice, "What would it take for you to come and work for us?"

"Mr. Benninger, I told you I can't even type. You shouldn't even be hiring me."

"What would I have to pay you to have you take this job?"

Out of the blue I said "$400."

"All right then, can you start tomorrow?"

My world spun around. What was going on? Was he just happy to get someone as honest as me, despite the sadness that came with the package? I thought he'd be concerned about my emotional state, but there was no sign of that, so I started the next day. They paid me $400 per month. I learned the job fast, wore a dress every day, and kept up the facade of the girl next door, straight as an arrow, well-adjusted as can be.

IV.

I lived near a community college and went to register as a part-time student. It was a tuition-free college, and the lines were long with the young and the old. I'd waited quite a while before my turn came and when I faced the woman at the desk, her patience had run out.

"What are you here for?"

"I want to register for a class."

"What are you matriculating in?"

"What am I what?"

"Matriculating in?"

A whoosh of shame raced through my body. Blood rushed up my neck. I had no idea what she was talking about.

"Never mind," I apologized. "I'm in the wrong line. Sorry."

With that, I left the college, abandoned my desire, and returned to my life as a victim of circumstances. The odds were against me, or so it felt.

I was not a young woman who had been trained in life-making. I was a young woman who failed plan A and never had a backup. I was an explosive mixture of fury and doubt, self-loathing and high hope. I still went to the mailbox every day hoping for a letter from the convent that said, *"We made a terrible mistake. Come back now."*

Of course, it never came. They made no mistake. But I couldn't get myself right with it. I started drinking more—Coors beer and lots of it.

I smoked dope, hash, cocaine, anything I could get my hands on to get into another reality.

I shot pool in a local bar, the Captain's Table, nearly every night. I won a lot, drank a lot, got home drunk, but always made it to work. I was a blue-collar kid in a white-collar job. Always there on time. Always presentable. Always pretending.

On my 21st birthday I rode my bicycle to the bar and spent the night celebrating. I stayed until closing, then staggered out to my bike and started home, riding along the oceanfront, listening to the surf pound the shore. I saw an abandoned bike lying in the sand and, because I knew someone who needed a bike, I picked it up and kept on going, pedaling mine and steering the other one with my left hand.

Everything was fine until I hit a curb and crashed to the ground, just as two policemen were driving by. I failed every sobriety test they gave me. Slurred my words. Couldn't stand on one leg. Couldn't walk a straight line. I was carted off to the Santa Ana Women's Jail in the back of their cruiser. It was a half-hour ride and the whole time I pressed my face against the grate trying to convince them I was a good citizen— used to be a nun, wanted to go to law school, interested in social justice and community action.

My mug shot looked as if my face had been in a waffle maker, with lines from the grate crisscrossing my nose. I'd broken my thumb when I fell on the curb, and it was beginning to throb. After the mug shots and booking, a guard locked me in a cell with four other women, there for offenses worse than mine. We raised a ruckus, shaking the bars, calling out for justice—all of us, just wanting to get out of there and back to our lives. A guard showed up, called me the ringleader, put me in handcuffs, and walked me down to solitary confinement.

My worst nightmare. Locked in a room with no way to get out. I pounded on the steel door until I wore myself out. No one came. I was freezing cold with a broken thumb, sobering up to a frightening reality. As my mom would say, "You made this bed. Now it's time to sleep in it."

I sat in that cell shivering and destitute until the door finally opened sometime around 6 a.m.

I'd made this bed. I'd gone down the rabbit hole all by myself. No one to stop me. This girl with so much promise, so much hope. No hero to save me. No superpower to save myself. What in the hell was I trying to prove?

I'd lost Rosie. I hated my job where I pretended to be straight because I was too full of fear to name who I was. I missed my family, the willows and maples, the cumulus clouds in the summer sky. I would not commit to a single thing—not a person or pet, not a place or a religion, because I had learned by then it never pays off. Twenty-one years old with a head of steam and a mind closed like a steel trap.

How in the world did it come to this? All I ever wanted was to be a light. And here I was locked in a cave of darkness.

Chapter 11
A Love Affair in Five Parts

I tell you this because I struggled with commitment for years.

I thought of it as a noose, a ball and chain. "What if something better comes along … I need my freedom … I can't be tied down."

As I reflect on it now, I see that I was afraid of committing to something that could go up in flames, disintegrate before my eyes, just as my life had after the convent. I lived on illusions well into my 40s, running away from anything I couldn't control (itself an illusion: this sense of having control).

This story is really about what we stand to lose when we fail to commit. Or more specifically, what I lost because I feared commitment. It is painted here in vivid colors and broad strokes, so you can't miss it.

The question is not, "What is worthy of your commitment?"

The question may be, "What makes you afraid to commit?"

It was too late for me when I figured out that answer. Hopefully, it will not be too late for you.

★★★★

—Syracuse, New York, 1971

I moved back to Syracuse with the hope of a getting hired as a community worker in a federally funded inner-city project. It was 1971. Nixon was president, though I barely noticed. My antennae for politics had not budded yet. I was still trying to figure out how to make a life.

The inner-city project was called PEACE, Inc., which stood for People's Equal Action and Community Effort. They were hiring for the summer and my friend Nancy said I'd be sure to get a job if I lived with her on Seymour Street, in one of the poorest, crime-ridden neighborhoods in the city. You had to live in the community you wanted to serve.

I jumped at the chance, interviewed, got the job, and for the first time since leaving the convent I felt some meaning attached to what I was doing. It wasn't long before I drove to Albany one weekend to visit Sister Robert Joseph, my high school English teacher, the one who tried to talk me out of becoming a nun. She was now teaching English literature at The College of Saint Rose in Albany, New York.

I hadn't seen her in two years, since a dreadful day in Syracuse right after my dismissal. As my sponsor, she'd received the news by phone that I was being sent home. It was June 6, 1969. When she got the call, she had just finished her master's program at the University of Chicago and her graduation was the next day. The news about me shocked her and she knew I'd be a wreck because of it, so she skipped her graduation and boarded a Greyhound bus headed to Syracuse.

I borrowed my father's car and picked her up at the bus station. I had only been home two days and was still in shock. We had no relationship to speak of, except that unspoken love she had for me as a teen and the total adoration I'd always felt for her. It had not been cemented by time together, casual letters, exchange of ideas, or gifts or poems. I hadn't seen her at all during my novitiate because she was so far away. Her role as sponsor evaporated in the distance between us, but something real remained—something buried and unspoken.

When she walked down the bus steps, she threw her arms around me. I was frozen and stiff, so broken I could barely speak to her.

"Let's go to a restaurant," she said. "Anyplace. Someplace cheap."

We got in the car and I stopped at the first one we came to—Valle's on Erie Boulevard, a family restaurant. We were some kind of family.

The waitress came and went. Food arrived. We both poked at our meal, but neither of us ate a thing. She asked questions, but I could barely answer in full sentences—traumatized by the shock, the suddenness—in disbelief, still, that it wouldn't be undone.

"Did they tell you why?" I asked her.

"Not exactly, something about relationships. Yeah, that was it. They always thought I got too close to people. Carnal, they called it."

I poked at the meat loaf and rich brown gravy.

She had known all those years before what would happen to me. She tried so hard to discourage me from entering, but I was resolute. I had a flash of us in the classroom, me standing by her desk when I was 17, pleading with her to be my sponsor.

"You're too big for them, Jan. You're too alive, too original. It'll never work."

I didn't know what she was talking about then. It was my only plan. It was all I ever wanted. It was safe. Sacred. No men.

She knew from experience what she was talking about, as she never fit in herself, in religious community. She was an outcast in every convent she lived in because she lived so large, said what she thought, breathed in Brontë, breathed out Brahms. She'd metabolized the classics in literature, music, poetry, and though it was only love for the arts she ever exuded, people afraid of passion in general would shake in their shoes at her commanding presence.

She stood out like a redwood in a Christmas tree farm.

"I tried to warn you," she said, stirring her coffee. "I'm so sorry I failed.

"You were always so independent. Your mind was always your own. They wouldn't let it stay that way. I knew you couldn't—or wouldn't—conform, and that's what I love about you, but that, too, is why this happened."

Her words were meant to lift me up, but the stark truth of them knocked me down. She wanted me to face the obvious, accept that I wasn't cut out for a vow of obedience, admit that it all made sense, despite the depth of my sorrow. I wanted her to make it go away, to change their minds, get me back in.

She had come all this way, skipped her graduation, spent all her money for a 16-hour bus ride to help me through this, but I was not responding.

"Why would they *do* this to me?" I asked, my voice a minor chord wailing. "If they really knew me, they never would have thrown me out."

I lived with everything on the outside. My love, my intentions, my passions—they were all transparent. My goodness *had* to have shown through. I couldn't believe they wouldn't have seen it.

"I went in there to save lives, like Helen Charles saved mine. She knew I was an outcast and whatever she did to turn me around kept me from killing myself. That's the kind of nun I was going to be. Now what?"

She stared into my eyes, nodding her head. I lashed out, angry and relentless. She sat in silence, absorbing my pain, honoring it in her own way.

I was inconsolable. I had lost my life. I was grieving my own death. Sister Robert Joseph agonized with me that day, but whatever love she sent my way failed to penetrate the walls I had built. By the time she'd disembarked from that dusty Greyhound, every entranceway into my heart was locked from the inside.

A couple of hours passed before we got up from the family-size booth, left our cups of cold coffee behind, and returned to the bus station three blocks away. We hugged hard, searching each other's eyes for what wasn't said, but the chasm between us could not be bridged. She boarded the bus bound for Albany, waving goodbye through a dirt-streaked window.

II.

Two years had passed since that grueling encounter at Valle's Restaurant and I was on my way to see her, eager to reconnect, eager to show her how far I'd come, that I'd gotten past my sorrow and was now doing something I felt called to do. It had taken time, but the crushing grief eventually subsided, and a phoenix had risen after all.

I pulled up in front of her Western Avenue house in my tan Chevy Nova. She lived in a third-floor attic apartment in a dorm for the nuns, right on the campus of The College of Saint Rose. When I arrived, she was waiting on the porch, reading a novel by Anthony Trollope.

"I always have a Trollope book going," she said as I bounded up the stairs, so happy to see her. We hugged and sat down in the wicker porch chairs. "I adore his mind!" she proclaimed, sounding like she did when she taught us English only five years before. "And by the way, call me Margaret—time to get over this Robert Joseph stuff."

Margaret Lalor was her given name and she appreciated Trollope's brilliance because she was brilliant herself. Though she grew up in the small factory town of Glens Falls, New York, the second of six children in an Irish family, both her parents had vast imaginations and traveled the world inside their heads. Every week, her father completed the Sunday *New York Times* crossword puzzle in pencil, then spent hours checking every answer in dictionaries and encyclopedias. Once he confirmed the accuracy of each, he returned to the puzzle to redo his answers in ink.

Her mother, a quintessential socialite, left town regularly for beauty pageants in Atlantic City, with suitcases full of outfits and little regard for the lineup of needy kids at home.

As a teen, Margaret took voice lessons with her sisters Marianne and Jane. They all read voraciously, loved poetry, and appreciated classical music in every form. When she was a high school senior, her younger sister Carol ran away from home, causing a scandal that was covered by the local newspapers. So when Margaret attempted to enter the convent—more because she was inspired by a nun than because of a religious disposition (just like me)—she was not accepted in the Albany province and had to complete her novitiate in St. Louis, Missouri.

I learned all these things because Margaret and I fell in love that weekend and spent the time unfolding our pasts, beginning a future that would chisel me into the woman I was born to be.

We lived two hours away from each other and both had jobs we loved, so we commuted every weekend to see each other. We had no name for what we were experiencing, other than love. Though still a nun, she no longer wore a habit or veil. In the streets we looked like two close friends, though she was taller, heavier, and 16 years my senior. I was 22. She was 38.

Her brother Michael lived in Albany, a few blocks away, and we visited him every weekend I was in town. He was an out gay man, the first I'd ever known. Shortly after we began our relationship, Michael invited us to Albany's Gay Pride Weekend, which included a rally in

Washington Park and a demonstration for gay rights on the steps of the Capitol building. Feminist/activist Kate Millett, most famous for her book *Sexual Politics*, was the main attraction. Three thousand gay people squeezed together to let the world know, "We're here and we're queer!" and to take in the messages of the poets, singers, and speakers who stood on the stage, giving voice to our hopes.

I was spellbound. "Margaret, look at them all!" I must have said a dozen times. "I can't believe this is happening!" My imagination had been so warped by homophobia that an unfolding like this felt like a miracle—so many thousands of us, out, proud, unafraid. It didn't matter that when this weekend was finished, some of us would return to lives of fear, go back to our communities and remain in the closet. The world was still against who we were at our core, and we weren't any safer in our towns and cities than we were before the rally, but our numbers mattered. Seeing so many daring to stand up, daring to say, "Silent No More, We're Here and We're Queer," was all I needed to claim who I was, to give it a name, and to create a life with that fact at its center. From that point, nobody had the power to keep me silent.

When we returned that night to Michael's apartment, he and a group of his friends provided the backstory for what we'd just experienced. Michael had been present at the Stonewall Inn on the night it became an epicenter for gay pride and political action. Because the New York State Liquor Authority penalized bars that served homosexuals, the Stonewall was operating without a license the night police raided it and started harassing patrons. "Harassment by police was nothing new to the customers at the Stonewall, but when it happened on June 28 in 1969, something shifted in the gay zeitgeist," said Michael.

After arresting 13 people, an officer hit a drag queen over the head as he forced her into the paddy wagon, and she shouted to the crowd to do something.

"When that queen shouted for us to *do something*, she probably had no idea she was starting a riot," said Michael. "People threw everything they could get their hands on at the cops—coins, bottles, stones. Trash cans up and down the street were set on fire and hundreds of people revolted in the streets.

"It took the Fire Department and a riot squad to disperse the crowd, and by the next night, Gay Power graffiti appeared everywhere along

Christopher Street. All night long you could hear people shouting out, *"Gay Power, Gay Pride."*

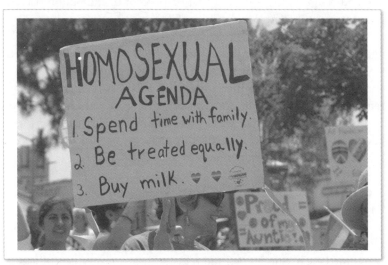

Photo by Jan Phillips.

For days after, protests continued around the Stonewall, sometimes involving thousands of people, and these uprisings galvanized the community and led to the Pride movement we were celebrating that weekend.

Though I had been gay all my life, I'd never had a moment of pride about it. I'd kept it secret, denying it even to myself. The church called it disordered and definitely sinful; the American Psychiatric Association called it a mental illness. In January 1966, *Time* magazine ran an article that referred to homosexual subculture as "a pathetic little second-rate substitute for reality, a pitiable flight from life ... It deserves no encouragement, no glamorization, no rationalization, no fake status as minority martyrdom, no sophistry about simple differences in taste—and above all, no pretense that it is anything but a pernicious sickness."

At the peak of my puberty, when I was most in need of support, when feelings for girls were surfacing that I had no idea how to handle, I didn't know where to turn. Four months after I left the convent, another *Time* article reported that America's 12 million homosexuals were one of the nation's most despised and harassed minority groups, "looked upon with disgust, discomfort or fear by two out of three people, with one out of 10 regarding us with outright hatred." A Louis Harris poll released about the same time reported that 63 percent of the nation considered homosexuals "harmful to American life."

As a young woman who had not yet learned how to defend myself against cultural assaults, these attitudes and writings had silenced me. Coming out was a dangerous act, but this Pride weekend in Albany changed my life. I had discovered my tribe—a community that had reached its tipping point and was not going to collude anymore in a culture of injustice. Now I was awake to a new reality, and now I would take my place in line, to speak out, act out, act up when necessary, hoping to make whatever change I could.

III.

Margaret left the convent after 20 years of religious life. We moved to California to start a new life, renting an apartment on the ocean in Newport Beach. She helped me register at a community college, and I began my journey toward a college degree. There were no jobs available in the teaching profession, so she went to work in a factory making dolls. I had some housecleaning jobs, but we weren't making enough to pay the bills, so we took a night job cleaning bars together, 2-6 a.m., then breakfast and sleep.

Knowing what a gifted teacher Margaret was, it was terrible watching her head out to a factory job every day. Terrible that we cleaned toilets in bars in the middle of the night. Terrible that we never had enough for anything other than bare essentials, and sometimes not even that. As poor as we were, we were never unhappy. We had the beach, I was finally in college, we were in love with life, in love with each other, and nothing came up that brought us down—at least for a while.

When summer came and school was out, we thought again. Were we okay with factory jobs and menial work? Was it enough that we fell asleep to the sound of the surf? Enough that we had perfect weather, blue skies, the Pacific at our door? What did we hunger for? Was anything missing? We were free to go and do anything we wanted, but what was it?

We were ready for work that mattered, that served the people. It's what we were cut out for, what we trained for and longed for. Like the lines of Marge Piercy's poem "To be of use" that Margaret had cut out and posted on our refrigerator.

> I want to be with people who submerge
> in the task, who go into the fields to harvest
> and work in a row and pass the bags along,
> who are not parlor generals and field deserters
> but move in a common rhythm
> when the food must come in or the fire be put out.

We wanted to be with people *submerged in the task*. That was it. But where should we go to be part of a community that needed what we had to give? We decided to go to Appalachia and see if our skills matched up with the needs of a community.

We saved our money, bought an old VW bus, and headed East, making it as far as Pennsylvania before the transmission went out in Easton. Luckily we were only miles from where Margaret's sister Jane lived—a single mom with five school-age kids at home. There wasn't much room for two more adults, but the estimate for fixing our van was $800, and our options were limited. We moved in and looked for work. By the next day, Margaret, Jane, and I were gainfully employed at the Lifetime Doors Factory not far from Jane's house.

It was grueling work every day from 7 a.m. to 3 p.m., gluing veneers onto every kind of door, cutting holes for locks and handles, hammering, stapling, hour after hour, faster and faster, with foremen checking your work and your time. After two weeks, we got a call from Bonnie in Syracuse, my best friend from school and Margaret's former student. She'd had a vision, or so she said. "I'm going to Europe. I saw it plain as day. I'm leaving in two months, as soon as I get $800 together. Want to come and meet me?"

It seemed a far-fetched idea to me, but I called out to Margaret who was sitting at the kitchen table, her blue denim jeans dotted with glue.

"Hey Margaret, Bonnie's going to Europe. She wants to know if we want to meet up with her."

"Tell her yes!" Margaret answered without hesitation, and I did, and three months later we were on our way to England with brand-new passports, one-way tickets, and $800 worth of traveler's checks to last forever.

Margaret had taken a class of English literature students to England and France, so she already knew how to negotiate a city. When we arrived, Bonnie was staying in the farmhouse of some new beau in Devizes, so Margaret shepherded me around London. We got the least expensive, highest balcony seats known to man, but we watched *Swan Lake* at the Royal Opera House, *Jesus Christ Superstar* at the London Palladium, and spent days visiting exhibitions at the Tate, National Gallery, the British Museum. Margaret cultured me with delight, as I was a newcomer to all things artistic. She mentored me in the arts, in theater and ballet, in poetry and literature—just by how she *was* with me. Her love of the arts was contagious and I caught it like the flu. I would never be the same and would always be enchanted by the works of great creators.

Margaret (left) and me on a hilltop in France. (Photo by Bonnie Boezeman.)

On December 31, 1972, we crossed the North Sea on a ferry to the Hook of Holland and made our way up to Amsterdam by train. Bonnie had joined up with us by now. She had her guitar and we brought it out often on a crowded street, singing songs by Bob Dylan and Joan Baez; Simon & Garfunkel; Peter, Paul and Mary, collecting guilders for beer and *bitterballen*, a deep-fried snack.

Our Bible was Frommer's *Europe on Five Dollars a Day* and one night we read about a pub we had to visit. It was owned by the former pianist of the renowned Dutch orchestra, the Concertgebouw, which Margaret had a poster of in our Newport Beach apartment. She knew everything about them, so we headed out one night to visit the pub, which was set up with a grand piano and hundreds of tapes of orchestral pieces with the piano track extracted. The bar owner/pianist, who had a mass of white hair and a handsome square jaw, accompanied the pieces, playing live on his Steinway.

We ordered some aquavit from the bartender and sat at a table near the piano. It was a weeknight and business was slow, so the owner came over and talked with us. He and Margaret got into a big discussion about music, which was way over my head and Bonnie's, so we kept downing aquavits and looking through *Frommer's* for other places to explore.

A few minutes after he went back to the piano, the pianist motioned to Margaret to join him. We were so busy we didn't even notice she left. It wasn't until we heard her singing that we realized what was going on. Margaret had asked whether he had the music for an aria she'd learned in high school. He did and what we heard was Margaret, in a voice as dramatic and powerful as Maria Callas's, singing "Softly Awakes My Heart" from the Saint-Saëns opera *Samson and Delilah*.

She stood next to the piano, eyes closed, hands folded at her waist, her face turned up in a sweet smile as the most unbearably beautiful notes left her lips. I had never heard Margaret sing like this before. I knew she told me she sang opera in high school but I couldn't connect, hardly heard it, had no room for it. But now, right here in that room, in that moment, it was too much beauty for me to even hold. It broke my heart open. I started to cry. I laid my head in my arms and sobbed, half for the sheer beauty of her amazing voice, half in shame that I'd not listened well enough to know the gift this woman was.

IV.

Our lives took different directions after a few years because of my fear of commitment. I wanted more than she could give me, stubbornly insisted on having it all: other relationships, secret affairs. I wanted to taste every wine on the shelf. She was as true blue as a summer sky and

I still blamed the past for its avalanche of sorrows, the reason I provided for my aberrant behavior. I was a tempest of emotion still, having only half-resolved my rage and shame. Margaret never asked for anything but honesty, and by the end, I was barely giving that.

After a tumultuous year of trying to separate, we finally accomplished the terrible feat. She got an apartment near her family homestead in Glens Falls, New York, and went through a variety of jobs as we evolved into the beings we strove to be. She finally found a job teaching English at a community college, and when that ended, she served as a docent in the Hyde Museum, worked as a ticket-taker in the Old Park Theater, and worked in admissions at the Glens Falls Hospital.

We wrote letters often, spoke on the phone, and I visited from the West Coast whenever I could. No matter where I lived or with whom I was living, we sent packages of poetry books, novels, CDs, and DVDs back and forth to each other from 1975 to 2018. She wrote once a week—keeper of the fire—notes usually written around *New Yorker* cartoons she'd copied onto a piece of paper in the library. Last was a Ted Kooser poem, "After Years," which she inscribed in the front of a small notebook. She sent me dozens of notebooks throughout the years so I'd always have something to write in. The poems she sent were secret code for how she was feeling. The Kooser poem left me reeling. It arrived in 2010.

> Today, from a distance, I saw you
> walking away, and without a sound
> the glittering face of a glacier
> slid into the sea. An ancient oak
> fell in the Cumberlands, holding only
> a handful of leaves, and an old woman
> scattering corn to her chickens looked up
> for an instant. At the other side
> of the galaxy, a star thirty-five times
> the size of our own sun exploded
> and vanished, leaving a small green spot
> on the astronomer's retina
> as he stood on the great open dome
> of my heart with no one to tell.
>
> *(printed with permission from Ted Kooser)*

I called her up right away.

"Oh my God, the Kooser poem. Are you okay?"

"Oh, Jan, was it my fault that we never made it? I try to figure it out but I can't make any sense of it."

We had lived together and traveled together for four years. We'd hitchhiked through Europe together, crossed the country in a VW van together. We worked together in factories and bars under intolerable circumstances, and we loved every minute we were together. But I was an unreliable partner. Just too young and immature. I ran away from commitment every chance I got close to it, afraid that I'd be rejected again, and my whole world would fall apart.

"No, it was never you," I said. "It was my fear that got in the way. Nothing logical. Nothing that makes any sense. I needed to be the one to get away before things blew apart."

"Did I do something wrong that you didn't tell me about?"

"No, never. I just wanted everything, so I'd always have *something* when the rug got pulled out from under me. I hadn't healed yet from the convent. I was a toddler emotionally. I'm so sorry I didn't stay, but it was never you."

"All right then, I feel better."

For 40 years we were full of love for the life in each other. She never got involved in another relationship, although I went on to one after another, until I finally let go of the past and focused on creating my life day by day—an act, I learned, that called for plenty of commitment.

In one of her last letters to me, which she always composed while listening to classical music on public radio, she wrote that "the requiems are part of my being now. They live in my cells. I have listened to them so many times—especially Mozart and Brahms—their notes have become me. We are one and the same."

When I visited on her 84th birthday, I asked to hear the story of her march to Montgomery. She was 32 when she left our homeroom class at St. Anthony's school to fly to Alabama. It was in March 1965 when Rev. Dr. Martin Luther King Jr. called for religious leaders to join him on his march from Selma to Montgomery.

When I sat to hear it at Steve's Diner in Glens Falls, I was 68. Her memory of it was as vivid as if it had happened yesterday.

"Sister Columbine wasn't at all in favor of me going, but Monsignor

Tom Costello knew I'd been working with Congress of Racial Equality (CORE), and he called Columbine to tell her he'd bought my airline ticket. There was no arguing with him."

"Did anyone go with you?"

"There were nine priests, a Franciscan sister, Sister John Joseph, and some other folks from our CORE group."

"How did you know where to go?"

"People showed up to take us to the march. It was on Highway 80. There were hundreds of onlookers lining the highway, screaming for the marchers to go back home. It was frightening to even be there. Four men from the Ku Klux Klan had just murdered Viola Liuzzo for having a young Black kid in her car. From what I heard, she was just driving him back to Selma."

"Did you feel threatened?"

"I was so afraid, I just wanted to get out of there, but we kept marching. The police were everywhere and they were eager to arrest us."

"Did any of them come up to you?"

"No, I think it helped that I was in a full habit. But the march was so tiring. I was exhausted by the afternoon. I'd have to sit on the curb every once in a while just to take a break."

"What do you remember most?"

"There was no feeling alone on that march. We moved like one people, one organism. But we knew we weren't safe. Anything could have happened to us."

"Were the cops everywhere?"

"Yes, but it wasn't just cops. The National Guard was there. Military Police were everywhere. Even in the airport, when the march was finished, the police harassed us. I went to a Coke machine to buy a Coke I was so thirsty, but a man put his hand over the slot, saying the machine was broken. Everyone just wanted us to go home. That was clear as a bell."

"Did you have to wait long in the airport?"

"It seemed like hours, but I think something changed for all of us. We had crossed a line and we'd never be the same. Now we knew what it felt like to put our bodies on the line, to turn the other cheek."

"But you were still afraid, right?"

"I was deathly afraid and huddled in a corner when an amazing thing happened. Coretta Scott King came over and took my hand. She walked me over to Martin Luther King standing with a group of men."

"Martin, disperse your men and make room for this Sister. She wants to meet you," said Coretta to her husband.

"Dr. King took my hands and asked me one thing: 'Where have you Catholics been?'"

"What did you say to him?"

"I said 'When you called this time, we came— and we'll come again,' and then it was time to board the plane."

"What happened when you got back to Syracuse?"

"Sister Columbine (the principal) told me not to say a word about it to the students."

"I remember, you didn't even mention it. We were dying to hear."

"I wanted to tell you kids all about it but couldn't. There was nowhere I could go with the hugeness of it all. That was one of the saddest things. Not one sister in the house asked me a thing about it. A few of them actually scorned me with their looks."

I flashed back then to that day in our homeroom when I told her I wanted to be a nun. Her negative response was so fierce, so protective. "They'll try to break you. You're too independent, too strong-willed. It's not right for you."

This was a warning about the dangers of community living based on her own experience as an iconoclast. She was treated like an outcast in her convent of 25 sisters and she would do or say anything to protect me from that kind of rejection. I now understood what I couldn't have understood as a 17-year-old.

After the march, some parishioners started calling her Sister Selma, mocking her for standing up in the way she did. Several of the nuns in the convent continued to shun her. No praise arrived from any direction. No curiosity. No inquiry.

"I kept up my relationships with people in the Black community," she said. "We met weekly to keep our spirits alive, to keep the work alive. That's where I got my sustenance."

Margaret went on to teach at St. Mary's in Amsterdam, New York, where she became notorious for circling between the convent and the church on her lunch hour, carrying an anti-Vietnam war poster. The mockery continued, only this time from students who threw items from their lunch at her in protest of her protest.

After being hired as English literature professor at the The College of Saint Rose, she continued to speak out against the war in Vietnam. Margaret had been 16 when the Nuremberg trials ended. She was aware of what atrocities occur when people do nothing and keep silent about what they see. She published an ad with a group of protesters in the *New York Times* on September 4, 1969, called "Individuals Against the Crime of Silence." It reminded readers of the history of Nuremberg—that even though men who committed crimes against humanity by following orders from their government were tried, convicted, and executed, thousands more got away who were guilty of the crime of silence.

Margaret, along with Fathers Daniel and Philip Berrigan, Thomas Merton, and countless other activists claimed in the ad that the war in Vietnam was immoral and that people of conscience were obliged to voice their opposition. Anything short of that could be considered a crime of silence, tacit approval to another human atrocity.

After our conversation, I wrote a *Huffington Post* piece about how Margaret's choice to march changed *my* life. How she passed the torch to me, instilled in me the confidence to stand up and stand out. I had followed in the footsteps of a modern-day prophet, a woman who called out injustice when she saw it, who bore the brunt of critics who ridiculed her and went on with her work no matter the consequences.

As a teacher, Margaret stood in our midst and showed us how to think and act from a moral core. She was not religious. She neither prayed nor encouraged us to. She did not suggest we do anything for Jesus but acted *herself* as he might have acted—speaking truth to power, speaking out against war, speaking up for the poor. I am who I am today because Margaret Lalor's love for life, for justice and peace, flowed through the canyons and crevices of my being. I learned how to think by watching her live. I learned how to live by diving into the lake of her and coming up for breath madly in love. For 50 years she taught me how to act in spite of fear, and my essay needed to reveal her power and carry her spirit between the lines.

When the piece was written, I googled "nuns in Selma" hoping to find an image I could include with the story. I scanned through dozens, some of which I'd seen in print decades ago when the story was live.

I'd settled on a photo but for some unknown reason, I decided to click through a few more. That's when it happened. A miracle. I could hardly believe my eyes.

A photo of *her* on the curb, resting, her in her habit, Sister Robert Joseph, afraid and exhausted, an icon for justice, the light in my life.

Sister Robert Joseph, CSJ from Syracuse, New York. In Montgomery, Alabama, after completing the march from Selma, March 1965. © Spider Martin. Printed with permission.

V.

Margaret died alone, because that's how she wanted it. Her last words to me, written on a postcard, undoubtedly dictated to one of her nurses, as it wasn't her handwriting: "Dear Jan, Don't feel that you must come. You know I love to be alone. I'm not afraid. Love, Your Margaret."

Her obituary read as follows:

> GLENS FALLS — Margaret Lalor, 85, died Monday, March 26, 2018 at the Granville Center for Rehabilitation and Nursing after a short illness. Born in Glens Falls on Sept. 2, 1932, she was the daughter of Robert Emmet Lalor and Myrtle J. Lalor.

No mention of the ripples of her life that still spread like tributaries across the prairies and grasslands, through the forests and mountains, in the cities and towns that we, her students and protégés, are populating. No mention of her impact as prophet, poet, teacher. No words from the hundreds of us whose lives were set on fire by the flame that she was. No mention of her 20 years of service to the Sisters of Saint Joseph of Carondelet. No mention of the marches, the rallies, the demonstrations she took part in—or of the mockery and abuse she withstood every time she held up her sign for peace, justice, gay rights, or voting rights for Black citizens.

Had I not been 3,000 miles away, had she not written to say she wanted to die alone, I would have been at her deathbed and proclaimed the sacrament of her holy passing with others around. We would have gathered in a circle, called out her name and her holy works. We would have sung to high heaven, giving praise and thanks for the way she breathed life into the world. But as it was, I was home alone when her sister called. "It's over now. She's gone."

She might be gone, but it will never be over. Like the requiems she'd become one with, I have metabolized her. She is in me like my cells, my blood, the marrow of my bones. And that within-ness is infinite, beyond time, beyond space. It is That Which Is. It did not come and it will not go.

For Margaret on the Day of Her Death
(after Emily Dickinson)

Because she could not stop for death
He kindly stopped for her—
She chose to face the night alone
and Night Itself concurred.

She spent her fuel on others' lights
when dimly did they glow—
She spoke out for the voiceless
standing up to every foe.

Her calling was to be a Force
that matched the Wind and Tide—
Her intellect and Love combined
to bridge the Great Divide.

She woke me up to Life itself
we fused, like yang and yin—
our souls will dance forever 'round
the Fire that burns within.

Some bonds they are Invisible
some threads cannot be seen—
like Magic she stills dwells in me
like salt dwells in the Sea.

Chapter 12
Yvonne's Wedding

I tell you this because my shame about it has kept me silent for long enough.

Events like these happen to women around the globe. We know how powerless we are, and we say nothing, for it will go nowhere.

No one will care, *says the voice in our head.* It will not matter. *Fewer than 40 percent of us ever mention the violence perpetrated against us, although 243 million women and girls have been physically or sexually assaulted in the last 12 months, according to a report by UN Women.*

It is an epidemic of its own, and so many of us are under attack. Now is a good time for speaking.

May these words wash away my shame.

★★★★

—Carthage, New York, 1973

It was a hot summer day in northern New York. Billie Jean King was preparing to trounce Bobby Riggs in the "The Battle of the Sexes" exhibition tennis match, Vice President Spiro Agnew would soon resign for bribery and tax evasion charges, the Vietnam War was drawing to a close, and the presence of the Watergate tapes was about to be revealed.

The temperature was rising toward 90 degrees in the small hamlet of Carthage, New York, and my cousin Yvonne, eighth of 65 grandchildren, was stepping into her mother's satin wedding dress. It was August 11, 1973, and I was 24 years old.

Close to a hundred people showed up at the farm, the family homestead, to celebrate the event. As usual, most of them were relatives. While a thunderstorm roused everyone in the early morning hours, the puddles soon evaporated and cumulus cottony clouds dotted the azure sky.

After the wedding, out came the fiddles, guitars, mandolins, and harmonicas. Out came the whiskey, the rum, the wines, and the beers—Schaefer, Schlitz, and Molson Canadian. Alcohol flowed like a river in spring and anyone old enough to want it lined up and got it. While Yvonne was kidnapped by her four younger brothers and whisked off to a bar to drink champagne from her shoe—a family tradition that all "good brides" went along with—several of us piled into my cousin's '67 Chevy and headed to Kings Falls, a local waterfall with a swimming hole and shale rock beach. It was a mile walk down a dirt path through a dense forest and was every teen's go-to place for unsupervised fun.

We loaded six-packs of beer into the cavernous car trunk, threw in some towels, and headed to our haven, dressed in our wedding clothes and already high. By the time we arrived, there were others in the swimming hole, skinny-dipping, drunk, and happy to see us.

We threw off our clothes and jumped in en masse. The others who were already there joined in and we spent an hour telling jokes and drinking beer. A young man I didn't know made his way over to me and put his arm around my waist. We were in water up to our necks and no one could see what anyone was doing. I let him touch my breasts but said no to any other probing. He was annoyed, but it didn't matter because by then we were out of beer and ready to go back to the music and the food.

We returned to the farm and everyone headed for the buffet table, blending right back into the party scene. Then there was more music, talking, or playing horseshoes in the back. It wasn't for a few hours that I noticed the guy from the Falls was at the party. He must have been a friend of one of my cousins because people there seemed to know him.

He approached me and said in a hushed voice that he wanted to "finish what he started."

"Nothing got started as far as I'm concerned," I said.

"You can't just let a guy do that and not follow through," he said, agitated at my resistance.

"I can do whatever I want," I said, leaving the room. I picked up a guitar and joined the musicians in our family favorites: "You Are My Sunshine," "Redwing," "Country Roads." We sang and played for hours, drinking as we played and loving every minute.

My mom and dad assumed their usual positions. My dad sat off in a quiet corner reading a newspaper or talking to one of his quieter in-laws, while my mother played fiddle and partied with her brothers and sisters. She was the second oldest of 14 children and my Dad was one of three. He was never comfortable in a rowdy crowd and my Mom wanted to play until the roosters crowed. This night was no different.

When the party calmed down, a few of my mom's siblings drove to town to find a dance hall. She went with them and they didn't return until 2 a.m. By that time, my father was a furnace of rage. He was jealous, sure that someone would take advantage of his wife. While he was famous for his mild-mannered demeanor, that night he did the unspeakable. Rather than wait, he got in his car and drove home from the farm alone. Left my mother high and dry. Unheard of, in my family where voices were rarely raised and arguments were quickly resolved.

In the meantime, I had fallen asleep fully clothed on a couch in the arena-size living room. This was a farmhouse built to accommodate a family with 14 kids and hired hands. Every room was the size of a small ballroom. The dining room easily held 16 for dinner. A few cooks could work side by side in the kitchen. Three couches barely made a dent in the living room, so five or six comfortable chairs filled in the space. The plush green carpet was thick enough to sleep on. I was only one of a dozen tired partygoers who crashed in that room that night, and I was neither the first nor the last to collapse.

In the middle of the night, I felt a body on top of me, hands grabbing at my skirt and pulling it up. I tried to get up but didn't have the strength. I tried to speak and a hand covered my mouth.

"Just shut up and don't move!" I heard him say.

I was not sober enough to have all my senses. It was completely dark and I couldn't make out a face. When he entered me, I felt a stabbing pain. I didn't scream out. I didn't move. And when it was over, I lay there silent until I fell asleep.

A few hours later, my mother woke me up in a state of alarm, shaking my arm.

"Your father's gone! He's taken the car and gone home. Come on, get up! I need you to drive me home."

When I sat up on the couch, my body throbbed. I looked around the room. Sleeping bodies covered the carpet. It could have been any of them.

I hobbled into the bathroom and sat down. That's when I noticed the blood. All over my skirt, my slip, my underpants. It hurt to pee. It hurt to walk. It hurt even more to feel that I had caused it. I had let that guy feel my breasts. I had gotten drunk. I had disobeyed the main rule for women: "Take responsibility for the situation because men can't control themselves." That was the only sex talk my mother ever gave me because I was the big know-it-all who said I didn't need it.

I'll never forget it, out on the front porch at 113 West Pleasant. I must have been 12. "Now those boys can't control themselves. It's going to be up to you. You're the one who has to say *no*." She talked as if their penises were sleeping snakes that became dangerous upon awakening. I knew even then that I wasn't going to have to worry about it because I never liked boys anyway. Why should I care if they can't control themselves? I didn't want anything to do with them.

I told my mother when I came out of the bathroom that I had been raped. I was a 24-year-old virgin who was violated and bleeding, but she was too upset to hear me. She had her own crisis to deal with.

"I can't believe your father did this," she kept saying. "He's so angry—he's never done anything like this before. I never should have gone dancing. I know how jealous he gets."

"Mom, did you hear me? I was raped, right there on the couch. I have blood all over me." It was as if she were deaf.

"I don't know what I'm going to do. He's never been this mad," she said, pulling her handkerchief out of her purse.

We were migrants uprooted from two different worlds and in that early morning light, we could barely comprehend what the other was saying.

When my mother tells the story, she stopped everything to comfort me. She was horrified at what had happened, helped me into the bathroom, fetched ice and rags to blot out the blood stains. She doesn't recall the wall between us.

I loaded our bags in the car, put my Chevy Nova in gear, and headed south on the county road. For the 90-minute drive, we hardly spoke. She fretted. Cried a little. Stared out the window trying to think up what in the world she should say to my dad. I knew why I was invisible to her. I knew the tentacles of patriarchy had us both in their grip, that we had both been wounded by the imbalances of power, and that once we regained our strength, recovered from these blows, we'd be the beacons for each other we usually were.

Maybe one day, I thought, *she'd be able to grieve with me.*

But on this strange and terrible post-wedding morning, we were two strangers, two women blaming themselves for the awful deeds of the men in our lives.

Chapter 13

Freedom's Just Another Word—Tales of Coming Out

I tell you this because it's happening all around you. Queers and transgender people are an endangered species. LGBTQ teens everywhere feel unsafe and contemplate suicide at three times the rate of straight kids. Forty-two percent of LGBTQ people report living in an unwelcoming environment. LGBTQ students say their worst problem is unaccepting families.

Though it seems as if progress has been made—and we have indeed moved forward as a nation—the hatred and condemnation we still face is unbearable and needs to be exposed.

My coming out story is similar to so many. There is rarely any affirmation, support, applause for standing up, speaking out. The more one risks, the more one loses; but the more one loses, the less there is left to lose.

At one point in my coming out odyssey, I'd lost everything. And then an amazing thing happened: I lost my fear too. What more could they do to me? I became fearless. I still am. Every single loss was worth that.

I share this story with some hope that it happens to you.

★★★★

—Orange County, California, 1975

I signed up for a class called Creative Slide Productions at a community college in Southern California. It was 15 years before the invention of PowerPoint and long before computers populated college campuses. I was shooting with a Pentax K1000 camera and had just finished an eight-week adult education course in 35 mm photography at a local high school. Photography was my new addiction.

The class offered an opportunity to produce two-projector automated slideshows that could be put to music. I already knew the power of an image. Now I would get to amplify that potential by adding words, music, and different dissolves between each slide.

We watched a variety of presentations to get our juices flowing, then we learned how to use the equipment. Our assignment was to create a two-projector presentation that was coordinated to music or narration. Each carousel held 80 slides, so we had a maximum of 160 slides to work with. We had the whole semester to decide on a theme, create the images, organize the slides on light tables and program the cassette tapes with inaudible beeps that would trigger the dissolve unit to advance the projectors.

By this time, I was immersed in the women's movement and had formed a collective with four other women called LIFE. It stood for Lesbians in the Feminist Effort—a name that says something about the mindset of the times. We ran weekly consciousness-raising (CR) groups, which were attended by about 20 women each week.

Three or four topics were decided on, rooms were labeled with the different subjects, and women chose which groups they wanted to participate in. Topics ranged from economic dependence to religion, assertiveness, childbearing, feeling silenced, marriage/divorce, coming out. Every week there were four new topics to talk about.

In small groups, each woman spoke to the subject and told how it influenced her life. It was not a therapy group, so there was no interaction, no feedback, just deep listening to whomever shared. It was in these CR groups that I learned one of the biggest lessons of my life: *I was not the problem.*

All my life, whenever I failed to fit in, it felt as if it was my fault. My fault that I was gay. My fault that I was a misfit in society, couldn't find a job, was thrown out of the convent, disconnected from my church.

As we explored our relationships with church, with men, with other women, as we talked about sexuality, spirituality, money, jobs—in every area women in the circles had common experiences. In a room of eight women, each woman had a story to tell about being sexually harassed. Each lesbian had been disowned or discredited by her family when she came out. Each of us was making less money than our male coworkers. Each had felt some form of discrimination in our churches. And each of us tended to blame ourselves when we experienced rejection or loss.

None of us knew how to express anger, to assert ourselves confidently, to ask for what we wanted in our personal relationships without feeling selfish. We each had a desire to be creative, but none of us believed we had any skill in this area, though we wrote poetry, composed music, painted, and drew and sang.

All the stories I listened to challenged the legitimacy of the beliefs I'd inherited and learned. Hearing our collective stories woke me up. An alarm went off in my head. Until then, I had trust in the institutions that had shaped me—family, church, society. I had never suspected they didn't have my best interests at heart. But now a new awareness dawned on me: The silencing of women had been going on since the beginning of the patriarchy. It was still going on and our stories were revealing its shape and size.

One by one, I let go of old ideas. I began to think my *own* thoughts, trust my *own* conclusions. It wasn't just me in those circles, it was nearly *all* of us—nearly all of us being harassed on the job, being silenced, striving for independence in a culture of domination. I sat in a circle of six women one night and five spoke about being violated sexually and never speaking of it.

Those kinds of experiences change a person. Week after week we grew closer, trusted more, imagined further. We grew braver and more committed to making change. We found our voices and spoke out. We organized conferences, created a newsletter, sponsored poetry and music events. Our "personal" had become political and we felt its power in our bones.

Until this happened, I had no reason to march in the streets, write letters to the editor, come out publicly, but now, knowing the magnitude of the problem, I was forced to act.

I decided to make my class slideshow a consciousness-raising production. I chose a ballad called "Sister" by Cris Williamson, an out, activist singer/songwriter.

I spent weeks photographing everyone I knew and loved, weeks making decisions about which slides to use, where they would go, what would come before and after, making sure that the dissolves were dramatic and elegant. I aligned every image with just the right words. The photos pictured my mom, my nieces and sister, friends and relatives, lesbians and non-lesbians in a beautiful montage from gay pride parades to singing circles, women at work, in church, in each other's arms. There was nothing erotic, nothing distasteful, but women only—shoring up, supporting, loving each other.

It was a painstaking endeavor, lining up 160 slides, timing the dissolves down to the second, so that every image came in at the right time with the right words. It was my first official creation as a photographer, my first coming out to my class. When my time came, we dimmed the lights, fired up the machines, and started the program. The title slide appeared, *Woman to Woman*, and Cris's angelic voice filled the room. For the next six minutes, images of strong, beautiful women filled the screen until the last one faded to dark as the song ended.

A terrible silence filled the room. There was no eruption of applause, as there had been with the other programs. The professor turned on the light and told everyone to take a five-minute break. He called me over to say how disgusted he was and that I'd be lucky to pass the class.

"What were you trying to do with that display anyway?" he asked.

"I'm just trying to show the rest of us—*my* people, *my* community," I said.

"Nobody gave you permission to do that. You don't just go exposing everyone to your private particularities."

"It was *my* presentation. Nobody else has the power to tell me what to show or not show. If you want to give me an F, go ahead. I don't even care. I'm not here for your stupid grade."

I walked out of the classroom and when I went to join the others, a few turned away from me. Nobody said a thing. They just shunned me. I was surprised, but I wasn't ashamed. I wasn't tearful or penitent. Outraged was more the feeling. The personal *was* about to become political, and I was about to take my power as an activist. I left the group and walked over to the office of the professor who taught a class in Human Sexuality. I had taken his course and knew he brought in guest speakers to share their experiences.

His door was open, so I knocked and walked in. He greeted me and asked what he could do for me.

"I want to speak to your class," I said.

"You do, do you? What about?" he asked, tamping tobacco into a curved mahogany pipe.

"I want to talk about being a lesbian—what it feels like to be afraid of coming out, and what it feels like to be despised when you do. I want to talk about being born gay and spending a whole lifetime feeling like a pervert. And I want to talk about finding my way *out* of that."

He nodded his head as I spoke, then struck a match and fired up his pipe. After a few good draws, a sweet-smelling smoke filled the room.

"Okay, sounds good," he said, searching for the schedule on his desk.

We settled on a date a few weeks out, and I talked to the students, explaining what led me to be there that day and why I finally knew it was time for me to speak out. I didn't know then this was the beginning of my life as an activist. I only knew I wasn't going to hide anymore, and if people had trouble with who and what I was, it would be their problem, not mine. At least that was my hope.

II.

That summer, I drove back to Syracuse to visit my parents. They had not seen any of my photography and I took my entire *Woman to Woman* production to share with them. The first night, when my Mom and I were together after my father had gone to bed, I came out to her.

"I think you should know that I'm gay," I said unapologetically. I was proud, actually. I had finally separated myself from the identities others tried to give me and defined who I was for *myself*. I did not aim to please anyone, to satisfy anyone's expectations, to fit into cultural grooves that were not my shape or size. I had outgrown my trust in external authority, particularly the Church, which had been the source of my self-hatred for so many years. Finally I was free of it all and that's what I wanted my mom to understand.

For months, I had been coming out everywhere, unabashedly, and feared no consequences. The day I was shunned for my slideshow was the birthday of a new zealot. That emotional beating led to a decision that was beyond personal. I would *always* speak out, come out, act out, not just for my own sake but for the sake of all of us—the millions of us—who were hated, shunned, beaten, murdered, and mistreated because of the way we were born.

I hadn't prepared myself for the tsunami that would follow my earthquaking announcement. No matter how proud I was to report that I had finally figured out my identity, it was not good news to my mom.

"What do you mean you're gay?" she asked.

"Homosexual. Queer. Lesbian. I'm attracted to women. I sleep with women."

"I thought you told me you weren't like that."

"Mom, I took forever to figure it out. I had it all mixed up with sin and perversion, and I never felt like that so I couldn't put myself in that box. But now I know I am that, and they've just been defining the box wrong. I tried everything to be straight, but I couldn't do it. It's just not me."

"Well, I think it's just terrible," she said. "Don't you dare tell your father! He'll have a heart attack and you'll be the one responsible."

"But Mom, I'm so happy. There's millions of people like me!"

"Happiness doesn't have anything to do with this. You know what the Church says about homosexuals and you're still a Catholic. What am I supposed to tell people when they ask about you? This is disgusting."

We argued for a few minutes about my right to tell my father and were getting nowhere. I finally told her about my slideshow. She asked what kind of photos were in it and when I told her, she said she wanted to see it first, alone, down in the basement.

I carted all the equipment down to the finished basement. The familiar smell of dampness mixed with the sound of the dehumidifier, turning itself on and off according to the humidity. The pool table, the old tweedy brown couch, my mom's Adler sewing machine looking like someone had abandoned it only seconds ago. The past blew through like a summer breeze.

The floor was littered with an array of threads, bits of material, dozens of pins pointing in every direction. The ironing board was up with the iron standing at attention, ready to go. I could paint the scene from memory. Nothing ever changed in this tableau but the colors of fabric, and there was comfort in that.

I hung a sheet for a screen, set up a couple TV trays, took out my slide carousels, the projectors and dissolve unit, and cued up the music. When it was all ready, I called her down. She took a seat on the couch and I sat on her sewing chair to run the machines.

When I turned down the lights and pressed *start*, the sound of Cris Williamson's voice faded in and the photos filled the screen, dissolving in perfect timing, transitioning in the fashion of life itself—from jobsite to home to pride parade to park, from solitary figures to couples to family gatherings, Black, brown, white, gay, straight, and in between. I thought she would love it, maybe even be proud of me. I thought my *Woman to Woman* offering might bridge some gaps that were erupting between us.

Right at the end, before the credits for music, the phone rang upstairs and she sent me up to answer it. It was a short call, and before I finished, she came upstairs and went right to her bedroom. I was so eager to hear her response. I had shown up in a whole new way, as an accomplished photographer, an artist and technician, with a skill set that no one else in our family had. It was the beginning of something new for me.

I headed back down to the basement to get the show ready to share with my father the next day and was horrified at what I saw. My legs buckled. Tears shot out of my eyes as I looked at the scene. Both carousels of slides had been turned upside down and my precious photos—the ones that took hundreds of hours to arrange in the perfect order—were scattered all over the dusty basement floor. The damage, on so many levels, felt irreparable.

III.

Word traveled fast about my coming out and before long my sister informed me that she didn't want me anywhere near her two daughters, who were about 7 and 5 years old. My mother and I argued terribly about what she perceived as a "choice" I was making that was tearing our family apart. She dreaded my visits home, fearful that I would blurt out the whole story to my father and he'd keel over and die on the spot. Occasionally she'd write and try to talk me out of who I was, as in this letter where she tried everything to get me to "straighten up."

Letter from Mom

Dear Jan,

I've been praying to God about your problem, hoping for some solution that will keep our family from breaking apart. God hasn't answered my prayers, except to comfort me, reminding me that at least you're not a cripple. There's hope in this if only you'd be willing to change your ways. You're being so selfish and I don't know how to change that, though I hope you figure it out and do it pretty soon.

Your father will have a heart attack if he finds out what you're doing and that will be your fault. I'm certainly not letting him know and you better not either. If you'd stop being so self-centered and remember what you owe to your father, you would keep your silence.

As for your brother and sister, they are both offended by your hairy legs. They are embarrassed and ashamed when their neighbors come over and you are there. Why do you have to be such a non-conformist? Can't you see how selfish that is? How can you hurt their feelings like that when we are such a loving family?

I don't know what happened to you that you turned out this way. We raised you to be polite, to make people feel good when you are around—now your whole family is ashamed of you for your strange behavior.

Not shaving your legs is bad enough, but you should also be ashamed of this whole homosexual thing. God never intended that and you know it's sinful. I thought since you went into the convent that you cared about your religion, and it makes me sick that you no longer do.

Your father would disown you if he knew and we'd never get to see you again. Don't you see how selfish you're being? Your own sister is afraid to have you around her girls and it will break their hearts to not have their Aunt Jan around, but this whole mess is all your own making.

I suggest you get through this phase as fast as possible. Grow up and stop thinking so much about yourself. This is not what we taught you. You are a good girl at heart but your behavior is tearing this family apart.

Love,
Mom

IV.

It was a conundrum, wanting to share my pride and joy with my family, but feeling such resistance from my mother and sister. There was nothing I could do to change their minds about how sinful the whole thing was, so I drifted away from them, emotionally and physically. And when I let my family go, I decided to let a lot of things go. I withdrew from the mainstream culture and retreated into a women-only world. I read only women authors, listened only to women's music, I worked and played with women and I did not traffic in ideas or institutions dominated by men.

I moved to Sonoma County in 1977 with my partner Nancy and her two small children. I learned to parent. I took courses from a university without walls, studied feminism, community organizing, and institutionalized racism. I continued to participate in CR groups and worked as a counselor in a residential alternative to prison for women. Everything I learned, I learned from the stories of the women I lived, loved, and worked with.

It was from Sonoma County that I wrote a letter to the Sisters of St. Joseph asking whether they would tell me why they dismissed me. Eight years had passed but I was still struggling with it, still depressed and anxious because it was all so unresolved. I had to get on the other side of that pain.

I couldn't put my finger on it, but there seemed some correlation with that rejection and my unwillingness to commit myself to someone. It was as if I had collapsed my pain into a neat little maxim that ruled my life: *Give yourself wholly to no one and nothing, for you will be stripped of it all in the end.*

I found myself being seduced away from my relationship and hated myself for the pain I was causing, so I sought help from a therapist. It didn't take long for the convent story to surface. Now I needed to revisit that event and get some clarity. By this time, though, my novice director, Sister Elizabeth Thomas, had died so I could not appeal to her.

I wrote a letter to Sister Joan Teresa, the provincial director, explaining that I had been dismissed in 1969 but was never told exactly why. Since I couldn't seem to get past my pain about the whole thing, I asked whether she could give me the official reason for my dismissal.

A few weeks later, a letter arrived from the provincial house. The reason for my dismissal: *a disposition unsuited to religious life, with excessive and exclusive friendships.*

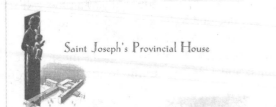

Saint Joseph's Provincial House

WATERVLIET-SHAKER ROAD
LATHAM, NEW YORK 12110

April 8, 1977

Miss Jan Phillips
15400 Bittner Road
Occidental, California 95465

Dear Jan,

It was a surprise to receive your letter. Though I did not have much interaction with you during your time as a novice, I remember you.

I am sure you realize that to reveal reasons for dismissal is not required by canon law, so I do not feel that those before me have failed in accountability. I have looked for the information you requested. The record is very brief, and simply states as reason, a disposition unsuited to religious life, with excessive and exclusive friendships.

I hope this will put your concerns to rest, Jan, that you may live your life, open to the Lord, and content to find his will shown you wherever you are. You will be in my prayer during this Holy Week.

In the Lord Jesus,

Sister Joan Teresa Groth, CSJ

Sister Joan Teresa Groth, CSJ
Provincial Superior

SJT:sl

That was that. I should have been fine now, having been given the very thing I asked for: the reason they sent me home. But I wasn't. I wanted what I couldn't have: the rituals of my canonical year. I longed for the prayer time; the hours of plain, hard work and service to others; the songs and meditations and Stations of the Cross; the silence, the solitude, the community gatherings. They were my pathways to joy and I couldn't seem to find them outside the Motherhouse walls.

I couldn't find them because there was no one out there blazing trails for me. Whatever pathways led to the happiness I sought, I would have to forge on my own. The life of my dreams wasn't going to simply show up for me. I had to create those circumstances, identify what I wanted, and gather those things around me.

At 28 years I knew little about making a life for myself. I was great at running away from what I didn't want, but not skilled yet at claiming what I wanted and heading straight for it. Plus I carried the weight of rejection and loss everywhere I went, singing my sad story like a country and western tune. I had years to go before I learned what it took to create a life, with lessons arriving from all manner of unexpected sources.

Chapter 14
The Prodigal Daughters

I tell you this because there is a price to pay for being real. When we go after what we really want, others often judge.

"So selfish," they say. "Always doing what she wants to do." "Tsk, tsk. Not following the rules."

From where I sit, those acts deserve applause. The courage to do what you want, the consciousness even to know what you want, is an accomplishment of the highest order. We are here to follow our heart's desire, to deploy it like a divining rod to sense our next steps. Is it fun? Head in that direction. Does it set your heart on fire? Rev up your engine.

Our species is evolving itself through us. It's complexifying through us, through our actions and choices. It's aiming for higher levels of diversity through us, so we find ourselves craving the "other" at times, wanting to merge with the unfamiliar, enter into territory that others call dangerous. All love wants is to find its other half and roll in the hay.

Whom we love is not in our hands. Love strikes like a lightning bolt out of the blue. No rhyme or reason. And yet we could lose everything if who we love is up for debate.

This is a beautiful story. I want all stories to end like this. I want every child who finds herself in the dark wood to have something magical like this happen to her. It's what we all deserve.

★★★★

—Stony Lake, Adirondacks, upstate New York, 1975

I come from a big tribe. My mother was one of 14 children. They all married and had big families, so I have 63 first cousins on my mother's side. It's no surprise that two of them fell in love and got married. It was legal where they lived, but nowhere in the world would it be condoned by the Catholic Church, and this, of course, was troubling to my Aunt Ruth, mother of the wayward bride.

This is my mother's family, minus her brother Roger who was already in the Army. My grandmother is in the middle, holding the last of her 14 children. My mother is between her and Ruth, the little girl in the print dress sitting on the end of the sofa. To Ruth's left is her sister Kay, standing. Ruth's daughter married Kay's son.

Aunt Ruth was a charismatic Catholic, which is like Catholic on steroids. The charismatic movement brought some emotional life into the church. Charismatics held prayer meetings outside of Mass.

134

They sang out loud, took part in faith healings, spoke in tongues. This group was moved by the Spirit. They took their relationship with Jesus seriously and bonded with him through Bible stories and faith sharing.

So being charismatic, Aunt Ruth rolled up her sleeves and put her faith in Jesus to work. She had to solve her spiritual dilemma. How could she reconcile that her daughter had just married her sister's son—forbidden by the Catholic Church—and would remain in good standing in the eyes of God?

Lucky for me, she not only solved the problem but shared the good news in a way that changed my life completely.

Coming out to my mother had been a disaster. She was petrified I was going to cause my father's death. As much as she loved me, she dreaded my visits home from California—on edge the moment I walked into the house.

"Now don't say anything to your father that's going to upset him."

"I hope you get through this phase fast and get back into the Church."

"I don't want you visiting any relatives on your father's side. I just can't trust you to keep quiet."

On one visit home, the day after I arrived, she woke me up early in the morning and said, "Come on, let's go up to the lake. Ruth's up there."

My mom was just sticking her toe in the charismatic movement and her sister Ruth had been involved in it for months. I think she needed a booster shot of Pentecostal Catholic. "The lake" was shorthand for a family camp my uncles built for hunting. Stony Lake was a small lake in Lewis County, in northern New York, 20 minutes from where my mom and her siblings all grew up. It was always crowded in the summer, but now that it was autumn, things would be nice and quiet.

I got dressed and we left while my dad was still in bed.

"Your father has a lot to do, so he's not coming with us," she said, grabbing her purse as she hurried out the door.

Before we were 10 miles down the road, we were yelling and crying—something we had never done in all our years of relating.

"I don't see why you have to do this to us!"

"Mom, I'm not doing anything. I'm just being me."

"Well, you're not being the kind of person God wants you to be."

"How do you know what God wants?"

"It's abnormal. It's sinful. I don't know why you can't be like your brother and sister. They don't give us any trouble."

"Because I wasn't born like them."

"This'll kill your father. I don't know why you want to tell him."

"I want to tell him because I'm happy to finally know who and what I am. I'm proud of myself. Why can't you be proud with me?"

It went on like this for two hours. When we got to the lake, Aunt Ruth and my grandmother were playing spades. After kisses and hugs hello, Ruth said to my mom, "Come on, let's go for a canoe ride."

Grandma was ready for a nap and I headed out for a walk in the woods.

I was sure that the God I communicated with was not troubled by my queerness. I gave up religion because the Church did not welcome gays, but they had nothing to say about what I believed. The Catholic Church considered homosexual orientation an "objective disorder" because they think of it as being "ordered toward an intrinsic moral evil," in their words. There's no sin unless we act on it. Once we cross that line and actually live like any other person responding to natural desires, our activity is considered a moral disorder, contrary to natural law. Intrinsically disordered, they say. I, on the other hand, never had one feeling or desire that felt immoral, evil, or unnatural.

I was not colluding anymore in a religion that not only discriminated against me but refused equality to women and maintained archaic positions on birth control. The Catholic Church's position on all things sexual led to untold deaths from AIDS and gay suicides and countless babies born to families unable to support them. The very church that prodded me toward justice and provided the impetus for my own activism was measuring up as a social justice nightmare. Nothing is ever as it seems.

I returned to the camp after a long walk and found Grandma reading a magazine and drinking tea at the picnic table that filled the kitchen area.

"Want to play gin rummy?" she asked.

"Sure," I said, sitting down across from her.

The smell of wood fire hung in the air and our feet ground into the sand that topped off the linoleum floor like sugar on an apple pie.

"So how are things going?" she asked as she shuffled the deck.

"Pretty bad," I said. "We argued all the way up here."

We are not an arguing family, so this piece of news came as a surprise, both to my grandmother and to me as it rolled off my lips. As tight as our family was, conflict was rarely mentioned. Our words floated in the air like balloons, strings dangling and unclaimed, until she broke the silence.

"What are you arguing about?"

"We're arguing because my mom doesn't want anyone to know I'm a lesbian. She's ashamed of me."

My mom and Aunt Ruth came through the door in the middle of my sentence.

"What's this?" asked Aunt Ruth. She turned to my mother and asked her, "Is that true?"

"Yes, I can't have her in the house," my mother said. "I can't bear her father finding out. I just want her to stop it."

My mother probably expected full support for her case given that Ruth was not only Catholic but hopped-up on the charismatic movement too. They were both deeply into the Bible now. They both had their prayer groups. They both participated in hands-on healings, mostly done by priests who traveled the charismatic circuit. But what she hadn't counted on was all the inner work Ruth had done regarding her daughter's marriage to Peter, the son of their sister.

Ruth had prayed long and hard on that one. She consulted Jesus, the gospels, and her own intuition. She did not appeal to an authority higher than her own faith. She worked it and it worked her, long and hard. She prayed for a way to see it through the eyes of Jesus.

The two of them had prodigal daughters who'd gone astray, left the sanctioned way for a path of their own calling. My mother was willing to abandon her daughter to spare her husband—from a possible health crisis, from his anger or grief or shame or whatever she imagined would be the consequence of finding out his daughter was a lesbian.

My aunt was not willing to give her daughter up. She was not willing to silence her, to insist she move away and not bring shame to the family. She used her faith. She deployed it in the service of mercy and kindness. Like Jesus, she chose the spirit of the law over the letter of the law. She saw religion as a ladder to a higher kind of love, and when she reached that higher ground, she no longer needed the ladder. It was love that consumed and guided her—not rules, not dogma, not what other people thought or said.

Ruth turned to my mother like a prophet in the wilderness. Rays of light streamed through the windows. The birds stopped chirping. I trembled in place.

"Marge, Jesus never said who to love or who not to love. Jesus only said to love them all. Love them all. That's what he wanted. That's what he asks of us. It doesn't matter who Jan loves. You should just be happy that she's loving people."

My mother stood still on the cracked linoleum floor of the camp hewn by the hands of her father and brothers. They were sons of Abraham and this was her burning bush. The revelation came in the simplest of words, as true revelations usually do. Nothing complicated. Just a gentle turning around for one who'd been looking in the wrong direction.

Her mouth hung open and tears poured down her cheeks.

"Oh my God," she said, staring straight ahead, as if beholding a beatific vision. "I can't believe I've lived this long and have been so stupid. How could I not have known what to do?"

Ruth's words pierced her like an arrow of truth. Time stopped that afternoon at Stony Lake. The three of us stared at my mother, bewildered. She was transforming. Something unpredictable, inexplicable was happening. Nobody moved. The light in the room grew brighter. Silence hung over the room until she looked at me and said, "You can tell your father anything you want. I've been wrong to keep you from him. I've been wrong to judge you. You're my daughter and I love you, no matter what."

This prodigal daughter was welcomed home that day. All thanks to a woman who took her faith into her own hands, who broke through the stone wall of religion to enter the mystery of absolute love, and from that place spoke a truth that transcends power.

Love them all, he said. Love them all.

Chapter 15
The Hundredth Monkey

I tell you this because it's about one small story that turned my life upside down. The day I read it, I made a decision that changed everything—my sense of self, my career, my entire future.

The story opened a doorway to a life I'd never imagined. It blasted open my imagination, fired up neurons, reminded me that every reality begins with an image of what might be. We think it, we see it, we speak of it, then we enter into it.

Had it not been for Ken Keyes Jr. writing his story, this book would not exist. That's how important our creations are. Just as his words caused me to think and act with new eyes, so might these words inspire you, and so might your words inspire others.

★★★★

—Syracuse, New York, 1982

By the early '80s, my spirituality had morphed into care for the world, and as a documentary photographer, I focused my lens on what mattered to me—cultural movements for justice, demonstrations for peace, common folks rarely pictured in the mainstream press, like gays and women who were not white, thin, and blonde.

My hope was to elevate the status of whatever I photographed. It was sacramental from the beginning. If I'm with you and we're about to capture a moment that says we care about something here, then there's a special quality to this experience. It's a holy moment. We give it our full attention. Trust grows between us.

Whatever we create together has its own life force. It can arouse feelings, provoke thought. It can cause someone to act. Our images have a latent power whether they're hung in a gallery or on a refrigerator door with kitty magnets. What we see, capture, print, and post communicate something about who we are and what we love. My photographs are code for *This is what I hold sacred, this is what I give my time to, this is what I cherish and will protect.* I want the pictures to stop people.

As a cultural creator in the early '80s, I made art that said *gay pride, women rising, end war, outlaw nukes, make peace.* Having grown up with *Life* and *Look* magazines, famous for photo-essays that brought the world into our living rooms, I knew the power of pictures. They'd been shaping my thoughts since my eyes first opened, and it was because of that power I chose the camera as my tool for change.

When I moved back to Syracuse from California, I went to the Syracuse Peace Council to see how I could contribute as an activist photographer. The Peace Council was founded in 1936 and is the oldest, autonomous, grassroots peace and social justice organization in the United States. It was there I met Dik Cool, who'd overseen publication of their Peace Calendar for 11 years. He was leaving the staff, so the Peace Council had decided not to publish a calendar that year. Dik was looking for other ways to keep it going. I was in.

A few nights later Dik and I met with three other activists over a $7 bottle of Chianti. We shared what we'd been up to, what our creative gifts were, what we hoped for, and by the end of the night we were the proud cofounders of Syracuse Cultural Workers, which would not only publish a 1983 Peace Calendar but would produce and distribute posters, cards, and datebooks that drew attention to the social justice issues of the time.

Syracuse Cultural Workers founders: Jack Manno, me, and Dik Cool, bottom row; Karen Kerney and Linda Perla, top row. (Photo by Ruth Putter.)

It was then 1982. The price of gas was $1.22 a gallon and a loaf of bread cost 55 cents. Ronald Reagan was president, and although he believed that world peace required the elimination of nuclear weapons, his approach to getting there was, to my mind, counterintuitive. He thought the U.S. should ramp up the arms race to bankrupt the Soviet Union, and his administration oversaw the production of massive numbers of nuclear warheads. Warhead tallies were often featured in the evening news, and dreaded anxiety attacks began to plague me.

A woman named Randall Forsberg initiated the Nuclear Freeze Campaign and drew attention to the fact that the U.S. and Soviet Union already had more than 50,000 nuclear weapons and planned to build 20,000 more. The campaign attracted massive support from peace organizations, churches, educators, activists, and hundreds of national organizations who had never taken a stand on national issues. The times were soon to be changing.

On June 12, 1982, concurrent with the Second United Nations Special Session on Disarmament, one million people demonstrated in New York City's Central Park for an end to the arms race. It was the largest antinuclear protest and the largest political demonstration in American history. Dik and I borrowed a friend's Volvo, loaded it up with catalogs and posters, and drove half the night to get there.

Since the other cofounders had jobs, Dik and I were the only ones who worked full time for Syracuse Cultural Workers. We developed a business plan, created a retail and wholesale marketing strategy, and reached out to artists around the country inviting them to submit socially relevant artwork. We paid ourselves $6 an hour, which was not enough to pay my bills, so I supplemented my income with a 20-hour-a-week picture framing job at Raintree Books in the Fayetteville Mall. This is where the magic happened.

One morning I noticed a small book on my work bench at the bookstore. There hadn't been any traffic through my area in the back and I hadn't waited on anyone, so it was a mystery where the book came from. The title was *The Hundredth Monkey* and it was written by a man named Ken Keyes, Jr. I stuck it in my bag when it was time for lunch and went out for a sandwich. As it turned out, I devoured the book, not my sandwich.

The main story was pretty short, about some research done on Japanese monkeys on the island of Koshima in 1952. Researchers provided the monkeys with sweet potatoes dropped in the sand, then they observed what happened. It seems the monkeys liked the taste of the raw sweet potatoes but found the dirt somewhat unpleasant.

An 18-month-old female named Imo solved the problem by washing the potatoes in a nearby stream. Her playmates also learned this new way and they taught their mothers as well. This innovation was picked up by various monkeys and between 1952 and 1958, according to the story, all the young monkeys learned to wash the sandy sweet potatoes to make them more palatable, and the adults who imitated their children learned this social improvement.

In the autumn of 1958, something startling took place as a number of Koshima monkeys were washing their potatoes. The exact number is not known, but someone suggested 99, so it's a hypothetical number. One morning there were 99 monkeys washing off their sweet potatoes.

Then, later that same morning, another monkey, *the hundredth monkey*, picked up a potato and washed it off.

By that evening almost every monkey in the tribe washed off their sweet potatoes before eating them. The added energy of this hundredth monkey somehow created an evolutionary breakthrough. Then, an even more surprising thing happened: The habit of washing sweet potatoes jumped over the sea and colonies of monkeys on other islands began washing their sweet potatoes before eating them.

At this point, the author suggests that when a certain critical number achieves an awareness, this new awareness may be communicated from mind to mind. When only a limited number of people know of a new way, it may remain the conscious property of these people. But there is a point at which if only one more person tunes in to a new awareness, a field is strengthened so that this awareness is picked up by almost everyone.

When I read that paragraph, bells went off. Lights flashed. I read it over and over. "This new awareness may be communicated from mind to mind ... [When] one more person tunes-in ... a field is strengthened ... this awareness is picked up by almost everyone."

I said right out loud in the middle of Friendly's restaurant, "I can be the Hundredth Person!" I was so charged, so penetrated by the possibility of it, I didn't give a thought to who was watching. I gathered my belongings and went right across the street to Key Bank where I sputtered the highlights of the story to a teller as I ransacked my purse looking for a $20 bill.

"I'm going to open an account so I can save for a trip," I said.

"Savings or checking?" is all she asked. Not a word about the whole incredible story.

"Savings," I said. "When I get $5,000 in here, I'm going to go around the world for peace. I'm going to talk to as many people as I can, in as many countries as I can get to. I'm going to communicate a new awareness!"

"Right!" she said, tweaking the glasses on her nose and avoiding eye contact. We waited for my receipt to print and she didn't say another word. Here it was, one of the most important days of my life, and I couldn't even get her attention.

That night I composed a 75-word ad for the *Pennysaver*, announcing all the odds jobs I was available to do. By the next week I had an early morning waitressing job at Howard Johnson's, a late-night dishwashing job at a French restaurant, two housecleaning jobs, and a three-story house to paint with a friend. All that plus my work at Syracuse Cultural Workers and Raintree Books. I barely survived.

It took nine months to save up what I needed. Whenever somebody from another country came by my workbench, I announced my plans and explored the possibility of connecting in their homeland. That led to relationships in China and Egypt.

I also put an ad in *Sojourners*, a Christian peace and justice magazine, which had a back page called "Connections," dedicated to just that. If people were moving from one state to another, they'd advertise on that page, hoping to find like-minded people in a new location.

My ad read: *Feminist photographer making peace pilgrimage around the world. Looking for Sojourner-like connections.* About a month later, a manila envelope arrived in the mail from Germany. Inside were 10 sheets of legal-size yellow paper, covered with annotated names and addresses of peace activists from several countries.

It was sent to me by a German man whose given name was Karl Mund. He changed his name to Amos when he went to Israel to work on a kibbutz and make amends for his father who had served in the German army. Amos lived and worked in Jerusalem for many years, participating in Israeli-Palestinian initiatives for peace in the area.

He sent me the names of people from India, Egypt, Israel, Italy, Austria, and Germany, many of whom I met and stayed with long before I met up with him in Berlin at the end of my journey one year later. Amos knew what I needed and he delivered it to me, a stranger, with no strings attached.

Neither of us were churchgoing people, but both of us dedicated our lives to peace. Our activism was our faith in running shoes, rooted in the principles of justice and mercy—a personal, emotional, and spiritual response to the political particularities of our times.

In preparation for my trip, I put together a five-minute slideshow called *Focus on Peace* with the International Children's Choir singing "Let There Be Peace on Earth" for a soundtrack. I would travel as an artist, not an educator. I would not speak about Pershing and cruise missiles or what our countries were doing wrong. I would speak about what each one of us could do as individuals to make peace in our own lives and have an impact in our communities.

I held to the possibility that a new awareness could be communicated from my mind to another person's mind, and that awareness could strengthen a field of higher consciousness. This was not a scientific experiment. It was a leap of faith. Whatever movement I made forward, like an evolutionary step, would not be seen, never be measured, but it would be real. I had enough love, hope, and faith to cause relationship, if people were willing to cocreate it with me. And fortunately, I was leading with pictures, each one carrying the freight of a thousand words.

Had Ken Keyes, a quadriplegic peace activist, not written his book—which landed so mysteriously on my workbench that day—I never would have heard of the hundredth monkey. My imagination never would have opened to the possibility of strengthening our global field of awareness. Had I not been exposed to the work of another dreamer, I would not have dreamed up an action plan like this. I would not have created Focus on Peace, which had its own impact on thousands of viewers around the world.

As it turns out, the hundredth monkey was a fictional metaphor for how ideas and behavior can abruptly change and grow. It was created by Lyall Watson, a South African scientist interested in telepathy, for his book Lifetide. But this is the power of story and myth.

As a cultural creator, I am inspired by the creators who go before me. Their ideas propel me. Their stories leave tracks on my maps. Their words make me cry, think, hope.

Public artists who work for the common good and speak to the social issues of the day do not wait till fear is gone, till answers arrive, to do their work. They jump right into the fray and offer what they can from their anguish, their confusion, from whatever vision they may have of a brighter time. It's an outpouring of who we are, an offering made from the tools at hand.

Whatever we make comes from the world we live in and the world within us. The daily news makes its way through our neurosphere, our bloodstream, our vivid imaginations, and what we make of it is our creation. The stories we tell, the music we make, the colors we splash on our canvases and journal pages—these artifacts are the evidence of our interior lives. They are our signatures—the sound bites we'll be remembered by.

Each morning in my meditation, I face the same questions: *What am I making of these times? How do I maintain my light? What energy am I offering to others?*

Everyone around the globe is now facing the same crisis, and it triggers different reactions in each of us. Reading *The Hundredth Monkey* probably never moved anyone else to make a trip around the world, but for me it was the only possible response. I never had a second thought. It took me nine months to save up $5,000, buy 200 rolls of film, and come up with a sketchy itinerary in my mind. As it worked out, the only thing I knew for sure was that I would land in Tokyo and start my work in Hiroshima and Nagasaki.

When we dare to jump off the cliff, wings sprout to support us. We are not left comfortless or alone, and help arrives serendipitously, like the book on my workbench all those many years ago.

Out of nowhere, voices call us in this direction or that.

"Come," it will say. "Someone needs you here," and you will sigh with relief.

"Yes, someone needs me," you will respond, your lips curled up in a wave of happiness.

And you remember then why you came here and what your mission was, and deep inside the cavern of you, you feel the heat of your own raging fire.

Chapter 16
Trials in Tokyo

I tell you this so you will take a chance, go out unprepared, try something new though you have no idea how it'll all work out.

I don't advise this level of risk and unpreparedness. It could've gone wrong, but it didn't—and it usually doesn't. The Universe is for us. It works in our favor if it's life and love and abundance we're up to.

Each new country came with its own surprises and twists. There was always some struggle at the borders—saying goodbye to the old, getting used to the new. I got better at it as I went along, but Japan knocked me out cold. I never saw it coming.

That's life. No seeing around the bend.

★★★★

—Tokyo, Japan, 1983

I landed in Tokyo on a drizzly day in November and made my way to the home of two women I had never met. Rita Harper and Akiko Terusaka had heard about my trip and knew I was looking for hospitality from people of like mind. Sight unseen, they extended an invitation to me and I landed on their doorstep after a long trip across the Pacific.

They had a small apartment and I had my own corner of a room with a tatami mat that I rolled out every night for sleeping. For the past nine months, I had been so preoccupied with working and saving for this adventure that I had failed to create a blueprint for actually doing it.

Akiko and Rita asked me about my plan and were astonished when I said I hadn't figured one out yet.

"You mean you don't know where you're *going*?" they asked in unison, their tone carrying a trifecta of emotions—disbelief, panic, and possible regret that they'd invited a ne'er-do-well for an unlimited stay.

"I know I'm going to start in Hiroshima," I said. I remembered reading John Hersey's book *Hiroshima* when I was 13. It told the story of six survivors of the American atomic bomb that was dropped on August 6, 1945. Hersey was a war correspondent and one of the first journalists to see Hiroshima after the bombing. More than 135,000 people died from the explosion—nearly half of them on that day, instantly.

I read his book in my bedroom on a Saturday afternoon. It made me nauseous. It filled me with rage. I read every detail of the survivors' ordeal from the day of the bombing to one year later. Hersey wrote the piece using all the storytelling techniques of fiction. He opened the door to every feeling I had. He invited me into the horror, the heat, the harrowing sounds and sights: people with melted eyeballs, vaporized, leaving only their shadows etched onto walls, children stumbling through the rubble, calling out for parents they'd never see again.

Reading the book, I did not have the imaginative capacity to place myself in Hiroshima. I was 20 years away from standing in the Hiroshima Peace Memorial Museum, too young and inexperienced at 13 to envision a future that I myself would create. I was still a believer then that life was happening *to* me. I hadn't discovered my creative agency, nor were there any adults in my life who spoke of such a thing.

But I did know one thing, or rather *believed* it to be true: There was an invisible thread connecting me to those people in Japan who experienced that nightmare. I read that book as if it were them and me, but all the while I felt *we*. Since my childhood, I never felt as separate from people as they made us out to be. I don't know if it had to do with religious training or intuition or a psychic sensibility that seemed so natural I assumed everyone felt it.

But it seemed to me there was a certain sameness about our experience as humans that made us part of all one thing. A phrase went through my head that helped me see it: *I am God to my cells.* And inside my body I imagined all the people in the world—*all of us*—held together by this kind of Idea (which people called God) that was really the sum of all our parts and the source of all our parts at once. And it was that notion of togetherness, or more, *reliance* on each other that led to my feeling of oneness in this tiny apartment in Tokyo.

In his spare 31,000 words, John Hersey changed who I was in 1962. His story woke me up, interrupted my life, and caused me to become the woman who was now in Japan, figuring out how to make a journey for peace.

I tried to reassure Akiko and Rita that I would have a plan soon, but we all went to bed that night minus any particulars about what to expect. Two days went by before my first clue arrived. I was beginning to panic, thinking I'd made a terrible mistake, when I saw a copy of the *Mainichi Daily News* on the kitchen counter. It was an English-language newspaper published in Tokyo. *That's it!* I thought. *I'll call them and get a story in the paper.*

I opened it up, found the number, and called the editor.

"There's an amazing woman here from the United States, just starting a journey for peace around the world," I said, as if delivering the hottest scoop of the day. "She's a photographer with a slideshow on the peace movements in the U.S. and Canada. She's talking to groups all over Japan. You should do a story on her fast, before she's gone!" I said, breathless with excitement.

My enthusiasm washed over him like a tsunami and he was ready to commit.

"Okay, where is she? I'll send a reporter over tomorrow at 2 p.m."

"Great! She'll be ready!" I said, giving him the address.

Rita and Akiko were excited when I shared the news, and none of us could have anticipated the huge response. *Mainichi* ran the story on the front page, included Rita and Akiko's phone number, and encouraged organizations, churches, and schools to call me if they wanted me to make a presentation.

I created a calendar and within a couple days, it was filled out for five weeks. Once I left for Hiroshima, I didn't see my Tokyo hosts for more than a month. It was in the process of *doing* it that I learned what I needed to know about communicating a hope. In the beginning, it was all a mystery unfolding. In the first few days, it was more a nightmare than anything else. I'd made a promise I didn't feel big enough to fulfill.

The things I had read in *The Hundredth Monkey*, the ideas that inspired me to even imagine such a thing as a world trip—communicating a new awareness, strengthening a field, behaving differently until the whole tribe picks it up—these were vague and nearly inaccessible ideas now. Their vividness was gone. The vitality that they stirred in me initially had faded. It had taken so long to actualize the dream that when I finally embarked upon it, I could barely feel the spark that ignited it.

Nobody back home knew how afraid I was. Nobody knew I was dragging my feet, though Akiko and Rita might have sensed it. Even before I arrived in Japan, fear kept me in Oakland for three months. I didn't know what I was going to do as a peace pilgrim, so I stalled. I started a love affair, convinced myself I needed more money and took on a house painting job, traveled up and down the state saying goodbye to friends and family—all the while not going anywhere.

When I got up the courage to leave California, even then I was too afraid to fly straight to Japan. I went to Honolulu to see friends, then to Maui, for weeks avoiding what I had committed to do. I never wrote home to say I was afraid. I never told anyone. I just kept on avoiding until the day finally came that I had to leave.

When I arrived at the Narita Airport in Tokyo, I broke down. All that fear and anxiety that circulated through my nervous system for months erupted in a thunderstorm of tears. Though I had an address where I knew I'd be welcomed, I had no idea how to get there. I had traveled through Europe in my 20s and was never challenged by the signs in train stations and airports. Though I didn't know Italian or German or Spanish, we shared the same alphabet. But the signs in Narita were all in Japanese, and I had no idea how to decipher them.

I stood in the middle of the bustling crowd and started to cry. I was overwhelmed, with a backpack I could barely lift, and a camera bag loaded with 150 rolls of Kodachrome film and 50 rolls of black and white. Standing at the intersection between East and West, between the known and unknown, between who I was and what I might become horrified me.

A kind Japanese man stopped his life for the afternoon and, several trains later, hand delivered me to the right address. And that's how I got to Rita and Akiko's. And that's why I was so paralyzed, prior to the newspaper idea, and before the filled-out calendar. Once I had places to go and people to see, my fear subsided. It seemed I might be needed then, if they called and asked for me. The idea might not have been foolhardy, grandiose, or too big for me. As I caught my breath and let life unfold, it appeared that I might be the perfect size, that this journey was cut out just for me.

I had translators for most of my talks, which was good. They slowed me down. I deliberated over my words, trying to stay with nouns and verbs. I aimed for simplicity, sincerity, communion. The slideshows carried the weight of fact and story, and the Children's Chorus carried the emotion as only music can. Thousands of people in dozens of cities with signs in all languages; hundreds of Buddhist monks and nuns marching together. Coalitions of peace groups brought together pacifists, children, university students, and union members. A demonstration in New York City was three miles long.

My agenda was simple: Create an occasion where people could come together, share our experiences, and speak and listen from our muscle and bones. I wanted us to go somewhere new together. I wanted us to *feel* together, ponder together, imagine something bold together. I didn't know how to be a public speaker, but I knew how to love. I knew how to share my feelings, and I knew it was good to be vulnerable, even if I cried, because people would know that it all mattered to me—the whole history, the whole dilemma of worlds at war, the whole idea of us saying, *Yes! We are the creators of these times and this culture!* I just wanted us to remember who we were in the presence of each other.

I showed my slideshows to dozens of groups, in schools, trade unions, international organizations. I never charged for any of my presentations, but someone would always take me home, feed me, put me up. Sometimes this was for a day or two. Sometimes for weeks. It was all organic. As I look back now, I'm astonished at how it worked out—that I was always cared for by people. And it was in their caring, as they fed and sheltered me, that their faith seeped out and entered me.

That is how I learned what Shinto means, what Buddhism is based on, how Catholicism shape-shifts in different cultures. I learned it from my personal relationships with those who believed in those traditions, for who we are is always evidence of what we believe.

I spent a few days in Hiroshima, honoring the pledge I had made as a teen after reading John Hersey's book. I went to the museum every day, dropped to my knees more than once in horror and shame. I cried in the arms of total strangers who were equally moved and unable to utter anything but tears.

Hiroshima is the place where the brain of my activist married the heart of my human. It's where the pieces came together for me, where all the reasons I stood there in that foreign land became crystal clear, where the meaning behind the metaphor of the hundredth monkey took my hand and led me on.

My time in Hiroshima was solitary. I was alone, breathing in the air, the history, the story as it was carefully revealed in the Peace Museum— in every tableau, every photograph, every piece of charred clothing, irradiated object, and survivor testimony. I would go on to discover many jewels in Japan, all of which sank deeply into a heart that had been ripped open in Hiroshima.

Chapter 17
Nagasaki: Fire in My Eyes

I tell you this because it's a story about the invisible threads that connect us, and how palpable they become when our heartstrings are involved.

I read John Hersey's Hiroshima *when I was 13. I cried for the survivors who lived with the imprint of a nuclear bomb on their bodies. I threw the book across my bedroom, running to the bathroom, needing to throw up. I wished I could do something, to make amends in some way, but I was powerless.*

Twenty years passed before my life's journey led me to Japan and into the living room of a Nagasaki survivor. We sat side by side on her couch. We drank tea and she relayed her story through a translator into my Sony recorder. Our eyes were locked on each other the whole time she spoke, and tears rolled down my cheeks as she described the haunting scenes.

My heart broke open that day with all the love and sorrow and conviction I felt as a teen. Her testimony riveted me. How she endured the nightmare and made her way in the world was a life lesson in moving on through the dark, no matter how alone.

I think of Tsuyo often, as a part of her is still with me. The connection we made was invisible, beyond language, strong as steel. It is a resource in the vault of my memory that steers me in the right direction when I near despair or abandon hope. She shared her story with me that day, but so much more was given than the facts of the situation.

★★★★

—Nagasaki, Japan, November 1983

Mr. Terumasa Matsunaga, the director of the Nagasaki Association for the Promotion of Peace, called me after seeing the *Mainichi Daily News* article. He was arranging an afternoon gathering of the Nagasaki survivors and wanted to include me in the program. In Japan, the survivors from the bombings in Hiroshima and Nagasaki are called *hibakusha*. It literally translates as "explosion-affected people." They were going to watch the premiere of a Japanese film, and following that, I would show slides and talk about the peace movement in the United States.

I asked Mr. Matsunaga if he could set up a morning interview with one of the *hibakusha* and provide me with a translator from his organization. He was happy to oblige and I arrived with the translator at the small apartment of Tsuyo Kataoka at 10 a.m. on the day of our event. She was a small woman, bent at the waist, who walked slowly, with tiny, quiet steps. She had tea on the coffee table and the three of us sat huddled around my tape recorder as Tsuyo revisited the nightmare from nearly 40 years ago.

She was 24 when it happened—an employee at the Mitsubishi Munitions Factory. On the afternoon of August 9, she and her coworkers were on a break outside the building when they heard the explosion. The force from the bomb threw her hundreds of feet. When she regained consciousness, there was no one alive around her—just dead bodies on the ground. These are her words:

"I made my way to the Urakami River to see the most horrible sight I can remember. The river was red with blood and filled with people washing out their wounds. They were groaning and calling out for their families. I was nearly naked and sick with the smell of my burning body."

Her words and images brought me back to the summer day I read *Hiroshima* at age 13. John Hersey's words broke my heart open and Tsuyo's were doing the same. I was in that room with her because of that book. When I read it, I felt the pull of whatever invisible threads connect us, and here I was, connected still to a woman who was telling the same

154

Tsuyo Kataoka in her Nagasaki apartment.

story, breathing her life into my air.

"Did you find anyone you knew?" I asked.

"I made it to where my house once was, but nothing was left. Everything had been blown away. I cried out for my family, but everyone was gone. Only my mother survived."

"Did you have a big family?"

"I lost over 50 people in my family. We could not even find their bodies. Right after I found my mother, I lost my eyesight, so she, at 69, had to care for me. Two days later, I lost my hearing."

I forced myself not to gasp, not to gulp for air. I looked beyond her scars, beyond the burnt flesh and raised lesions. I drifted into the sky of her eyes and flew into the heaven that held us up.

"Where did you go for help?"

"For days we wandered, looking for shelter, until we found St. Francis Hospital. It was nearly destroyed, but we found a place to lay our mat. A terrible thing happened then. It began to rain very hard and blow in on me—an oily, dark rain that covered my whole body. Flies gathered in my open sores and maggots hatched in the wounds. There were hardly any doctors and so many wounded."

"Were you blind for long?"

"On September 20, my eyesight came back like a miracle. I was happy to see again, but the sight of my body was disturbing. I found a broken piece of mirror on the ground and wanted to die when I saw my face. I didn't even look human. My skin had melted everywhere."

"Did anybody come to take care of you?"

"My brother came back from China and found us. He built a little hut and the three of us lived there. I got well enough to walk and most of my hearing came back. In 1951, I got a job as a scrubwoman in a tuberculosis ward. I was so deformed it was hard to have people see me. I had tuberculosis myself but was too poor to go to the hospital."

Tsuyo had an operation on her hands and face in 1958. Her internal organs were all damaged from the radiation and she endures the pain daily. We went together to Mr. Matsunaga's event following our interview and gathered with 40 other *hibakusha* who meet monthly as a community. They are all frail and disfigured, walking with canes, leaning on each others' arms. They do what they can as activists, speaking at schools and organizations, repeating the same mantra: *Never again another nuclear weapon*. But I didn't learn until later how alone they felt in their mission.

We all met in a large meeting room, with long tables that faced the screen in the front. Mr. Matsunaga introduced the film, explaining that a Japanese filmmaker had acquired recently declassified footage from the U.S. military and incorporated it in this film on Nagasaki. He had not previewed it, so no one knew what we were in for.

When it was time for the movie, the lights went down. Mr. Matsunaga sat on my left and Tsuyo Kataoka on my right. The film began with a slow pan of the Peace Park, Nagasaki's memorial to the victims. Colorful flowers and paper cranes filled the frame and the lens widened for an aerial view. From the sky it looked like any city, glittering gold in the afternoon light. Mr. Matsunaga proudly described in English what we were seeing of his native city and all was well.

Then the film flashed back 40 years. With a sudden cut, our vantage point changed to the cockpit of a U.S. bomber plane moments before it dropped the atomic bomb on Nagasaki. The sound of gasps reverberated around the room. People froze in their places. No one had any idea this was coming. We watched the bomb drop. We saw the cloud form into a mushroom shape. We witnessed the firestorm. We saw the driving black rain of sticky, dark radioactive water penetrating the ground. We saw a beautiful city destroyed in seconds from our perch in the plane.

Then it got worse. Another jump cut and we were on the ground, looking through the lens at the remains of a disaster. Thousands of people lay dead on the ground, incinerated by the blast. Some were walking through the rubble, charred, dazed, calling out names of their family members. Mr. Matsunaga collapsed into tears beside me. He buried his head in his arms on the table, his shoulders shuddering in sorrow.

I looked at Tsuyo and we were equally horrified. There was nothing any of us could do but stare ahead, take it in, try to breathe. I would hear an occasional shriek as one of the *hibakusha* recognized him or herself in the film, burned almost beyond recognition, but not quite. Gasps, sobs, and wails filled the room as they relived a nuclear holocaust.

When the movie was finished, we sat in darkness. No one moved. The sounds and sighs of unbearable pain, irresolvable loss, quieted in time and the community regained its composure. There was no process. No leader jumping up to facilitate next steps. Like a multicellular organism, all the parts joined together to form a more perfect union. And it wasn't until that had happened that the lights were turned on.

It's never about individuals in Japan. It's always the whole that's considered, and this whole, this community, unified and healed itself, right before my eyes.

Once the lights were on, Mr. Matsunaga walked me to the podium and introduced me. My slideshow was ready to go, but I wasn't. I hadn't yet recovered from the trauma of that experience. I stood before that whole group of survivors and started to cry. Now I was the one who was bent over.

"I'm so sorry this happened," I blurted out. "I'm so sorry it ever happened to anyone, and I do everything I can to keep it from happening again."

I spoke every sentence slowly, every word deliberately, and the translator delivered my sentiments and ideas to the best of her ability. The crowd of 40 *hibakusha* sat quietly before me, nodding their heads, affirming me collectively. When the slides came up, their eyes widened. When the sound of the International Children's Choir broke into our silence, they smiled. Now there was image and music to carry us away, and transport us it did.

We watched slides of a million people marching through New York for nuclear disarmament, including the delegation from Japan that had flown in to participate in the largest march in history. When they saw the photo of an aging Buddhist monk, his wheelchair lifted above the crowds by young monks in saffron robes, they called out his name in respect. They bowed from their seats, their heads down, their shoulders thrusting forward. So much reverence.

Several Japanese flags were flown in that parade, all carrying the same message in Japanese and English: "Never another Nagasaki! Never another Hiroshima! Never another nuclear war!" I saw several *hibakusha* wipe their eyes.

That sense of inseparability returned to my chest. No time. No distance. Only the one thing—this energy connecting us. Only love shape-shifting into billions of forms all day long. Mystery was afoot.

When the slideshow was finished, I asked whether any of them would like to speak into my tape recorder and share what they were feeling. Every one of them lined up. We bowed to each other, then they uttered their words into the microphone. Later, after the translator listened to the tape, she was amazed that so many said the same thing.

Their singular message was this: "We thought we were the only ones who cared until we saw your pictures. Thank you for letting us know we are not alone. Thank you for working to prevent another nuclear war."

Those pictures *were* worth a thousand words that day.

Chapter 18
The Roads Both Taken

I tell you this to remind you of the hurdles you'll find on the path.

Obstacles come in many forms: other people, the written word, the voice of our own inner critic. It feels like a test. Do you really mean what you say? Will you fulfill that commitment? Are you in this for the long haul?

This destination was the site of one of the most liberating experiences of my life. And I almost didn't get there because people tried to discourage me. A smart man told me I wasn't worthy of it. He made fun of my intentions, negated my intelligence. He implied that I would be wasting the precious time of the man I wanted to see.

And there were other obstacles: It was a long distance away; the cost of getting there was high; I didn't know where I was going or what it would be like.

There is a price to pay for life-changing experiences. It requires courage, always; a willingness to make peace with the unknown; an indefatigable confidence in oneself. These are virtues, spiritual muscles we need to keep in shape. Had I let people talk me out of this, I would not have learned a lesson that is critical to this book. This book would not exist. Your life would be a little different. And my life would be vastly different. This is what I mean by "we are all connected."

★★★★

—Takamori, Japanese Alps, December 1983

I first heard about Father Oshida from the Sisters of St. Joseph in Tsu-shi. They told me about his visit with the Dalai Lama, where both men sat together in silence for an hour. At the end of the hour, the Dalai Lama asked if Father Oshida would return again one day and honor him with another meeting.

After hearing the story, I wanted to meet the man. He lived far away in the Japanese Alps, the sisters said, on a small retreat that he built with a few others. Legend had it that as a Dominican priest in Tokyo, he was a social activist, always advocating for the poor, insisting that the Church dedicate more funds on their behalf. In general, a thorn in the side of the hierarchy. So they missioned him in the mountains on a small patch of land and sent him a few seminarians. He was to be their novice director. Together they built Takamori, a ragtag monastery of crooked thatched huts that was designed for simplicity, communal living, contemplation, and hard work in the rice fields.

The sisters of Tsu-shi were enthusiastic about my visiting Takamori. They tracked down the phone number. They brought out a map of Japan so we could see how far away it was and how high in the mountains. "A good hundredth monkey place," they laughed. "Buddhist *and* Catholic, already enlightened!" As if it were a done deal that I'd be going, they mapped out an itinerary for me, which trains to catch and where. They visualized the whole trip, and their joy overflowed.

The next day I gave a talk at a high school in Nagoya and ended up staying overnight in a rectory that housed a few priests from the Nanzan Institute for Religion and Culture, which was near the school. The community of scholars at Nanzan dedicated themselves to dialogue among different religions and philosophies, East and West. One of the scholars who lived there, a priest only five years my senior, welcomed me and took time to show me around the temples of Nagoya on a bicycle trip.

He had two master's degrees and a doctorate in religious studies from Cambridge and was an unabashed intellectual. When he asked why I was on this peace trip, I told him about reading *The Hundredth Monkey* book. I shared that I was inspired about how consciousness evolves, and that I was hopeful that something positive would occur as a result of my interactions with people and my intention for peace.

"I'm never going to know *what* got changed or *how*, but I don't care about that. I have faith in the possibilities of this experience," I said.

"That's so naive," he responded. "Monkeys don't have a class system. Some don't have automatic dishwashers in their kitchens. It's economics you should be talking about if you're interested in peace, not monkeys and sweet potatoes."

As bright as he was, he couldn't accommodate the mystical. It was all facts for him. Research, information, theory. For me, the engine of change is in the heart—it's fueled by risk, relationship, compassion, invitation. I enter into the sanctity of one's space with love as an offering. I sit and inquire with no judgment. I listen deeply. My heart and brain pour out their gifts—thoughtfulness, appreciation, empathy—and what grows in that fertile field of consciousness is a sense of oneness.

That is what I know from my lived experience. That is what I believe causes peace to take root. And that is what I was out to achieve. I was not a teacher out to change minds about Pershing missiles and nuclear stockpiles. I was an artist hoping to break hearts open, hoping to ignite imaginations to new visions for the world.

But the young priest would have nothing of it. For him, the brain was the locus—think about it, analyze it, report on it. It was all information, no inspiration. Sitting in his kitchen with our teacups between us, we personally embodied yin and yang.

He had already written a few books. I had already founded a few organizations. He imagined and wrote; I felt and acted. His thoughts circulated around the world; my body was circumnavigating it.

He wrote books and articles about Christianity being converted to Buddhism, about using our technology to converge religions, not convert people. He gave me his article on the selfishness of the Christian mission—how many resources are dedicated to individual conversions while the global spiritual community is being neglected. With astute and scholarly reasoning, he argued for different faiths coming together to be changed by each other, to experience a new fullness and share in our responsibilities as global citizens. He was designing a highway; I was forging a path. Different windows, all one light in the room.

When I asked him whether he'd heard of Father Oshida, of course he had, and had written about a delegation of Buddhists who had visited there. When I said I wanted to visit Takamori, he discouraged me, as if Father Oshida were too busy for me, or that I wasn't important enough, or shouldn't bother him.

"I'm going to call him anyway," I said. "The nuns gave me his number."

"Go ahead, but I'm telling you, he won't have time for you. He's got a lot on his plate. He spent time with the Dalai Lama you know."

This is how to silence a woman. You demean her. You do everything you can to assault her dignity. You do not acknowledge her intellect, her contribution, the power of her energy. You mock her ideas. You repeat again and again that thought trumps feeling.

His words were kryptonite to my Superwoman. I felt myself weaken. I reconsidered calling Father Oshida. I felt my confidence, my self-worth wane. Though I respected the priest's intellectual attempts to connect Buddhism and Christianity, what was happening emotionally did not feel unifying in the least. I'm sure he wasn't aware of the impact of his words, as he lived and worked solely with men, rarely crossing the landscape of emotion. It was up to me to protect myself.

I didn't have the chutzpah to say that I was feeling bombarded by his negativity, that I missed the presence of women and their emotional support, that I didn't think it mattered at all if someone thought lofty thoughts if they weren't kind and considerate to the ones they're with. I simply excused myself and retired to the small, masculine room where I would spend the night.

When I woke up the next morning, I called Father Oshida. He invited me up immediately. "Yes, yes, come visit us in Takamori. You work with us. You pray with us. We feed you. Come soon. Stay long. Okay? Okay?" It took several trains and buses to get there from where I was. I arrived in the early evening and was greeted by Father Oshida and a sister from the Philippines who had lived there for many years.

Ten people were living at Takamori at the time, three nuns, three seminarians, and some itinerant retreatants. After tea and some sweet treats, the sister showed me to a little room with a tiny bed.

"Bell ring at 5:30," she said. "We meditate and pray, then Mass, then eat. See you then. Chapel next door."

I slept like a baby and woke with the bell calling us to prayer. The chapel was hand-hewn like all the buildings, slightly crooked, see-

A seminarian working in the rice fields.

through cracks in the wall, straw mat covering the floor. The temperature was 24 degrees Fahrenheit the first morning. It was early November in the mountains. We sat in a circle around the altar, which was simply a cloth on the floor in the center of the room with a chalice, candle, plate, and water bowl on it.

For 30 minutes, we sat in silent meditation. Cushions on the floor, people sitting cross-legged. I was tortured. I could see my breath. Being there was a disaster, was all I was thinking. No stillness in the brain. No silence. Thirty minutes, constant complaining. Then Father Oshida rang a bell and we sang Gregorian chant for a few minutes. Following that, he said Mass, then we shared a simple breakfast and went to the fields to work in silence. We worked morning and afternoon tending to the rice, then met for meditation before dinner.

It was always vegetarian fare. Rice, miso, vegetables, tea. One night, a neighbor came bearing gifts. They lit up the barbecue, grilled up what the neighbor had brought, and we all stood by the fire feasting on the delicacy. It was the most delicious thing I had tasted in months. When I asked Father Oshida what it was, he said eel. We were eating barbecued eel.

"I thought we were vegetarian," I said.

"Only vegetarian until neighbor bring eel," he said, as serious as could be.

Every night after dinner, people gathered round a small fireplace and Father Oshida gave an evening talk. Mostly it was in Japanese, but he translated the important parts into English for me. I had been reading books on Buddhism every night before bed and was facing a growing dilemma.

When he asked one night if any of us had questions, I asked him mine.

"Father, as a Christian, I have always learned to be a social activist. Jesus said to go out and teach all nations. I have tried to be an advocate for the poor, a maker of peace. But when I read the Buddhists texts, they seem to say the opposite: 'Be still and realize that everything is unfolding perfectly.' One says be quiet, the other says speak out. Now I don't know what to do," I said.

"Don't know what to do about what?"

"Well, I see the rightness in both of them, and I don't know which one to choose. I just started this journey around the world and I don't want to go home, but if it's better to just meditate and think of everything as perfect, I probably should. I'm so confused!"

"Both!" he said immediately. "Both way right way! No choosing! Be both! Do both!"

"But Jesus and Buddha say different things," I said, hoping for a longer answer. "Which one should I follow?"

"They same," he said. "Buddha the thought. Jesus the event. Same! Same!"

When he spoke of Jesus as the *event* of Buddhist thought, something clicked for me. Nothing I could talk about or claim that I understood or could explain to anyone else. It just resonated down deep. It felt true. It connected things in my mind.

We're simply evolving, from stardust to matter to conscious matter to whatever the next steps are after that. We're participating in the evolution of consciousness itself, mind-at-large, coming to see and reflect on itself from a variety of perspectives. My body is here in the service of that, and though it will not survive, the consciousness within will continue to thrive.

We are all improved versions of the ones who came before, and though the masters of consciousness whom we know as our teachers may have reached a perfection unknown to us, we have the capacity for a higher intelligence than the Neanderthals, the people of the Dark Ages, the Renaissance, the Enlightenment period, and any era before us, by reason of our timing and our place in the evolutionary scheme of things. We don't have to keep referring to the sacred texts of the past, which were written by people for the people of that time. We are the prophets and mystics of *this* time, and we are the writers of the new sacred texts.

After referring to Jesus as the event of Buddha's thought, Father Oshida urged me and anyone there who could understand English to stop trying to make literal sense of things and pay attention to the event.

"Experience your life and everything around you as an incarnation. Do not think with your mind. Go down to the depths. Experience wisdom. All religions are the same, except Christianity is responsible for most war and death," he said.

I tried to practice what he said in the morning meditations. Tried to pay less attention to my thoughts of being in pain and just experience the whole crazy deal of sitting in a freezing cold chapel in the Japanese Alps with a renegade Catholic Buddhist priest and several other strangers working at being the brightest lights we could be in the world.

I was blessed to be there, that's all I knew—and happy that I didn't have to choose between Jesus and Buddha.

Chapter 19
Amazing Grace in the Himalayas

I tell you this because what happened here offers a glimpse into evolution. At least it felt that way to me in retrospect. It used to be that we had to compare fossil records to see how a species evolved over centuries. Now, in real time, we see evidence of birds evolving in response to present-day climate changes. Forbes, National Geographic, *and* Nature Canada *recently reported on how different species are changing their breeding times, their migration schedules, and even their birdsongs when urban noise becomes loud enough to mask the lower frequencies they usually communicate in. They switch to a higher pitch to rise above the din and attract their mates.*

Our place on the web of connectedness is not just a spiritual assertion. It's a biological fact. We are interdependent in ways we can't even see. And this was pointed out to me by young students in Nepal, who were more tuned in to our reliance on each other than any of the adults in the room. As I travel now, witnessing the minds of millennials processing information and connecting dots, I am astonished at their ability to synthesize and articulate ideas beyond my imagination in my 20s and 30s. Evolution *is what I call it. See what you think.*

✖✖✖✖

—Kathmandu, Nepal, 1984

I met a woman who taught at the International School in Kathmandu, a school for the children of U.S. personnel working in Nepal. When I asked if I could show *Focus on Peace* there, she agreed to check with the principal and let me know. It wasn't as easy as I thought. The principal and a few teachers wanted to preview the show to be sure it wasn't "subversive."

I explained to them that they were all photographs of the peace movement, except for four slides from Hiroshima. After looking at my slides, the principal said the slideshow "failed to address the issues, was propagandist, and the children should not be exposed to it."

The science teacher backed him up and asked me whether I was for unilateral or bilateral disarmament. I told him I was traveling as an artist representing the peace movement. I was not there to debate about military issues or discuss how many times we could blow up our planet.

I was there to fill in the details about the growing movement for peace in the United States and Canada. My job was to let viewers know how many people were showing up, saying "No more!" to nuclear weapons, insisting on other ways to settle disputes. I was there to get people thinking about how else it might be. To start a conversation about where peace begins, how it feels, and our right to have a say about weapons since our taxes and our lives are part of the equation. I said all this as calmly as I could.

The science teacher grew red in the face. "You must love the Russians!" he shouted, his fists pounding the air.

"I do my best to love all people," I said.

"Then you should go there where you belong!" he yelled back. I stood there numbed by the chill in the room, while the principal and teachers argued among themselves whether the students had anything to learn from seeing the slideshow. I excused myself to use the restroom and while I was gone, they decided I could present it to the seventh, eighth, and ninth grade classes, and after the show, someone from "the opposition" would debate me so the students could get the whole picture. All this would happen the very next day.

At 9 a.m., I stood before the group of students and described why I was there and what they were about to see. I told them all the images were taken in the United States and Canada except for the few they'd be seeing from the Hiroshima bombing. I shared a little about my meeting with the survivors and how they'd asked me to include photos showing the actual impact of an atomic bomb. Aside from that, all the people they'd be seeing in the slideshow were people who were demonstrating for disarmament.

The lights went down, the sounds of the International Children's Choir singing "Let There Be Peace on Earth" faded in, and images of a movement for peace appeared and dissolved into each other for the next five minutes. The kids witnessed images of hope and horror. When it was finished, the light exposed their tender faces—some in tears, some with their heads in their hands, some looking bright-eyed and eager to talk.

We took a short break then reconvened in a big circle on the floor. The science teacher sat right across from me. I asked if anyone wanted to share their feelings about what they'd seen. A few students raised their hands and spoke about how afraid they were of war. The science teacher brought up the dangerous Russians and how important it is that the United States have more weapons than them.

A red-haired, freckled boy spoke up. "No, don't you see?" he asked, directing his attention to the teacher. "The weapons we have are too dangerous. They will kill too many people and even kill our planet."

A girl across from him chimed in, "Something new has to happen now. We can't do what everyone has always done. We have to find a new way to disagree."

"We have to make up a new way to argue," said another. "Countries will always disagree, but we can't let them have nuclear bombs. I agree with all the people in the photographs. I want to be one of them."

The science teacher remained silent while each student in the room shared their feelings about nuclear weapons and future wars. He listened intently. His anger subsided. Each child spoke gently, honestly, directly to him. He received them like leaves receive the sun. Something was happening to him. He never looked at me, but he melted into the eyes of the students who addressed him. His entire demeanor changed. His face softened. His hands opened, his body relaxed.

When he spoke his words were kind, soft. His bluster was gone. "I've come to understand something very important today and it has to do with what we believe," he started. "All my life, I've held to the beliefs I grew up with. Whatever I learned from my parents, my ministers, my teachers—I believed because I trusted them. But this is not that world and things have changed and each of you are teaching me how."

He took a deep breath and looked around at the whole circle. "I can't say that I think we should destroy all our weapons and have no defense against Russia. But I can say that I agree with you—we have to find a new way to disagree. I know I am part of the old way of thinking, and I know you are bringing us somewhere new. I appreciate your thoughts today and I thank you for being such bright young thinkers and for making a difference in my life today."

The students clapped and cheered and stood up to go to their next class. The science teacher walked over to shake my hand. "Best of luck on the rest of your journey," he said with a smile. That was it. A metamorphosis had occurred and this is what it looked like. Nearly invisible.

I'd just been a witness to something evolutionary. The children insisting on original approaches to conflict, on finding new solutions to global disagreements—this was an embryonic, evolutionary thought taking root in the human species, I thought. Maybe I was right that day in Friendly's restaurant when I devoured Ken Keyes's book in one sitting. Maybe we are the hundredth persons. Maybe we just have to think out loud, share our thoughts in order to strengthen the field that will change all minds.

Chapter 20
India: Mystery, Madness, Magic

I tell you this because it's about the arduousness of self-transformation. We're caught off-guard by situations we have no control over, like a surfer barreling down the face of a killer wave, knowing how badly it could go, and yet hanging on, choosing it, daring the worst.

The world I wake up to these days sometimes feels out of control. It feels tempestuous, unpredictable. And that's how India felt to me when I first entered the subcontinent after a long but luscious trek in the Himalayas.

It was so chaotic and impenetrable, I battled the culture every day. I gave it power over me. I had a huge life lesson to learn, but rage and judgment clouded my vision.

It took three months of mental labor to get my mind right, but I finally did, miraculously.

This is how it happened.

★★★★

—Patna, Bihar, 1984

Travel through India ripped me open. Every character strength I prided myself on disappeared before my eyes on the great subcontinent. On the spiritual path, each baby step forward was followed by a giant step backward. My commitments to be joyful, kind, and generous fizzled by noon when I'd find myself on a street corner, flailing my arms and shouting at someone who was impervious to my rage.

The street typist who promised to type my letter with no errors and expected full pay when he turned over a sheet full of typos. The rickshaw driver who wanted me to pay an extra 500 rupees because he got lost on the way. The waiter who delivered my wonton soup to the table next to me and tried to correct his mistake by giving it to me after half a wonton had been eaten. Another server who cleaned my glass by spitting on it and wiping it with his handkerchief. What horrified me at first became a curriculum for consciousness, but in the weeks between, I was a stranger unto myself.

I had always heard of the amazing "spirituality" of India. Travelers who'd returned from a visit there would speak of it as if they'd been to Shangri-La. Where I expected to find beauty, order, some reflection of ancient wisdom, I found chaos, inconceivable reasoning, unacceptable behavior. I didn't know then that India was my mirror. Though I seemed to be looking outward, it was my interior that was being revealed. Every scene I participated in offered a ringside seat to my shortcomings.

I walked into a store to buy a can of beans. Two clerks showed me the beans and another one wrote the ticket. A different clerk arrived to take the ticket to someone who would wrap the can. Another showed up to walk the ticket over to the cashier. Someone else ushered me to another counter to pay. My beans mysteriously showed up at a different counter where a young woman held up the can and smiled. Each of them were most likely proud of themselves for the part they played in my purchase, while I was on the edge of exploding. *How could they be so inefficient?* I wondered.

Were I the woman I thought I was, I would have found it quaint, or even amusing, but I was agitated instead—I thought I knew a better way.

On a bus ride to Baroda, there was a flurry of activity on the road and the bus pulled onto the shoulder to wait. An hour went by. I had finished my book and was now getting edgy. I left the bus to see what was going on. Hundreds of people were getting out of buses and walking toward a large hill on the side of the road. They each carried a small bucket and a serving-size spoon.

"What in the world is going on?" I asked a person standing near me.

"Oh, they are widening the road. These people are here to get rid of that hill."

"People? You're using people to get rid of a hill? You have a space program in this country. Where are the bulldozers and Caterpillars?"

I was infuriated.

Had I been in India a few weeks longer, I would have had a different response, but I hadn't yet had my crash course in Indian culture. That would occur soon.

I was staying at a Gandhian ashram founded by a man who'd lived with Gandhi since his teenage years. When I woke up one morning, I learned we were going to build a barn that day. The whole community of us. By now it *was* monsoon season, and the temperature was well over 100. The rains would be arriving soon, and the air was thick with humidity.

"How does this work?" I asked Nayan Bala, an English teacher visiting from New Delhi, whom I'd befriended.

"Looks like we just take our place in line," she said, pointing to a crowd that was beginning to take shape by the creek.

We formed a long line from the creek to the building site. There were about 40 of us. Teenage boys filled up tin bowls with water, sand, and pebbles at the creek. They handed them off to other boys who carried the bowls up a ladder, then handed them off to the women in the field, who passed them along to the men at the foundation.

I looked around to find other options that weren't so backbreaking. A few water buffalo ambled around the creek bed. A tractor and a couple flatbed trailers sat idle in the field. There it was, the answer to my dreams.

"Nayan Bala!" I shouted to get her attention. Her sari was drenched with sweat but she had a smile on her face when she turned my way.

"This is ridiculous!" I yelled, pointing my arms at the lazy buffalo. "Look, we can hook them up to the flatbed, fire up that tractor, and automate this whole process. It's stupid for us to be doing it by hand. *Don't you know time is money?"*

Nayan Bala (right) and another woman building the barn bowl by bowl.

Those final words tumbled out in slow motion, echoing through the caverns in my brain. Time stopped and we stood frozen, staring into each other's eyes.

Oh my God! I thought, *The Ugly American has outposts in my head.* I was ashamed and she knew it. Before I could utter another word, she touched my arm, leaning toward me to say, "I don't think you've been in India long enough to know that we try to give work to as many people as we can. Everyone is happy to be here. They'll be able to say to their children and grandchildren when this barn is built that they helped build it. You wouldn't want to take that away from them, would you?"

"No, I wouldn't," I said, full of shame.

She picked up the tin bowl and passed it on.

In that one moment, I understood everything about the grocery store, the bus, and the people on the mountain.

I understood how programmed I was, despite my illusions that I had overcome it. For the next two hours of passing bowls, I had time to reflect on why I was so judgmental, why I thought my way was a better way.

Yes, it was true that I had overcome my conditioning in some areas: I had outgrown my religious indoctrination and created a spirituality of my own; I had disinherited the notion that I, as a woman, was a second-class citizen; I had accepted my gayness and was proud of myself and my gay community. But whatever cultural baggage I carried as an American who learned we're the best country in the world, that our way is the right way, well those illusions get dropped by grace, with the help of others who cast a light on our blind spots. I needed Nayan Bala to help me with that one.

By the time I'd passed the last bowl of stones, I'd made a decision—I was not going to leave India until I'd managed to have an anger-free, judgment-free day. That would turn out to be quite a feat.

Nayan Bala and I stayed up half the night talking, our cots side by side, our eyes staring straight up into the hot blackness surrounding us. In the distance the sounds of tribal drums and flutes punctuated the silence, announcing the wedding that would take place soon. Nayan Bala interpreted the sounds and sights that were alien to me, and that night she shared something intimate.

She'd been a singer, in love with music, doing what she'd dreamed of since she was a child. She studied music, performed it, taught it.

"I loved singing more than anything else, but I had to give it up," she said in a whisper.

"Why give it up?" I asked.

"My husband died when I was 30. I had to mourn him. I could sing no more."

"What about when the grieving was done? Couldn't you sing then?" It had been 20 years since he died.

"It would not be proper. A woman cannot return to singing if she is a widow."

"That's not right," I said, shifting back into my *right vs. wrong* mode. "You should be able to carry on with your life, do what you want. That's terrible. What did you do when you gave up singing?"

"I went back to university, got a Ph.D. in English. Now I teach there, at the University of Delhi, and every day I am sad not to be singing."

We went back and forth a little before drifting off to sleep—me talking about women's rights, freedom, how things *ought* to be, and Nayan Bala defending her culture, succumbing to a sadness that I judged to be unnecessary.

How would I ever teach myself to be nonjudgmental? How could I possibly get through one day without feeling angry in a country that, through my cultural lens, offered so little freedom to its women? How could I manage my emotions so they'd pass through me without generating a cloud of negativity and a storm of words I'd later regret?

I started with my "time is money" remarks in the field and worked backwards. Where did *they* come from? My thoughts that something was wrong. Where did they come from? My feelings of being uncomfortable, not in control. It started with my thoughts and feelings. I felt a certain way, separated myself from what was unfolding, projected onto that separate reality a judgment, then uttered a string of words that reflected that judgment. Had it not been for Nayan Bala's kindness and good will, had I spoken those words to someone agitated like myself at that moment, I might have created an explosive situation. Nayan Bala deflected my negativity, but it could have been otherwise.

What I learned from looking back is that my thoughts were the culprit, not the circumstances. I had to change my thoughts, not the environment. I didn't enter into a reality created by someone else. I entered into a reality I created with my own thoughts.

So how do I prevent myself from becoming angry when I confront something that appears unjust? That was my challenge. I was quick to jump into *my right vs. their wrong* mode. I would have to retrain my brain. I would have to remain part of the whole, not separate from it. I would have to abandon the habit of polarizing, stop thinking in terms of us and them, right and wrong.

The whole challenge brought me back to the Japanese monastery months before and the crisis I experienced when I thought I had to choose between Buddhism and Christianity. Father Oshida's words ricocheted off the sides of my brain: "Both! Both! No choose! You both! Buddha the thought. Jesus the event. You ongoing event. You incarnation! It happening now!" He said it with such urgency. Nothing separate. All one thing. Everything unfolding perfectly.

That was the state I had to enter. The state of wholeness, oneness, awareness. I had to go on a negativity fast, a nonduality marathon. I had to stop talking until I became aware of every word I uttered. I had to see myself, my thoughts, as creative agents and start directing them toward what I wanted. And when I found myself in a situation that didn't appear to be my own creation, I had to respin it with no duality in my words or ideas.

I embarked on a campaign of mental discipline unlike anything I had done before, reminding myself over and over that the events I entered into physically were the materialization of my thoughts and feelings. Every situation became a reflection of my consciousness, mirroring in vivid detail whatever my mind was projecting. Practicing what felt like a reversal of reality consumed me. I trained my brain day after day— failing and falling, failing and falling—life isn't happening *to* me, it's happening *through* me. If I wanted something changed, I had to change my thoughts.

It took three months of concentrated focus, absolute attention to see through the apparitions into reality itself. Three months to learn how to stay curious, joyful, intrigued in the face of India's complexities and cultural disparities. I had a track record of no wins when I started. Every day I got angry about something—from the caste system to the beggars to the bedbugs.

I continued to work and travel throughout the land, visiting Delhi, Calcutta, Bombay, Baroda, Pondicherry. I stayed in ashrams, in homes, in Salvation Army hostels, and the international community of Auroville, encountering situations that tested my ability to stay calm in the face of chaos. Over and over I failed until it finally happened—I made it through a day in complete peace. I encountered chaos and laughed in its face. I was good to go and ready to leave.

Egypt was next on my journey, and I went to a travel agency to book a flight. Rajiv, a handsome young Hindu dressed in Banana Republic clothes, made the arrangements for a one-way ticket. It would be ready in a few days, he said. I went back to my Salvation Army Guest House and packed up my backpack.

My flight was a week out so I had seven more days. Every day brought a plethora of hurdles to jump, and every day I missed a few and made a few. On day six, I went to the agency to pick up my ticket. I was never more eager to leave a country.

When I asked for Rajiv, they said he had left for America.

"Yeah but ... he must have left a ticket for me. He said he would."

A woman looked through his desk and came up with nothing.

"No, sorry. Nothing here."

I felt it coming up, the blood rising up my neck. The pressure mounting. Disbelief at this level of inefficiency. An old voice I thought I'd rewired crept into my head, *How could he do this to me?*

Another voice spoke up. *Nobody did anything to you. Someone just did something. What you make of it is up to you.*

I wanted to scream. I wanted to shout and cry and flail my arms. I wanted to get physical, pound things, break windows.

I stared into the face of the woman and deliberated. I chose peace that day.

"Okay, then," I said, taking my seat in a rickety chair. "I need a one-way ticket to Cairo."

Chapter 21
Sacrament-Makers of Today

I tell you this so you will ordain yourself a priest of the imagination and bestow blessings wherever you go—blessings on the people, blessings on the creatures, blessings on the maples, the pines, the rivers, the lakes.

We are called now to take it upon ourselves to proclaim the holy moments sacred, to stop the action and raise our hands and bless it out loud, joyfully, communally.

The old days are gone when you waited for a priest, deferred your own authority as a Child of the Cosmos, a Knower of Things, a Bestower of Grace. I ordain you right now if you are hesitant. I have powers given to me by the Spirit that blows through us. The world is hungry for our blessings. We cannot withhold them any longer.

Children are being born, people are being healed, lovers are committing, the sick are letting go—they need our words, our tenderness. They need us to risk not getting it right but getting it real. That's all we want. We want to nuzzle up against the real, to be with people who say raw, honest things, who are wise enough to know this minute here, this calls for a blessing.

I ordain you and ask you to speak out when the others have no words on their tongue. You need not try and remember old prayers. They were for time gone by. We are the ones now. We are the sacrament-makers. We are the writers of the new sacred texts.

✶✶✶✶

—Antiparos, Greece, 1985

The first time I said Mass for my mother, we were in Greece on the tiny island of Antiparos. I hadn't seen her for more than a year when she arrived in Athens, and after a couple days at the Parthenon, the Acropolis, and Olympia, we were ready for the remote—sandy beaches, no people, no museums. A quick boat ride ferried us to our fantasy land.

We rented a small bungalow for a few nights and spent our first day hiking through fields and encountering a recently widowed farmer who wanted to marry my mother. We shared some bread and wine with Theo, who begged us to stay and live with him in his little hut overlooking the sea. After looking at all his family photos, we bade farewell and continued our hike to a secluded beach where my mother planted her towel on the powdery white sand, lay down, and fell asleep immediately.

I waded into the turquoise waters of the southern Aegean to dive for stones we could use for checkers. I'd make a life-size board while she slept and we'd have a game when she awoke. *I had lived and gone to heaven.* After collecting 12 fist-size stones in black and white, I searched the beach for a branch to draw my lines in the sand. Just as I finished the 64 squares, mom rolled over and stretched, waking up slowly from her midday nap.

That's how the days went in Greece with my mother. A lot of miles, a lot of fun, not much talk, joy unbound. I woke early on Sunday morning and decided I'd say Mass to begin our day. I walked to the village for a bottle of wine, fresh baked bread, candles, and flowers, which I arranged on our kitchen table altar. While mom still slept, I brewed some coffee, tuned my guitar, and lit the candles, pondering how to create a sacrament we would bestow upon ourselves. I'd been away from the Church for 16 years since being refused the sacraments in 1969, but parts of the Mass surfaced in my memory: entrance song, readings, homily, offertory, consecration of the bread and wine, communion, exit song.

180

I took Mom coffee in bed and said when she was ready we'd have Mass in the kitchen. A big question mark took the shape of her face. In 20 minutes we sat together at the kitchen table, about to enter a territory we'd never explored.

My mom and me getting ready for Mass in Greece.

Though we'd had trouble in the past about my gayness, our rifts were healed by time and love. Now we were so happy to be together, here in Europe where she'd never been, that she handed me the reins and trusted whatever direction we moved in.

She saw we had all the makings for a Mass sprawled out on the brightly covered table and she didn't ask one question. According to the Catholic religion, this would have been a sacrilegious act—a woman preparing to say Mass. But whatever went through her mind, I never questioned.

"Okay, Mom, for our entrance song I'm going to sing the song I wrote you for your birthday, okay?"

She smiled and nodded her head in agreement, already into a sacramental silence. A warm breeze blew into our sanctuary, ruffling the curtains and fanning the flames of our burning candles. I strummed a G chord and started to sing:

When I'm walking down the road some days
and see the setting sun
there's a question in my mind sometimes
'bout what I've left undone.
I wonder if I've made it clear
to those I've left behind
just how very much I feel you here
and hold you in my mind.

And I want to say thank you for your kindness,
thank you for your dreams,
the love that you are sending
rushes through me like a stream.
It flows into my morning hours
and takes me through the day;
at night it's like a candle
lighting up my way.

I'm heading toward the mountaintop,
moving toward the light—
the truth that I was seeking
is moving into sight.
I know I had it with me long before I started out
but I'm learning from the bottom up
what faith is all about.

And I want to say thank you for believing,
thank you for your love
I'm soaring on the breezes, flying like a dove—
if it weren't for all you've given me,
the strength you handed down,
I never would have found the wings
to get me off the ground.

And though I'm often by myself
I never feel alone
the Spirit's here inside me

and I feel like I'm at home.
When I hear the songs we used to sing,
I know you're doing well
and it feels just like a miracle
near as I can tell.

And I want to say thank you for your goodness,
thank you for your care,
there's some who call it Energy
and some who call it prayer,
but there's something to this Spirit
that's holy as it's free
and this journey that I'm making
is for you as well as me.

We both cried some at the end of the song. It was then time for readings, but we had nothing to read, so we shared about something we read that made a difference in our lives. My mom went all the way back to *Little Women* by Louisa May Alcott, saying how nice it was, when she was a child, to imagine a life like the March girls had instead of her own—oldest girl of 14 kids on a dairy farm in northern New York, her mother so often sick in pregnancy, she the one called upon to mother the rest who needed care. How she wished she could have been Jo or Amy, living an exotic life away from the farm.

I shared about the power of Doris Lessing's *Shikasta*—how it opened me up to new ways of thinking and provoked a reimagining of the culture that shaped me. We gave thanks to the authors, evangelists of a kind, and acknowledged that sacred words arrive from every direction.

After that, in lieu of a sermon, we each told a story about something we'd learned from someone real in our lives. She spoke of her boss Fred who gave her more and more responsibility until she finally realized her own worth and knew she was capable of just about anything. I spoke about the ways that Margaret Lalor shaped me as a cultural activist and creative force by believing in me the way Fred believed in my mother. We gave praise and thanks to the two of them.

Then it was time for bread and wine. I poured wine into our tiny juice glasses. Mom took the bread into her hands and broke it.

We did not repeat holy words or replicate the actions of priests we'd watch do this all our lives. We just looked each other in the eyes and smiled.

"I'm so glad you're here, Mom. This day is blessed and I'm grateful for it."

We sipped some wine and ate some bread, then my mother spoke:

"I'm so glad to be here with you, honey. And I'm grateful to God for making it all happen."

"Amen," I said.

We wiped our lips and our hands with little napkins, then it was time for our final hymn.

"What shall it be, Mom? Got a favorite?"

"How about 'You Are My Sunshine?'"

I picked up my guitar, played a C chord, and we ended our sacrament with a song that to my family is as important as the "The Star-Spangled Banner" and "America the Beautiful." It's a song of homecoming, a hymn of belonging that says no matter where you are, no matter what you've done, you belong to us and we will never let you go.

With that, the Mass was ended and we went in peace to plan our day. It was only later, after giving it some thought, that she asked me never to tell anyone what we'd done. While I was awash in joy at the power we took to celebrate a sacrament of our own making, she was worried we might be judged by people or priests who considered this a sacrilege.

I honored her request and kept it a secret, though I wished I could have shouted it from the rooftops. Thirty years later, when she'd moved to Oceanside, California, to be near her children, I'd often spend Saturday night in her apartment and wake her up in the same way: "Okay, Mom, wake up. It's time for Mass." She grew to love our ritual and by the end had no trouble admitting her daughter said Mass for her on many a Sunday.

CHAPTER 22
PILGRIMAGE TO THE HEART CHAKRA

I tell you this because I learned a lesson I never knew I was missing until I went to Iceland. I went to find one thing and found another instead: a common occurrence, as every traveler knows.

It's a magical tale with a surprising end—one that I would never have imagined. I understand better now what Robert Louis Stevenson meant when he said he traveled not so much to get to places but to "come down off the feather-bed of civilisation."

The best lessons are rarely found in books.

✭✭✭✭

—Reykjavik, Iceland, 1995

When I saw the ad, my heart somersaulted: a pilgrimage to the "heart chakra of the planet" for women writers. I had no idea how anyone could map the whereabouts of our planet's chakras, but someone had convinced Hannelore Hahn, founder of the International Women's Writing Guild, that this had been done and she promptly organized a trip there with two Icelandic women as leaders.

On our first night in Reykjavik we sat around a table to introduce ourselves, and hardly anyone could say clearly why they were there. We were like the characters in *Close Encounters of the Third Kind* who'd encountered UFOs and become obsessed with images of a mountain-like shape. They couldn't get the mountain shape out of their minds, and when photographs of Devils Tower in Wyoming showed up on the nightly news, they left their homes in droves to drive there. Iceland's heart chakra had become our Devils Tower. We simply had to be there.

Thirteen women writers flew to the Kentucky-sized island from four corners of the United States. Our guides were Sunneva and Hildur, who had grown up on the Snæfellsnes Peninsula, home to the 700,000-year-old Snæfellsjökull, a glacier-capped stratovolcano, which is nearly 5,000 feet high with a 656-foot deep crater. We traversed Snæfellsnes for days to reach our destination, the mighty glacier.

Sunneva and Hildur had grown up in the area and were familiar with all of the enchanted spots. They both had the ability to see energy fields and colors emanating from the land masses around them. I'd not researched Iceland and had no idea that belief in elves and other varieties of "hidden people" was prevalent throughout the country.

Folklorist Terry Gunnell, who teaches at the University of Iceland, claims there are 13 types of elves that are as tall as humans. In an *All Things Considered* radio show, Gunnell, explained that elves help Icelanders make sense of nature. They make their homes in crags and rocks and are said to dress in old-timey 19th-century outfits. When plans are made for new roads, elf advocates often team up with environmentalists to prevent elf habitats from being disturbed.

Gunnell surveyed 1,000 Icelanders about elves and found only 13 percent said it was impossible that elves exist. Thirty-seven percent said it was possible they exist, 17 percent found their existence likely, and eight percent were absolutely certain that elves populate the land.

Maybe Jules Verne had heard of this when he began his subterranean *Journey to the Center of the Earth* here. Snæfellsjökull National Park and Snæfellsjökull volcano are both claimed to be an opening to the underworld. A trail cuts through lava fields to the black-pebble Djúpalónssandur beach and on to the white swooping seabirds at the cliffs of Dritvík. These are the trails we hiked.

We stopped often to rest on the way, sitting in a circle like preschoolers gathered for stories. Hildur and Sunneva shared tales about the strong women of Nordic sagas and the giantesses who live in the cone-shaped mountains. We stopped at sites along the way where, we were assured, the energy was powerful and the colors (unseen by me) brilliant. "Here there are great waves of energy. You can pick stones that will help you on your journey, some from the lava rocks and some from the pebble beach. They have different qualities and can be used for different things," said Hildur with absolute authority.

We climbed up red hills of cooled lava, sinking into the ash that blanketed the craters. We walked on carpets of lichen-covered rocks, through blossoming heaths toward the delft blue sea where the dragon rocks lay. We drank from the waters of a sacred spring, marked by a statue of the Blessed Mother after someone reported a vision of the virgin there. Sunneva and Hildur led us through centers of male and female energy, past statues to the gods and into grottoes of the goddesses. We snaked along the cliffs in a long line of color, our hiking clothes bright against the pale blue sky.

At night, we sprawled out in sleeping bags on auditorium floors, traveling from school to school as we made our way through the mystical land. It was high summer, the season of the midnight sun, and darkness never intruded into the night. Each evening at midnight, we formed a circle, shared stories from the day, and sent our spirits into the heart of the glacier. I often ventured out into the pale gray night, photographing the silhouettes of cattle and craters, listening to the night birds and the gentle winds.

Along the way, we plagued our guides with questions about the heart chakra, wanting specifics about the sacred mysteries of the land. How would we know when we got there? What happens at the heart chakra? Would we feel different vibrations when we arrived? Were we almost there? Like tourists focused solely on the destination, some of us were in jeopardy of missing the journey.

Sunneva and Hildur were patient with us, meeting our questions with cheery smiles. After three days of hiking, we arrived at the base of the glacier. Sunneva led us to a sparkling blue stream, naming it as a source of power that ran from the glacier southward, along the ley line that aligned Snæfellsjökull with Glastonbury, Stonehenge, and the pyramids of Giza. We gathered in a circle around Sunneva, squinting into the snow-covered mountain with our private thoughts about sitting on Mother Nature's heart chakra. With a handful of heather in her palm and her red hair blowing in the Arctic breeze, Sunneva explained how it was determined that the glacier was the heart chakra for the planet and why she hadn't been willing to answer our many questions about body chakras and earth chakras.

"In the East and in the West," she said, "the mind is an important part of spiritual discipline. Whether one is engaged in emptying it or filling it up, the mind is primary in Eastern and Western spiritual experience. In the North we find our spiritual power in Nature. To us, spiritual wisdom cannot be taught, only experienced. It is not something we think of, but something we feel. And we feel it with the earth and in the earth. You had to walk these paths, hear these birds, climb these hills in order to take in the power of the North, to feel the energy of this glacier. And now you have it in you. It is yours forever."

Sunneva left the circle and knelt down to drink from the stream. Others followed, sipping the crystal blue water from the cup of their hands—the final rite of passage in our journey to the heart.

Norse paganism, known as Ásatrú, was the primary religion among the people who settled Iceland in the 9th century. It encouraged intimacy with the earth and regarded the wisdom acquired by people through their lived experience as more significant than that acquired from religious books. Today, about 42 percent of Icelanders describe their religious viewpoint as pagan, humanity's ancestral religion. There is no sacred text, but rather a set of precepts that encourage tolerance, honesty, and respect for the natural world.

In spite of all the religious dogma I had disentangled from, and regardless of the global faiths that moved me forward, on one level I was still a spiritual child when I traversed the lava fields of Iceland. My brain had been colonized by the church of the Roman Empire—a church that had no reverence for the earth, that separated human from divine, secular from sacred, that did not abide nontheist myths or magical elves. So wandering through the heather fields of Snæfellsnes as Sunneva pointed out elf habitats or commented on radiant colors I could not see, I was at a loss. I stood at a threshold, looking into another dimension of reality. I could suspend my disbelief or open doors to new possibilities. If my imagination had been frozen in time, might it be possible for me to thaw it out?

Spirituality in Iceland had nothing to do with patriarchy or apostles' creeds or sins—venial or mortal. Spirituality there was an experience of communion, of our oneness with nature. It was an immersion in beauty, in the Sacred Heart of a living planet. People can say what they will about earth's chakras and families of elves, and none of it matters, but had every child born from this soil been introduced to the land like Icelandic children, I think our planet would not be endangered.

Journey to the Heart

We walked alone through wild terrain,
searching for stones that called us by name,
leaving pieces of ourselves in the red rock swirls
always to be one with the heart of our world.

Two by two, three by three
we climbed the black cliffs, brave and free—
holding hands, stones, feathers, dreams,
we circled the mountain in a colorful stream.

Winding through heath and black-pebbled beaches,
the pulse of ourselves ever increasing—
our quickening breath on the uphill path
preparing our hearts for the glacier at last.

We drank in water at the sacred pool
letting go of what we knew,
each one kneeling all alone
making room for the Great Unknown.

A ritual steeped in power and grace,
a great light streaming from every face,
we absolved ourselves from fear and pain
forgiveness flowing like a cleansing rain.

Making our way to the Mother's heart
to the white-capped glacier with the gifts we had brought,
we lay our bodies down, touched our lips to the ground
ever moved, ever grateful for the magic we had found.

What we'd come so far in search of
was a mirror to our might,
a reflection of our grandness,
a reclaiming of our sight—

and there She stood before us
the Heart of all the earth
saying *yes*, my daughters, all power is yours—
I rejoice in your rebirth.

Chapter 23
Finding My Balance

I tell you this because it is about your power—our power—to feel unity though everything around us feels torn asunder.

I tell you this because I want you to rethink some words—mystic, prophet, divine, creation—and redefine them so you see yourself in the picture.

I am trying to open some doors here. I'm handing you keys. I'm saying it, right out loud, the kingdom is not what they said it was.

You have turned your back and it was right to do so because what they called "truth" was an insult to your magnitude.

I am only one person writing here, but there are millions of us, everywhere, trying to piece together words that say this same thing: You are that which you have sought all along.

We are singing our hearts out. Can you hear us?

You are already home.

★★★★

—Syracuse, New York, 1992

I had been working as a photojournalist for the Syracuse *Catholic Sun* for about a year, writing stories, creating photo-essays, winning awards. It seemed a match made in heaven until a Syracuse University photojournalism student approached the editor and said he'd do my job for free. The next day I got my pink slip.

I went into a tailspin and did what I often do in a crisis: I called my psychic astrologer friend Paula for a hit of her wisdom. She has a knack for tuning into Mind-at-Large and actually understanding what it's saying.

"This is great, Jan. You're in Syracuse. It's time for you to go to graduate school."

"Graduate school? How am I going to do that? It's already August. School starts in three weeks."

"Don't worry," she said. "It'll work out. Just go up there and show them who you are."

I went through my books and found a copy of *Making Peace: One Woman's Journey Around the World*, which had been published a few years earlier. It was a soft-cover photographic chronicle of my peace pilgrimage. I didn't have time for GREs, but this book would give the committee people an idea of what I was capable of. With my book in hand and a few copies of my best work from the *Catholic Sun*, I marched off to the Newhouse School at Syracuse University and found Professor David Sutherland sitting in his office, surrounded by towers of photography books.

When I introduced myself and explained what had happened at the *Catholic Sun*, admitting that I wanted to start right up on my master's degree, he smiled and reached for my book. His wire-framed glasses teetered on the end of his nose and he said nothing while he flipped casually through the pages. He never looked at my photo-essays from the *Sun* but squinted my way and said, "I think we can make something happen."

They accepted me right away and my hopes loomed as I imagined myself in Socrates' Circle with a band of other curious minds eager to expand. This, however, was an illusion. I was already in my mid-forties and old enough to be everyone's maiden aunt or grandmother. No one was interested in sitting in any circle with me, and a lot of them were busy driving around in new Jeeps and planning trips to Cancún for spring break. I just didn't belong.

I gave it two months then decided I had to quit. It was not fun enough and life is short. I woke up one morning and called Paula to let her know, since the whole idea had originated in her head. It only seemed fair to inform her it was over.

When I gave her the news, she spun into alarm mode.

"Wait! Wait! Don't do anything," she said in a panic, then left me hanging. I imagined her dialing in to her private wisdom channel. How *did* that work with intuitives anyway? Did they hear voices? Feel a hunch in the body? In less than a minute, she was back on the line with three questions, none of them very relevant in my opinion.

"Okay, Jan, answer these questions," she said, launching right into them. "Are you eating and drinking moderately?"

That was the *last* thing I could be accused of. I confessed immediately. "No, I'm not. I'm drinking cheap wine every night, I never cook, and all my pockets are stuffed with Almond Joy Miniatures. I do sugar like other people do supplements."

"Oh dear," she said. I could just see her shaking her head at me, worrying over my bad behavior. "What are you doing for your body? What's your exercise routine?"

"I don't have one."

"Oh my, this isn't good," she lamented. "What about a spiritual practice? What's your spiritual practice?"

"Paula, I don't *have* a spiritual practice."

That was it. She put her foot down.

"Jan, your life will *never* work out if you don't take care of these things. It's a requirement. Now give yourself three weeks to make a plan, get these things handled, then call me back. And don't call *before* then."

Damn it! I thought, hanging up the phone. *What the hell am I going to do for a spiritual practice?* That was my biggest concern. The others I knew would be easier—exercise and moderation—at least compared to the spiritual practice. My relationship to religion was complex.

I decided right away that this wasn't going to be painful. I wasn't going to sit on the floor. Wasn't going to sign up for a yoga class. Wasn't going to go to church. Or get up before dawn. It had to be comfortable. This had to suit my disposition.

I settled on 20 minutes of silence every morning. I'd light a candle to make it feel special and wouldn't allow any distractions. No phone, no magazines, no newspapers, no TV. Door closed, candle burning, me in the bed. That ought to do it. The thought of it yanked me back 20 years to my convent training when we meditated every day for 30 minutes, sandwiched between our spiritual reading and community vespers. The memory of it was like a shoulder massage. Those 30 minutes of contemplation each day had been a slice of heaven. Maybe it wouldn't be as hard as I thought to carve out some time for emptiness.

I started the very next day, all pumped up, hoping for magic to happen. It didn't. I swatted errant thoughts away like flies. Twenty minutes felt like an hour. Mundane concerns hijacked my imagination. Grocery lists. Friends to call. Oil change to set up. Days passed and I never improved. *If others can do this, I can too*, I told myself, thinking of all the mystics I'd read about over the years, sure they weren't any smarter than I was. I burrowed in, trying to concentrate, as if effort would help. That only made things worse. My brain was unmanageable.

I came across a line in a Deepak Chopra book: "Effort is the problem, not the solution." I needed another strategy but didn't know where to turn. So I decided to relax. No one was judging me. I wasn't going to be graded on this. The only thing that mattered was that I showed up every morning.

Once I calmed down and stopped trying to control the experience, things improved. How things turned out was more a matter of grace than will. My job was simply to breathe and be aware of it. When thoughts invaded my space, all I had to do was reel my mind back to my breaths. I remembered that from my convent training and also from the classes I'd taken in Transcendental Meditation in the 1970s. I'd had several periodic brushes with a spiritual practice over the years, but never settled into one with any commitment. This would be my first and there was no reason I couldn't make a go of it. I might not have been religious, but my sense of spirituality had remained horizonless since Father Grabys pried my mind open in Theology 101, back in my novitiate days. I was not one who believed in a geographical expanse between heaven and earth. It all pretty much boiled down to the one moment we had right in front of us. The eternal now. "The kingdom is within and all around you" is the biblical phrase I stood by.

So I kept lighting the candle every morning. The only effort I made was to stop working at it. When I had a thought, I explored it for duality. If it was dualistic, I converted it. I defended both sides of an argument. I practiced atheism a few days a week. It was all good. I was rewiring my brain, and since I couldn't build a wall to keep thoughts out, I mastered the thoughts that came in. I printed out quotations that took me beyond right and wrong and put them on my altar.

> When the ax comes into the forest
> the trees, upon seeing its wooden handle, say
> "Look, one of us."
> —Hasidic saying

> My barn having burned to the ground, I can
> now see the moon.
> —Japanese saying

> If you don't share your wealth with us, we'll
> share our poverty with you.
> —Nigerian chief

Surrender and fulfillment happen simultaneously. It is all one unfolding, one event, like moss and the tree, fire and heat, oxygen and air. For the meditator, there is only the awareness that there is nothing to seek, the moment at hand contains the universe. Divinity is the air we breathe. Our bodies are saturated with the sacred.

As I relaxed more into my morning meditations, I began to feel less alone. The experience felt more visceral on some days. One morning I seemed to float into the silence like a parachuter drifting through cloudless skies. The quiet wrapped her arms around me like wind around a sail. I felt a presence, a counterpart—a yin to my yang. I had an invisible dance partner, and she had a gift for me: a gift of words. They fell from her realm into mine, lining themselves up in colorful couplets in the pages of my journal.

Now is the time to be mindful of light,
to keep the flame going, to give up the fight;
for life is a pleasure, it's not meant for pain,
let go of the struggle and dance once again.

For you all have an angel who sits at your side,
who waits for your calling, who hears every cry;
she's there at your service, there as your guide,
so call her, she's waiting with arms open wide.

The God that you're seeking needs not to be sought
you're already one like the sea and the salt—
the Source is within you, the force is at hand;
it's been in your soul since your life began.

So rejoice, my child, in the gifts that you have;
the light of the world is the torch in your hand,
and if you get beyond your fear and your pain,
you'll see God in the being who goes by your name.

It was a song. I never would have known. I sat down with my guitar later that day, and sure enough, it had a beautiful melody. *What shall I call it?* I asked no one in particular, and a name, like an aroma, drifted up from the lined sheets. Call it "Rebecca's Song."

By week three, I'd extended my morning time to 30 minutes. Miraculous creations did not drop from the heavens every day, but I wanted to be there just in case. I imagined myself a satellite dish to this Super Muse, my hands and mind open to whatever intelligence was being broadcast my way. I was *in communion* with that beautiful source, that font of creativity.

Over the years, I had not established a spiritual practice despite the spiritual nature of my journey and was only doing this because I trusted Paula. If she said my life couldn't work without it, I was in. What's 20 or 30 minutes when you're weighing it against a life's chance to succeed? And the practice *was* changing me—though I can't say what mattered more, the moderation in food and drink, the physical exercise, or this silence in the morning. I just felt happier, healthier, and less lonely than before.

That I was just a tiny dust speck in the vast scheme of things, an amalgam of stardust and clay, never changed, but I felt connected by consciousness to everything around me. My former notion of God as a masculine deity shape-shifted, and images of the divine feminine sprouted from the newly tilled soil of my soul. I thought of myself as matter *mattering*, part and parcel of the whole thing, one piece of the cosmic puzzle—and I was making something of it. I was in cahoots with Creativity Itself. Songs bubbled up. Poems drifted in. Anxiety walked out the door.

Every morning I woke up happy, eager to see what the Silence brought. Some days ideas arrived out of nowhere, curiously connected to questions bubbling up on the inside. Other days came with lavish litanies of distracting thoughts. It was always like that—back and forth. Something, then nothing. Predictably unpredictable. On Monday, a profound awareness of my oneness with creation; on Tuesday, a meaningless cacophony of chaotic voices. My meditations were a constantly changing weather system of events.

When three weeks had elapsed and I called Paula back, I was like a new person. I'd been biking to school, eating mostly plant-based meals, drinking only a couple glasses of Chardonnay on the weekends.

"Paula, you're not going to believe what happened!" I said when I heard her voice.

"Oh yeah? What happened?"

"Everybody on campus has changed dramatically!"

We had a good laugh, knowing that no one had changed but me, and that change made all the difference. I stayed on to finish graduate school and have maintained my spiritual practice for 30 years, still going through the same ups and downs as I did in the beginning. Elegant blessings some days. Barren deserts other days.

I've aged in the process like a nice Cabernet, and the major thing that's changed is the time I spend in silence. I still light a candle and sit in my bed, but I might be there for an hour or two if nothing else calls me. By now, scientific research has come up with a rationale why the whole process is so satisfying. According to neuroscientist Andrew Newberg, more of our brain lights up when we attach ourselves to the Infinite, so it's no surprise that a spiritual practice leads to higher levels of creativity, intuition, and happiness. When we limit our reception of noisy information, we stop feeling overwhelmed by petty facts and open ourselves to immense possibilities. It's like an automatic update of our personal operating system.

"Religious and spiritual contemplation changes your brain in a profoundly different way because it strengthens a unique neural circuit that specifically enhances social awareness and empathy while

My altar today—a piece of the Chelyabinsk meteorite that landed in Siberia in 2013 with a photograph of it moving through space, a wooden chalice turned by my friend Terry, a book for the names of people I'm praying for handmade by my friend Irina, a hawk feather, and two candles representing masculine and feminine.

subduing destructive feelings and emotions," writes Newberg in *How God Changes Your Brain*. In the past few decades we've learned that the art of connecting with the Absolute—or whatever one perceives the Boundless Silence to be—is a physical as well as a mystical phenomenon.

In a spiritual practice, one often thinks of the experience as *union with*. There's a measurable social impact. I do not feel alone in my morning meditation, although as a post-theist I have long since given up the notion of a personal deity. I do not subscribe to the idea of a God in the heavens who intervenes in human affairs.

One does not need to believe in God to be a practicing mystic. A mystic is one who has an unmediated experience of the Unknown, considered by some to be sacred or spiritual. I have that every day and so do millions of others around the planet. It doesn't take a priest or rabbi or imam to get you there. Anyone who wants to have a connection to the invisible forces we collaborate with *can*. But it takes practice—a spiritual practice.

You can read a hundred books on mysticism and never get close to being one if you're not willing to sit in solitude for a few minutes every day. That's the nut of it. Mysticism is an experience of *being*, not *knowing*. It belongs to the body. You can't get there by thinking about it. You have to sit your body down and *not* think about it. That's why Meister Eckhart called the process one "not of addition but of subtraction."

There's no need to add to what you *have* or *are* or *know*, but there's a lot to leave behind. For one, a belief that it takes effort. The only effort is the effort of *being there*, sitting there, every day, with no judgment, no expectation, no disappointments if nothing seems to happen. The process is an inward alchemy, a raising of one's self to a condition in which union with the Infinite is possible.

Another thing to release is the idea that you're a seeker trying to find Something or Someone. Be a finder. Sit there long enough to feel light making its way into your bones and marrow. A fish doesn't seek water. A bird doesn't seek air. A mystic doesn't seek God. There is no longing. Just the union. Different each day, like love itself. Sometimes subtle, barely there. Sometimes all riled up, full of fury. Sometimes a stream of loveliness, quiet and pulsating.

The experience of oneness is incremental. It grows in intensity. One's relationship to divinity, to the Invisible Force, deepens and expands interiorly. It grows from the inside out. What *you* bring to the table—your level of commitment—is quintessential to the outcome. It's like the difference between a New Year's resolution and a wedding vow. You commit and you do not waver in that commitment. Each day you grow more familiar with the quiet; you begin to crave it; you may even sit for longer periods, just for the lusciousness of it—and as you lean into that cavern of darkness, something inside you changes.

The Silence feels fuller, the emptiness more fertile. The dance becomes more animated. The connection is complete. Nothing to achieve. What was always true is true forevermore. *I am one with the Beloved.* Every person who knows this relationship comprehends it as *connectedness.* I am not separate—not from the earth, not from the multitudes of people, not from the stars, not even from the Divine. As Jesus once described it, "I and the Father are one."

Alan Watts, in *Behold the Spirit,* wrote that "the whole point of the Gospel is that everyone may experience union with God in the same way and to the same degree as Jesus himself." Jesus, the Jewish preacher and spiritual teacher, reminded the people, more than once, that whatever was true for him was true for them as well. *What you see me do, you, too, can do and even more.* And the path he laid out was simple: prayer and kindness. Go to the desert for solitude and prayer, then go to your communities and feed the poor, heal the sick, call for justice.

As cocreators of the cultures we belong to, it is our job to renew and refresh the spiritual teachings, to keep them relevant to the minds evolving in consciousness. Isaiah, Daniel, Amos, Hosea—the prophets of old—spoke to the people of *their* times, in *their* terms. Now, it is up to the prophetic voices of this century to call people to prayer and action, to reimagine divinity in new forms, and to create prayers, poems, and new sacred texts that close the gaps between heaven and earth. It is the work of the faithful to go beyond those dualities and make of the earth a sacred living organism worthy of our reverence, our awe, and our love.

He Is, She Is

He is Cosmic Intelligence, Mind at Large
She is Wisdom, making soup and bread
from his stellar ideas.

He is nighttime, twilight, dawn and daylight
She is the Serengeti, the rain forest,
Lover's Lane and Death Valley.

He is silence, stillness, a cavern of nothingness
She is birdsong, lovemaking, the laughter of children.

He is the heat of the Sahara desert
She is the sand in the palm of his hand.

He is space, all boundless and infinite;
She, a galaxy wrapped in his arms.

He is the fire, She the volcano,
spewing new earth from his molten seed.

He is the sea, and She the wave,
He the wind, She the wheat fields.

All day long they rise and roll,
lean and bend, like teenagers
locked in love's embrace.

Life begins with the union of the two
From that One, the New is born.

These times are conditioning us for a new world, one that we conceive of and shape with our own minds and hands. It is a threshold time, a portal into a culture of kindness and justice, if we make it so with our thoughts, our prayers, and our actions.

What Is a Mystic?

Someone who has mastered abandon.
Someone who is mad for mystery,
who seeks out uncertainty,
who picks doubt for a dance partner.

A mystic is someone who lights the candle
and cries for joy,
crazy in love with No One.

A mystic doesn't argue about God,

defend God,
crusade for God.

A mystic is a burning bush,
a spark of the Holy Bonfire,
the one in the corner
laughing at Nothing.

Don't look for bruised knees, bowed heads,
hands clasped or beating breasts.
Don't listen for *mea culpa*,
talk of sin, right or wrong.

If you're looking for a mystic
look in the forest, not a church.
Look for someone with an apron on,
with work boots and gloves.
Look for someone who's pitching in,
helping out,
someone doing something
to set this world aright.

A mystic makes breakfast
of the Great Beloved
and all day long
metabolizes love.

Chapter 24
Nothing to Forgive

I tell you this because it's the jewel in my velvet pouch. Because it's a story that holds the desert and the springs, the midnight sky and the purple dawn.

I tell you this because there's something in here for all of us, no matter how far into the dark wood you've stumbled, no matter how deep into the cavern you've slipped.

Hear this like a birdsong, like your favorite sonata, like waves outside a cottage bedroom. The words flew into my ears but they are meant for the family.

I'm telling this story to break open your heart, that it can be emptied of debris and unforgiven faults, that the light can return.

That the Light can return.

✳✳✳✳

—Syracuse, New York, 1990

"Hey, Marion Ripski's at John the Baptist now," my partner Annie called out from the living room. "Maybe she'll be your witness."

It was now 21 years since I'd been dismissed from the convent and I still hadn't figured out how to get closure. At 41 years old, I had a lot yet to learn about my own role in the events of my life. I carried rejection around like a lead weight, injustices that were thrust upon me by my Church and community. But that was about to end, finally. Sister Marion Ripski had been the provincial director at the Motherhouse during my novitiate. She'd rotated out of leadership and was now living in a convent 10 minutes from where we lived. Annie and I had both been novices during her tenure, and Annie thought she might be able to help me resolve my turmoil once and for all. I looked up the number for the convent and called right away.

"Sister Marion, I don't know if you remember me, but I'm Jan Phillips and I was a novice at the Motherhouse in the late 60s. I was dismissed right before vows and haven't been able to heal this hole in my heart after all these years. I wondered if you'd be willing to sit with me and let me share my story to see if that would help."

"Oh yes," she replied. "I remember you. I'm sorry you've been carrying the weight of this. I'd be happy to set up a time to see you."

Within a week, we were sitting knee to knee in a small, dark parlor of the convent on Court Street.

"How would you like to do this?" she asked.

"I'd like to start at the beginning, at age 12 when I decided to become a nun," I said. "I'll tell the whole story, right up until today, and the only thing I ask is that you don't interrupt. When I'm done, you can say anything you want."

"Okay, that'll be fine," she said graciously, getting comfortable in her chair.

"I'll probably cry through the whole thing, but don't worry. Just let me have my feelings."

"Whatever you need," she said.

I began with the terror I felt at age 12 when I realized I was gay. I went on to share about Sister Helen Charles' response to my despair, how she healed me, the whole positive reinforcement thing with my mother, why I decided to become a nun, how much I loved the convent even though I wasn't obedient.

I talked about my relationship with Sister Marie Catherine, how important it was, how awful it felt to be told I couldn't speak with her anymore, how lonely I felt, and the same thing happening again with Sister Rose, being silenced, misunderstood, how I longed for relationship, needing it to balance out my hours of prayer and contemplation. I described the night of my dismissal in minute detail—the surprise of it, the taking of the veil, no chance to say goodbye, not knowing what to tell my parents, my descent into hell, the years of praying and hoping they would write and say, "Please come back, we made a terrible mistake."

I cried through it all and she kept her eyes on mine the whole time, leaning into me, nodding her head in compassion, listening as if her own life depended on my words. I spoke of my shame and why I ran away to California. Told her about the drugs and drinking and that night in jail, and the rage that was all mixed up with grief and the therapy I'd tried, and all the times I'd moved thinking it would go away if I just lived somewhere else. I told her what it felt like to get the letter from Sister Joan Theresa explaining it away as "excessive and exclusive relationships." How unseen I felt for who I was. I think in the long run I just hoped to be seen and respected by someone in the community. It was a matter of pride for me that people did not think I just up and left.

When I was done, we sat in silence for a short time before she said, "Thank you, Jan," and continued with a response I never imagined.

"Sister, will you forgive me for this terrible injustice that was done to you under my watch?"

I was flabbergasted. In a hundred years, I never expected an apology, nor did I think I deserved one. And yet, here she was asking for forgiveness.

"Of course, Sister. I forgive you for this terrible injustice that was done to me under your watch."

And then she asked, "Sister, will you forgive the entire community of the Sisters of St. Joseph of Carondelet for this terrible injustice that was done to you?"

My heart nearly broke open. How could this be happening? I didn't expect it to go like this at all. I was so visible to her. She made my pain her own. It felt as if there were only one of us in that room.

"Yes, Sister, I forgive the entire community of the Sisters of St. Joseph for the terrible injustice that was done to me."

She nodded her head then and closed her eyes, and in that moment, the heavens opened and the greatest grace I have ever felt surged through my entire being. It was over. The rage, the grief, the shame, dissolved like bubbles into thin air. The weight lifted. The dark night turned to dawn.

Then something happened in my brain that I'll never forget. The whole story reversed itself. The entire trauma transformed into a feeling of thanksgiving. An era of suffering was transfigured right then and there. We sat quietly as if nothing was happening, but the entire world shifted beneath our feet.

"Oh my God," I said, as if witnessing a beatific vision.

"What is it?"

"I shouldn't be forgiving you. I should be thanking you, and the entire community for giving me the privilege of spending two years in a monastic environment. It was never the right place for me, but you gave me the chance to feel it, to get my spiritual underpinnings, to understand the balance of solitude, prayer, community, and service. You gave me the time to see what I needed out in the world and then you let me go. Like I was an eagle in a canary cage. You released me."

She sat perfectly still in her chair, her eyes glued to mine.

"Did this work as you had hoped?"

"Oh, Sister, it couldn't have been more perfect," I said, feeling the nightmare was finally finished. It was resolved. It had a happy ending.

We hugged and I got in my car for the short drive home. And then another awakening, like a bolt of lightning.

I saw every move I had made to create that reality. I saw every choice, every disobedient act, every secret I participated in that led to their decision to send me home. It had not happened *to* me any more than it had happened *through* me. I was the agent. Geppetto, not Pinocchio. Nothing happened that should have been a surprise to me. I knew the consequences. I took my chances. I made it happen.

I knew that all along, but knowing it was not helpful. For some reason, I needed a witness, and thankfully, Sister Marion Ripski was a relevant one. She'd been there when and where a part of me died. She knew how it happened. My history was recorded in her body.

I did not walk into that convent parlor imagining how it would go. I never thought forgiveness would enter into it. Never imagined being asked to forgive anyone. And then to hear those words, to have that feeling—*nothing to forgive*—enter into me like air into my lungs, like breathing in grace. It broke the fever. And it lives in me still like a pearl in an oyster—a precious, wild, and beautiful thing.

Every harvested tragedy leads to some wisdom. That is the point of it, the value of the turbulence. Once we get up on our feet after the initial blow, once we circle round the story, see it from different angles, tell it from different perspectives—processing our pain all the while—we get to a point, if we're lucky, of finding the gift in the grieving. The timeline for this cannot be determined. It is a process of Nature, happening to us as earthlings, coming and going on its own time, as does spring, winter, fall, and summer.

I feel I was given a universal truth. *There is nothing to forgive.* Things happen. We get hurt. We fall down. We get up. I remember standing in a kitchen once in Philadelphia with a woman who was telling a story about someone who'd done her wrong. "I'm never going to forgive her," she shouted. "Never! I'm never going to forgive her!" I kept seeing an image of her thrusting a knife into her own gut every time she said it.

"This is killing you," I said. "It's not hurting her, it's hurting *you*."

Next I knew the subject was changed and we never returned to it, but I've remembered it for decades. And even though it feels to me like a truth, I can't assert that it's true for everyone that there is nothing to forgive. The idea must be mapped across the contours of each individual life. Each person must decide for themselves where they stand on the matter. For me, it has held up for 30 years, against every injustice in my life.

As John Updike once said, "Confusion is just a local vew of things working out in general." Hard to see this when we're in the thorns and thistles, but some height and distance really changes the view.

Chapter 25
The Great Betrayal

I tell you this because it shines more light on the subject of forgiveness.

In this story, I am the one confessing my sins, my grievous misdeeds and harmful acts, and I am the one who must forgive myself—an act of love that opens doors to higher consciousness and deeper understanding. A Course in Miracles *says that forgiveness is a healing of the perception of separation.*

My fear of being queer caused me to divide myself into parts, to divide myself from others, and to divide a beloved friend from the only community she had. Fear had become a scythe in my hands.

A short story can cover a day, a week, a year. This one covers a lifetime. It took my whole life to learn the lessons woven into these lines. It took every fear, every failure, and every force from beyond and within to forge my human being into a woman of wisdom.

I think it's the same for most of us—if we're alive and well, the seats we're in are the winners' seats. And it took every mistake we made to get where we are and know what we know. I know that forgiving myself healed whatever perception of separation I had from others. My memory of connectedness returned.

That's what I hope for you. That this story revives your memory and returns you to the One from which you came and to the whole to which you belong.

—Syracuse, New York, 1967

In 1963, I entered high school. I'd stopped fist-fighting, stopped hating girls, stopped beating up on my brother and calling him a sissy. I now had a best friend, Bonnie McHale, who was, like me, an outlier and an athlete. We'd been blood sisters since sixth grade.

Bonnie lived a mile away from me, and every day after school we'd meet up for softball, basketball, tennis, ice-skating—whatever sport was in season. She was better than me in archery, ice-skating, basketball, and the backstroke, but it was my job to keep her from thinking so. She was superior in all sports, but I had the psychological edge—I could *get* to her.

I prided myself on being a leader and joined every group in sight so I could rise to the top. I needed the spotlight. It was my way of proving that I was a good person, haunted as I was by the dark shadow lurking within. Bonnie's insecurity had other sources, but we were equally besieged and had a need to stand out in the crowd. Her family put her down for not being smart enough, for being so tall (almost six feet), for having strange toes and thumbs, for ears that stuck out. They were merciless.

We both hated ourselves in different ways. I was beginning to be attracted to girls and knew this was an abomination, so I tried everything to compensate for what felt like a fatal flaw. I went to daily Mass, joined the Legion of Mary, performed charitable works every week, read the *Imitation of Christ* and *My Daily Bread*, but I was in an impossible predicament.

On one level, I knew myself as a child of God. I was a good person—kind, fair, fun to be around. I didn't doubt that. But I also carried the weight of being *predisposed to evil*. Even though I was headed for the convent in a few years, according to everything I'd learned from the catechism and the pamphlets we read in religion class, I was guilty of the worst crime ever. I hadn't committed any homosexual acts yet, but I knew I *was* one, which caused me constant turmoil. Inside me dwelt a mystic and a misfit who were always at war. I was rarely free of it and the battle manifested outwardly in terrible ways. One was a betrayal of my best friend.

Despite our competitiveness, Bonnie and I were as close as two girls could be, until one fateful day when she put her arm around me in a way that made me feel uncomfortable. I thought for a second that she might be homosexual. That triggered in me a series of actions that are nearly inexplicable.

Me, Bonnie (center), and Mary O'Connor (right) practicing our guitar licks.

I didn't ask her anything about the incident. I never said how it made me feel. I simply leapt to the conclusion that if she was queer, something had to be done about it. My own self-hatred was about to turn outward. Here it was. My first crusade. My own personal Inquisition.

Behind her back, I organized a secret gathering of our friends. I confided my suspicions to the group and whipped up a frenzy of emotion. Then, with the most fervent righteousness, we shunned her. Not one person spoke to her. When she came close, we simply turned our backs or walked away. This went on for days. Then I wrote her a two-page letter and delivered it on the last day of school, right before I went away for two weeks.

I couldn't have done anything worse to a good friend. I couldn't have been meaner if I tried to be. I left town and there was no one there for her. None of the other girls called or came around. She read the letter in her backyard, leaning against the peeling red wood of their two-car garage. Over and over, she took in the stinging sentences, trying to make sense of this terrible paradox. I had been her best friend. What had she done? Why had I turned everyone against her? What should she do now? She sat on the ground crying for more than an hour. Weeping, grieving, despairing.

I am the one on the left. I'm wearing white gloves and a hat with a veil that circled around my head and half-covered my forehead. I have no idea how to carry a purse. I can barely walk in my high heels. I am a tortured soul, trying to fit in. It's Easter Sunday. All I want to do is die and resurrect as someone else.

She hid the letter in an old tin box in her closet and prayed no one would find it. She read it a hundred times, wondering why? What was I talking about? How could I do this to her? She didn't even understand some of the words I used, they were so remote and unfamiliar.

When I finally came home, she wanted to talk with me, but I refused. I was cold. Distant. Mean.

"We're not discussing this," I said. "I don't want to talk about it."

That was the edge I had.

That whole sorrowful disaster had nothing to do with Bonnie. She never tried to be affectionate. She didn't have a homosexual bone in her body. I was the one who was queer. I was the one falling in love with girls, ashamed of myself but unable to help it. I was the one who had internalized every message I received about the perversity of homosexuals and grown to hate myself. That's why I tried to make everyone think I was so outstanding—star student, president of the Glee Club, president of Charity Guild Sorority, editor of the school paper, yearbook committee. Textbook. A classic case of projection.

Last month, 50 years after the incident, Bonnie and I sat in my living room trying to understand how such a thing could happen between two teenage girls who truly loved each other.

Lines from that letter are still in Bonnie's head, seared in her memory forever:

> "Dear Bonnie,
> I'm sorry I have to tell you this ... We've had discussions about you
> and your behavior ... We think you are queer, a homo ... We don't
> want you to be part of our circle anymore ... You're not one of us ...
> We can't be friends ..."

Neither Bonnie nor I could recall how the upset was reconciled. Weeks passed, seasons changed, and there we were, pitcher and shortstop, forward and guard, alto and soprano, right back in our favorite positions again as if nothing had happened. We finished high school, traveled through Europe together, found her husband together— she a heterosexual hippie and me and my partner beside her, gay as can be. Once she became CEO of Time Life Warner in Sydney, Australia, she even sent me a round trip ticket so she could tromp me on the golf course of her country club. Still competing, as always, though I no longer have to have a psychological upper hand.

I shared the story with my friend Barbara, a psychoanalyst who's had a therapeutic practice for 40 years, hoping for an insider's insight into my actions.

"How ironic that I spent so much energy to combat in Bonnie the very thing I was suppressing in my life," I said. "I hated myself for being gay, so I projected the whole ugly mess onto her. I tried to make it her problem."

Barbara reminded me of our body's remarkable ability to protect us

Bonnie and me after our reconciliation. The black eye came from a basketball game, not her fist, though she certainly had the right after what I had done.

from what we're frightened about.

"Everything you learned about being gay was interpreted as a threat to your health. And it was, potentially," she said. "So that denial and projection, that cruelty, was all in the service of defending your self-system."

My self-system was under attack from every direction—church, society, peers, parents. I did know it wasn't safe to be that way, but luckily, I can say now and I *do*, frequently in my prayers, that I'm grateful for being gay, and for more reasons than one.

Had I not been born gay, predisposed to being an outcast, I could not have felt its burden, would not have felt the empathy for others enduring similar kinds of judgment that I now feel in the company of those who are discriminated against.

Had I not been born gay, I would not have developed skills in transcending self-hatred or hatred from others. I would not have had to work on loving myself, enter the dark forest of despair, feel my way into a self-love that is extravagant, overflowing, that can be felt by others.

Had I not been born gay, I would not have learned to advocate for change, speak out for justice. I might not have become a social activist, might not understand the workings of other ideologies besides homophobia—racism, sexism, capitalism, patriarchy—and see how they rely on each other for their own self-preservation.

I might never have learned to think originally if it hadn't been a requirement of my own survival to banish ideas of anyone's infallibility, any church's authority over my life, so I could proclaim my own sanctity on my own terms.

Had I not been born gay, I might have missed the signs to the path of the heart, following the masses unwittingly into consumerism and consumption; had I not been at the deathbeds of brothers with AIDS, witnessed the violence against gays in more countries than my own, watched the transition process in a cousin's transgender partner, been sent home from the convent because of my queerness, then my heart would not have broken in half, would not have opened itself to Love Supreme, would not have been tenderized by life's bitter pounding.

I would not have understood *disempowered, debilitated, dismisssed* in the ways that I do, through the pores of my flesh, the chambers of my heart, the elegant cells of my cerebral cortex. Life wouldn't have washed over me like a tsunami and I might not know the feeling for the word *survivor* as I know it now.

I have confessed my sins to Bonnie McHale. I have knelt at her feet and said, "I'm sorry." I have forgiven myself as she has forgiven me. And that's all we can do when we make mistakes—mine them for meaning, see how they happened to prod us forward, confess and admit, then continue on resolute as can be. Every tragic incident we participate in has lessons for everyone who shows up at the dance.

As human beings, we can only learn from our human errors.

Chapter 26
Death in the Valley

I tell you this because it's about death, and something about death gets our attention.

I want your attention here more than anywhere, because this is where you'll face the temporality of your life—its tender vulnerability, its unpredictable horizons. We're leaves on a tree and can be blown off at any moment by any storm. No say in the matter, though until then our words are fire. They ignite. They light. They can burn.

Most of us will not have a chance to look out over our life's topography and get it raked into place before we die. Most of us will die with unwritten letters, unspoken gratitude, unforgiven trespasses. Those things take determination, commitment. We don't tend to things like that unless we really mean it about living a full and complete life. Easier to let opportunities for greatness run through our hands like powdery white sand. And how will they speak of you when you are gone?

This chapter is a nudge on your shoulder. It's me pushing you from behind. "Come on, you really want this, get it right." I can't preach about it. I can just say I was part of a miracle one day and it woke me up. All I can do now is tug at your comfy blanket. "Wake up! It's beautiful out here!"

✶✶✶✶

—Lone Pine, California, 2004

I pulled my car into the breakdown lane and grabbed my video camera. A flock of birds above Highway 194 plunged and ascended as one unit, performing a sky ballet. When I first looked up, they were all white, soaring in perfect unison. Then they swooped down, rolled over, and turned silver in the early morning light. When they sailed off toward the mountains, their feathers turned black in the changing shadows. They returned and repeated the whole dance again. White to silver to black. Mesmerizing.

I had to record them. It was an unbelievable sight. Leaning up against my hood for stability, I turned on the video camera and zoomed in. Pavarotti blasted through the open windows, the desert breeze gave lift to the flock, and I was in my glory as a creature on earth. In the past three days I had visited the lowest place in the U.S., Badwater Basin in Death Valley; the highest peak in the contiguous states, Mount Whitney; and Big Pine Forest where I sat in a grove of bristlecone pines, the oldest trees on earth at 4,500 years plus. I had also spent time at Manzanar, one of 10 American internment camps where more than 120,000 Japanese Americans were incarcerated during World War II.

I had just focused my lens on the birds when I heard the sound of metal crashing into metal, a horrific sound that lasted a split second before everything went black and absolutely silent. In one brief flash of light, I saw my camera, my car, and myself flying through the air. Then back to the empty void.

When I became conscious, I was underneath my car, lying prostrate and facing the rear wheel. I lifted my head enough to see my outstretched arms and feared immediately that I was paralyzed. I tried to wiggle my fingers and was amazed when they moved. Then I tried my feet and my toes. They moved too. *I can get out of here*, I thought. *I just have to shimmy out.*

I tried to drag my body forward but couldn't move. I was under the exhaust system, impaled. The searing muffler burned through the flesh on my back and hip. I tried to dig my way out, but the hardscrabble desert land was impenetrable. I couldn't make a scratch in the dry, hard dirt.

Floating in and out of consciousness, I knew I was about to experience my own death. A wave of sorrow rumbled through me when I thought of my mom hearing that I'd been killed in a terrible accident. Then came the worry of what I'd made of my life. Did I have regrets? Was anything unfinished, unforgiven? What about the trail I left behind? Had I contributed my gifts? Had I said thanks to everyone I was grateful for?

Yes, I thought. *I did the best I could do.* Flashing back to a childhood image of St. Peter at the Pearly Gates, I heard a voice in my head say, *If there's anyone to report to, I'll be proud to report.*

It was time to let go, but how could I do this? I wanted to live. Though barely conscious, I remember the anxiety. I was afraid, not so much of the unknown, but of the end of everything I knew. I remembered hearing about Native American elders who went to the mountaintop when their time had come, waiting for the moment, letting go, offering their bodies to the creatures who could use them. And Inuit elders doing the same: lying in a snowdrift, braving the new, letting go, offering up.

If they could do it, I can do it, I thought. I closed my eyes, took one last breath, and whispered to no one, *Here I come,* before slipping into the silence and heading back to the Source. I was on my way home. As my soul departed through the soles of my feet, I heard the *whoosh* of its exit. Then the black void again. The spaciousness. Safety. No lights. No people. Just space and freedom and peace.

Then I heard the frantic voices, "Is anybody there? Is anybody alive?"

Suddenly I reentered my body. Right in through the soles of my feet. *Whoosh.* I was back under the car again. The voices got nearer, "Is anybody there? Is anyone alive?"

I answered in a voice barely audible, "I'm here. I'm alive."

I heard the sound of running feet coming toward me.

"Where are you?"

"Under the car, by the back tire."

I looked up and saw their legs. Two men.

"Oh my God!" they cried out. "Wait there! We'll go get help!"

If they left me, I knew I'd die. A strange, strong voice boomed through my body. "You *are* the help. Just lift up the car."

"We can't!" they shouted back. "We need help!"

"You are the help," I cried again. "Lift up the car now."

And in one miraculous moment, they became the gods they were capable of being. They put their hands under the fender, and on the count of three, lifted the car as if it were an eagle's feather. Then two hands reached down to pull me out. They belonged to the man who had hit my car, who was bruised but able to walk. The four of us merged in that moment, melded into one movement, one miracle.

They called an ambulance and I never saw them again, though I lit candles for them and prayed for their well-being through my months of recovery.

I've always felt the events of our lives happen in order to bring us insight, to ground our wisdom in the flesh and bone of us, readily accessible. And now, after skin graft surgery, after months of healing and therapy, after finally overcoming PTSD, I was left with the question, *What wisdom did this yield? How was I a greater person because of it?*

The gift, I decided, was twofold: First, it gave me the chance to assess my life as a whole to see whether I needed any midcourse corrections. Second, and most important, it taught me the great lesson: *We are the help.*

When those men approached the wreckage, the first thing they felt was their helplessness. They didn't believe in their own powers and wanted to run off in search of help. They were caught in the story we've been told all our lives: Help is somewhere else, power and strength are somewhere else, the solutions are somewhere else, beyond us, outside of us. But when they heard that voice bellowing out from under the car, "You are the help," something happened. Illusions dropped. Doubt disappeared. And in rushed a huge and mighty force, a new belief that rippled through their minds and muscles, giving them whatever strength they needed to do the impossible.

Whatever is needed at this time in history to right this world, to right our own personal and precious lives, we have these things *within* us. Science and technology will not save us. Government and religion will not save us. More information and faster computers will not save us. It's our thoughts, our actions, our moral will that will save us.

If I look at my life and find it lacking in adventure or challenge or joy, the solution to that is right inside me, dwelling as a potential, awaiting a decision, a decisive action. If I look at my business, my affiliations, my family and feel uninspired, unseen, or disconnected, the way to wholeness is inscribed on my heart, written on every cell, waiting for me to look within and learn from the silence.

No one becomes a visionary who does not first look within. And none of us can inspire another until we first learn how to inspire ourselves. Coming to grips with the power we have is a first step toward our true magnitude. Dropping our illusions ("We're not strong enough to lift the car") is the first step in thinking originally, living authentically, seizing our power. It takes courage. It calls for reflection. It means letting go of the mediocre to create the magnificent.

All those voices in your head—let them go like a bunch of balloons. Then remember those men coming upon the wreckage, thinking themselves powerless until they heard the voice rising up from below— "You are the help"—and then lifting that car without a thought.

This is us. This is what we're capable of. *"What you have seen me do, you, too, can do, and even more."*

Chapter 27

Making It Happen: A Case Study

I tell you this because it's easy to forget how we create reality. Life happens so absurdly fast sometimes, it seems as if we're caught in a maelstrom of someone else's making. But the truth is, we have a hand in shaping the circumstances of our lives.

No matter the forces against us—poverty, prejudice, patriarchy—we have a say. We have a voice, two hands, two legs, and a mind to make a plan.

Usually, it starts with desire. That, and heartbreak. Those two things collide, and passion kicks in. The imagination shifts into high gear, a proper future is envisioned, and the body is deployed in the magnificent undertaking of creating something from nothing.

At least that's how it happened for me in this story. Desire met with heartbreak and erupted in a creative outburst that altered reality. An outburst that's still going on. That's changing the world one small spark at a time.

It could happen to you.

✯✯✯✯

—San Diego, California, 2009

I woke up and lit my candle just like every other morning, but a few minutes into the quiet a thought penetrated my brain. *Time to do international work.* That was it. One sentence. No directions. No map.

Okay, where shall I do it? I asked nobody. Since no response followed, I went through the continents in my mind. Asia, Africa, North America, South America, Europe, Australia. I decided on Africa. The place where it all started. Where humans first stood up, had thoughts, learned to communicate. The Cradle of Humankind, some like to say. The place of ruthless colonization, brutal injustices, and indefensible invasions is what I was thinking.

What shall I work on? I inquired into nothing. A few words floated in: *women, children, education.* All right, now I'm getting somewhere.

I dove into the murky waters and surfaced with a sketchy plan that required action. The first step was to find a collaborator. The days of the Lone Ranger were over. I knew it would be trickier to have a partner in the endeavor since I'm bullish on having my way and stealthy enough to succeed on my own. After all, my peace pilgrimage around the world had positive outcomes and I did that alone. But 25 years had passed since then and I didn't need anyone to remind me that partnership and teamwork yield better results because of the novelty of ideas diversity evokes.

The only way I knew to attract a collaborator was to mention my idea everywhere I went and see if I could entice anyone to join me. After casting out a few months in San Diego with no bites, I found my collaborator in a Cleveland restaurant, friend of a friend who had retired from Ursuline College and was ready for action. Cathy Hackney was her name and feminist leadership was her focus. A Ph.D. and a social activist walk into a bar …

"I'm in," she said. "What do we do now?"

"Okay, now we have to visualize. Keep thinking Africa. See yourself over there. Imagine yourself making a difference. We do that until we're called into action," I said.

A month later she called. "A nun in Nigeria wants to know if we'll come and lead a visionary leadership retreat for the Dominican Sisters." Cathy was on the board of Our Lady of the Elms, a Dominican high school for girls in Akron, Ohio. The sisters there were our connection to Sister Rita who lived in Nigeria and invited us to come. I had recently written a book on thought leadership, *The Art of Original Thinking*, and had been facilitating visionary leadership groups around the country. Cathy had been teaching and writing about feminist leadership for years. We were a dream team, and somehow Sister Rita caught wind of it.

Sister Rita Schwarzenberger was a trim, white Dominican Sister of Peace from Kansas who was at the helm of the Hope for the Village Child Foundation, a nonprofit that delivered services and care to five villages around Kaduna, Nigeria. They had a building in Kaduna that was a healthcare and training hub with a steady flow of people getting immunizations for their babies, vision testing, entrepreneurial training, and care for their children with rickets. The work never ended.

By March 2010, when we arrived, Sister Rita had already spent more than half her life in Nigeria. It was more home to her than Kansas. Cathy and I offered to volunteer our facilitator services for the Dominicans in trade for visits to the tribal villages after our retreat, hoping we'd find the clues to our next steps there.

After a six-hour drive to the Motherhouse in Gusau, we met for three days with 20 nuns to reimagine leadership and address the obstacles they faced as women cultural leaders, healthcare administrators, social workers, and visionaries. The sisters were between the ages of 30 and 60 and some had traveled up to 10 hours on dusty, hot, crowded buses just to get there. When they shared their hope for the weekend there was a general consensus: They wanted to change traditional thinking about women in leadership and challenge the male-dominated structures that kept women subordinate.

We asked for some examples of how male domination manifested, and the first response brought laughter and hoots from the whole group. Every one of them knew the seriousness of the claim: "The man always gets the gizzard." It seems Nigerian girls learn early that the important things, the delicious delicacies, the most desired objects will never be theirs. Men always get the goods. This ideology was rooted in family structures and followed every girl on her path into school, marriage, the workplace, and church. There was no escaping it. The glass ceiling was made of brick.

As the women went around the room calling out directives they'd heard all their lives, Cathy and I wrote them on the board. Here's a short list they came up with in the first few minutes:

Women should only speak when spoken to.
Women do not possess good reasoning.
Women can't make decisions.
Women are baby machines.
Women are meant only to be mothers.
Women must always submit to men.
Women must get married.
Women are weak.
Women must not compete with men.
Women should not get involved with politics.
Education is wasted on girls.
Women must never challenge authority.
Women are the property of men and need their protection.

Two Dominican sisters at the Leadership Retreat.

The sisters were exhausted by the injustices confronting them every day. They spoke of having to deal with *big men,* their word for men in authority, men who would dominate, censor, restrict, penalize, and intimidate them at every turn. The leaders in that room were driven by aspirations for justice, concerns for social issues, a hope of transforming their institutions into centers of high moral and ethical standards. They knew changes had to be made and those changes needed to be made by *them* if the young women coming up were ever going to experience equality. They wanted to create new messages for their younger sisters, messages of liberation and personal power.

So we looked at those expressions on the board and reversed every one, coming up with what they called a Women's Bill of Rights that began each line with the words "Young woman, you have the right to":

- Speak when you want, wherever you are
- Believe in your own strengths
- Participate in politics to build a better government
- Have your thoughts, feelings, and words respected
- Choose your future on your own
- Work in any profession you want
- Not marry if that is your desire
- Attain the highest level of education you choose

What they had come up with had the power of a national anthem. We said it together more than once, and each time the volume, the power, the commitment behind it rose in intensity.

"We should raise money and put this on billboards!" I said. We imagined that and cheered. "Yes! Yes! Billboards around the country, to empower girls everywhere!"

Then one sister brought us back down to reality. "The Bishop would not allow it. He would punish our community. He would destroy our Motherhouse. We would be left with nothing."

A terrible silence came over the room. This is what was true for them. This was the poison sea they were swimming in. They had so much work to do, but they committed to do it. On the last day, four midwives in the group assumed leadership, and Cathy and I sat down. They were about to use midwifery as a metaphor and collectively create a template for the new. *It may be a difficult and long labor, but they would confront the chaos, birth the gifts in each other, push and pull and struggle together.* We ended the weekend with a frenzy of music and dancing, then began our long, bumpy journey back to Kaduna.

Sister Rita lived up to our bargain and secured a Jeep, a driver, and a staff person to accompany us on our visits to the villages. The roads were barely navigable, but luckily we had sunny days and no rivers to forge. Each village we visited had one building designated as the school. They all looked the same architecturally. One long cement structure with four classrooms each. Some had desks, blackboards, a teacher's desk, a few books around, and class was actually in session when we arrived.

But later in the day, when we drove into the isolated rural community of Ikuzeh, I was stunned to see rows of children in crisp green uniforms lined up outside their school waiting for their teacher. When they saw the Jeep pull in, a swarm of kids ran to meet it. After opening my door, they pulled me by the shirtsleeve into a classroom, sat down on the dirt floor, and pleaded: "Be our teacher! Be our teacher!"

A blade ripped through my heart. I started to cry right away, touched by every part of this scenario: that they had waited all day for a teacher who was not coming, that they were so hungry to learn, that they had no desks nor any books, that they believed I could teach them. Smiling through my tears, I asked, "Okay, what's two plus two?"

"Four!" they shouted in unison, raising their arms in the air, full of pride.

"Oh my!" I said, surprised and delighted. "What's seven plus eight?"

"Fifteen!" they cried out, every eye on my face, looking for approval.

"Well, this is your lucky day!" I said, my voice trembling. "You need a teacher and I'm going to do everything I can to help you get one. Now will you show me around your village?"

They leapt up at once, grabbed my hand, and led me to their huts, their goats, their gardens.

I couldn't get them out of my mind. When we returned to Sister Rita's that evening I asked about the teacher at Ikuzeh.

"They rarely show up," she said. "There's so much nepotism here, they'll have a job whether they go or not. Plus, you can't get up the hill without a four-wheel drive or a motorcycle, and usually they have neither, so those kids rarely see a teacher."

"We have to fix this," I said. "I promised those kids."

Sister Rita and I brainstormed some possible solutions and came up with an idea for a learning center with an apartment on each end. That way we could house two teachers and have a decent space for education and community learning. She made some phone calls and the next morning we were in the car heading to the home of the chief, known as the Paramount Ruler, the *Agom Adara*: leader of the Adara people.

He was excited with us about our idea and went to the village people to see if they'd be interested in a learning center with teacher apartments attached. They were excited about it, too, so we had buy-in from everybody concerned. We each had our work cut out for us. Cathy and I would return to the U.S. and create a nonprofit foundation to raise money for the center, and Sister Rita would talk to a builder and get a cost estimate.

Since there was no electricity and plumbing in the village, the cost was quite low. Two apartments with a large room in between would cost $25,000. That seemed manageable.

We had the Livingkindness Foundation established within six months, then Cathy was hired to teach at Kent State University and had to drop out. Now it was up to me to raise the money. I decided to raise consciousness as I raised cash, so I organized a three-day conference at Skidmore College called *Women's Voices, Women's Visions*. We had daily classes to support the creative work of cultural activists—from art to poetry to journalism, technology, and advocacy in social justice.

At night we listened to EVE Talks by women, which were similar to TED talks but feminist in nature. The acronym stood for Expressing

Values that are Evolutionary. Each evening Livingkindness presented an Art & Activism Award to a woman who'd dedicated her life to igniting action and awareness through her creativity. These awards came with a $1,000 check and an invitation to share her journey with the rapt audience.

My commitment was to honor the work of women of color and indigenous women, whose incredible work so often goes unsung. Some of the awardees were Atlanta playwright Dr. Shirlene Holmes, drummer and teacher Ubaka Hill, longtime rock and roller and cofounder of Institute for the Musical Arts June Millington, Chickasaw Nation poet/writer Linda Hogan, Barefoot Artists founder and community transformer Lily Yeh, and Grammy Award winner/musician from the Oneida Nation Joanne Shenandoah.

For three years, hundreds of women gathered at *Women's Voices, Women's Visions* in support of our Nigerian project. I also received a grant from the Sisters of Charity of the Blessed Virgin Mary in Dubuque, Iowa, and by 2014 the building was under construction.

Livingkindness Centre for Learning, Izukeh, Nigeria.

Now it is outfitted with 20 computer stations, solar power, and laptops loaded with culturally relevant software for the students to learn English before they enter secondary school. Since the community is involved in animal husbandry and organic farming, the adults use the computers as well to learn more about agricultural methods and marketing their products. There are two teachers living in the apartments so the children never have to worry whether a teacher will be coming or not.

So this is how it happens that you manifest reality. You wake up with a dream that becomes the nebulous impetus. *Africa. Women and children. Education.* You decide if you want to go solo or attract a partner to work with. You plant the seed in the ground and nourish it. Envisioning, speaking about it, praying on it, opening to Spirit are all forms of fertilizer for your seed. Now listen carefully: The process is organic, fluid. You are working with invisible forces. Clues about next steps will be on their way to you. You will feel them in your body. *Heart's desire. Heartbreak.* When these two forces collide, something new is ignited. We are led by the fire.

When my heart broke open in that little schoolroom, all heaven broke loose in the realm of infinite potential. Doors flew open. Ideas flooded my mind. Energy surged through my bones and blood. The steps necessary to build alliances were laid out before me. Livingkindness Foundation was born with the help of a hundred midwives and it is alive today, being reinvented as a force for racial justice in my own country.

—San Diego, March 4, 2021, update

I just received word from Sister Rita that the *Agom Adara* was recently abducted and assassinated. The Adara chiefdom was dismantled by the present governor who also declared that the Adara people, the Agom's house, and the Livingkindness Centre for Learning would be under the rulership of an emir whom he appointed.

Kidnapping is rampant, and the village head of Ikuzeh has been kidnapped and missing for 20 days. The kidnappers demand a lot for ransom and it does not always guarantee safety. Agom Adara's people paid a ransom for him but he was murdered anyway.

The teacher who lived at the Centre has left because women who are kidnapped are usually raped. The last two meetings that were held at the Centre to determine its direction were disrupted by abductions of two members.

These are the times we were born for. To face such desperation and not lose hope is our supreme challenge. Whether we're dealing with First-World or Third-World problems, every one of us has some role to play in the solution. Alexandria Ocasio-Cortez said during her congressional campaign: "Justice is about making sure that being polite is not the same thing as being quiet. In fact, oftentimes, the most righteous thing you can do is shake the table."

I'm shaking the table right now about white privilege and systemic racism. I'm shaking the table about the unwillingness of white Americans to delve into the part we play in the matter. I'm shaking the table about criminal injustice, out of control capitalism, the climate crisis. I light my candle every morning still. I fuse myself to Mind-at-Large, opening like a satellite dish to receive my bulletins from Supreme Intelligence. I've come to rely on this pipeline of communication. I close the door. I put my mind at rest and announce my presence. I open my hands as a gesture of readiness. *Okay, I'm listening now.* Then I sit there, knowing the two worlds are connected.

Infinity communes with me, the finite one, in mysterious ways. I don't know its language, but I know how it feels coursing through me. It's the wind in my lungs, the oxygen in my blood, the sound of my song. I have nothing to seek, for there is no distance between us.

This is a mystical truth. Its home is the heart, not the brain. Our solutions are here on earth, not in the heavens. We are mortals in communion with Immortality Itself. Messages are coming to us directly, not from a pulpit, not from an ordained authority, but right into our own consciousness anytime we sit and open ourselves. This is the discipline that changes everything—our habits, our self-confidence, our neural circuitry, our imagination.

This openness, this daily practice of receptivity, is the one practice that trumps all others because it creates the pathway for everything you're wanting to make its way to you. Your sitting there—even for 10 minutes a day—sends the signal that you're open for business. There is no other evidence. Your entire body has to be in on it. You have to mean it.

Look. I'm really here, listening with all I've got. Look. My cell phone is nowhere in sight. My dog is not here. The TV is off. I have lit a candle. Look. I mean it. I'm ready now.

That is the very first step in conscious creation: Establish a relationship with the Cosmos-at-Large. Stop thinking of a heavenly father who hears your prayers and makes things happen for you. See yourself as creation unfolding in human form. You are *that which you seek* in shorty pajamas, in a flannel shirt, in slippers or work boots. You have the whole world in *your* hands. You are the mind opening to Intelligence itself, the eyes and ears and hands of Original Light. You are the sentient being that Love itself longed to become. This is mystical stuff, but you can feel the truth of it, can't you? You are capable of everything. We can put things together again. But not while we're still stuck in the old paradigms.

This is our time to burst out. Beyond religion. Beyond polarities and dangerous dualities. Beyond capitalism and cronyism and nonsensical America first ideology. We can create extraordinary lives, dream up and manifest incredible miracles—not like raising Lazarus or ascending into heaven (old paradigm)—but like tuning into what's breaking our hearts and knowing that's a signal for where to turn, what to do next.

Of all the things that break you open, what is the one that really hurts? Rainforests burning? Puppy mills? Plastic in the ocean? Hungry polar bears? Just allow yourself to admit it to someone. Let yourself hear your own voice saying what tears you apart. And then listen. You'll feel your way into next steps. You'll feel yourself less alone. You'll sense the connection, strange as it is, to Infinity itself, and that can be the beginning of the relationship you've longed for all your life. Think big. Let yourself feel. Open your heart. Know what you want. Want it hard. Then enter into the world you are creating. This is how to manifest reality.

Chapter 28
Leaving God for God

I tell you this because it's good to be aware of the words we speak. We create our lives with them. The word became flesh. If you think it's impossible to pay attention to your words, that they slide off your tongue like an alligator slipping into a swamp, unbeknownst to you, then stop speaking. Stop speaking until you retrain your brain.

Go on a word fast. Nothing at all until you progress toward mindfulness.

Then, when you are awake, when a word on your tongue yearns like birdsong to be expressed in the world, break your fast, and speak. But stay alert.

Pay attention. Be deliberate. Yours is the voice of the One Breath.

Stay true to its raging fire.

★★★★

I was in an RV with two other women heading for Santa Fe when one of them, my friend Jane, came out as an atheist. We were on our way to a workshop I was going to lead called *Divining the Body*. I was sure Jane would be the only atheist in the group and I felt protective of her, knowing how often people bring up God at events like this. Though I had left behind my notion of a personal deity by then, I hadn't replaced it with anything else. I was lingering in the liminal space between theist and post-theist, but Jane's announcement jolted me toward action.

"How does it feel when everybody talks about God like they do?" I asked Jane.

"Oh, I'm used to it now. It won't matter. You can forget about it."

But I couldn't forget about it. I drove hundreds of miles wondering how I could make this feel as good for Jane at it was going to feel for everyone else. I didn't want her to feel excluded. My job is to create connection, but I imagined a gap of light-years between some of these women.

We stopped at the Albuquerque airport to pick up three women from Missouri who started talking about God the moment they arrived. Every time I heard the word, my ears burned. I'd look at Jane and she'd just shrug her shoulders.

"It was raining, but God got us a great taxi driver who got us there on time."

"I was married to an alcoholic, but God set it up that way, so I'd learn patience."

"God helped me find just the right man on eHarmony ... God gave me a child with disabilities ... God gave me cancer because ..."

I wanted to shout out, *Who exactly are you talking about and how does this work?!*

When we arrived at the retreat center, we had two hours before our first gathering. I still had no idea how to handle things, until a thought occurred as I entered our meeting room. When we convened in a circle I made the announcement, "There's only one rule for the weekend. You can share anything you want, but you can't use the word G-O-D."

"Can't say *God*? Why not? How are we going to talk?"

"Because we're trying an experiment," I said. "If we have to come up with new ways to describe what we're talking about, we'll get clearer about what it really is. It's a global world now and we have to practice relating to people who don't share the same notion of God."

They weren't happy about it, but they agreed and we kept the rule all weekend with just a few slips. By Sunday lunchtime, I felt a palpable energy in the room. Women spoke in concrete terms and their words radiated with self-authority. They grounded their wisdom, rooting it in real terms and real stories. They took responsibility for the lives they were creating. *I did this. I chose that. I moved this way and not that.* They claimed their agency in the matter.

By the end of the week they spoke likewise, women warriors. No one reached up to the heavens for answers. No one credited God for courage that a woman herself had exhibited. They praised themselves for heroic acts, of which there were many, given the lives women lead in patriarchal times. And this was not a challenge to anyone's faith. We believed what we believed. Our words were as real as our flesh and bones and the upshot was like the difference between a Mary Oliver poem and a Hallmark card—power, not platitudes; lightning, not a match.

This is the value of diversity. Diverse perspectives open doors to new perceptions. Had Jane not offered me a challenge as a leader or had I not leveled the playing field, we would not have evolved in such a wholehearted way. What might have been *more of the same* turned into *like nothing before*. We pushed forward, disciplined ourselves, spoke mindfully, changed our brains.

This power is in our hands every minute of the day. It is a matter of paying attention to our thoughts and words. It's how we evolve ourselves and move beyond the poles of heaven and earth, spirit and matter. Meister Eckhart wrote in one of his sermons that the "highest and dearest leave-taking is ... leav[ing] God ... for GOD." That means leaving our *idea* of the sacred for an *experience* of the sacred. To me it means embodying divinity, acknowledging *I Am That*. I am a salt crystal in the sea of God. There is no separation. Everything that *is* is God unfolding, divinity materializing, yin yanging. Divinity is the wave, matter is that wave in particle form—two versions of the *one thing*.

After that weekend in Santa Fe, I asked people in all my workshops to refrain from using the word *God* while we were together. I encouraged them to say whatever they wanted to share with the group, but to use only concrete terms, to speak in such a way that listeners could see pictures of their words and enter into their story. Initially there's some resistance, since it forces thoughtful and slower speaking, but it also offers a way into our creative power. When we stop saying God made everything happen, we place ourselves in the picture and see what *we* did to cause the reality we're describing. It doesn't detract from anyone's faith. It provides us with a lens to see ourselves as cocreators, a requirement of this hour with the fate of our planet in human hands.

Since I had been asking folks not to use the "G-word" in my workshops, when I was invited in 2018 to cofacilitate a spiritual retreat with Michael Morwood in Nova Scotia, I knew I had to let him in on it.

Michael had been a priest in Perth, Australia, until resigning from his ministry after then-Archbishop George Pell banned Michael's book, *Tomorrow's Catholic: Understanding God and Jesus in a New Millennium.* Michael was an evolutionary thinker who would not be silenced, and he'd gone on to write several more books, marry his wife Maria, and teach throughout the U.S. and Canada. We sat across from each other at a bed-and-breakfast in Truro, Nova Scotia, buttering our homemade scones at 8 a.m. when I came clean.

"Michael, I hope you don't mind, but it's my practice to discourage people from using the word G-O-D during my seminars."

He looked at me, put down his scone, took a sip of coffee and said, "Jan, I hope you don't mind but it's my practice to discourage people from using the word C-H-R-I-S-T during my seminars." We laughed out loud and knew right then we'd be a good team, though neither of us knew the rationale behind each other's thinking.

We'd been invited there by a group called Atlantic Seminar in Theological Education, begun in 1969 by five college chaplains, that wanted to create an event for clergy that furthered their thinking on faith-related topics. The group came up with the idea of an annual five-day seminar led by scholars who spoke to the biblical, theological, and practical aspects of whatever topic it decided.

As time passed, more laypeople started to attend the seminars and that changed the dynamic of the group, which was initially quite conservative. As these newcomers became part of the organization and joined the steering committee, discussions within the group expanded.

Joanne MacIntosh, registrar and participant for more than 30 years, shared her thoughts with me in a recent email:

> People long for the truth and, in 1986, I was starting to believe that the "church/clergy" were withholding the truth from us commoners. I was not alone. We were few in number in the beginning, but the committee listened. They heard that we were looking for truth, because the truth in the pages of scripture is often spoken in "church speak" and it is elusive. There were voices that we wanted to hear, like Marcus Borg, Diarmuid O'Murchu, John Shelby Spong. They came to speak to us and the numbers rose, the interest grew, and the hunger was apparent. We hunger for truth, and when we hear it and see it, we know how to find truth in the rubble. We as churched people do not want to leave our church family behind, but we need a reason to stay.

I had asked her previously what possessed the group to hire Michael Morwood and me, a silenced ex-priest and a lesbian ex-nun post-theist, to lead them in their seminar. Her insightful answer was heartening:

> People like yourself offer us a truth of being that helps us know that we are all part of the one great family—diverse, real, honest, loving, caring, and inclusive. It is what we want to hear and when we hear *your* backstory, and the backstory of an ex-priest, and so many other honest stories, we say Amen Brother and Amen Sister.

It's that diversity and backstory that people desire now as they reexamine the relevance of their faith and create spiritual communities that sustain them. We are a more complex people than the masses who listened to Jesus speak from the hillsides. Most of us reflect on new ideas before incorporating them into our belief system. We let them mix and mingle with the experience of our lives and the wisdom of our bodies before concluding they are tenable and worthy of our allegiance.

Thought patterns that have dominated us for centuries are in a state of disruption, and upticks in social consciousness are seismic. What

Black communities have known for hundreds of years is just now seeping into the white imagination: The systemic nature of racism is not just happening *outside* our white bodies but is so deeply imprinted *within* us that every cell is contaminated with its poison. The expression *If you're not an anti-racist, you're a racist* has risen up out of tragic times, after George Floyd, Daunte Wright, Breonna Taylor, Tamir Rice, Eric Garner, and the litany of others killed by corrupted police policies and law created by white men that we as Americans sustain.

People are triggered by statements like these because we need to enter into the land of our shadows to reckon with racism, which *has* to happen before we have any hope of righting the wrongs. I am saddened and astonished every day at racism's long tentacles, and I have worked in communities of color much of my life. But this is a time of volcanic eruption, a point of bifurcation. It is an evolutionary moment and every one of us is on the road, choosing moment by moment which way to move—toward each other or away.

People in power rarely question the power structure. They hardly notice it if it's working for them. Whites deny the institutional nature of racism because we are rarely the victims of it and therefore don't notice it. Men rarely comment on patriarchy or sexism as institutions that perpetuate injustice. They benefit from it and don't notice the destruction that comes with it. But women can tell you the harm it causes.

Men have to *work* to understand and undo sexism. White people have to *work* to understand and undo racism. Christians and Muslims have to *work* to understand and undo anti-Semitism. And religious people have to *work* to keep the spirit of their religion more elevated than the laws of their religion, just as Jesus worked to do in the Jewish community—preaching love and mercy and justice over food customs and codified traditions.

That is our *real* spiritual work. Though we may light candles and pray novenas and attend online or in-person church every day, the holy work of this hour is to align ourselves with people who open doors to change and direct the public discourse. We can participate in any number of groups to educate ourselves and come to terms with how racism is metastasizing in the body politic. It's upon white people to do our homework and create diverse coalitions to build a new era, rooted in fairness toward all people. Any spirituality that does not bring about more justice, more social awareness, more right action in the world is a lame and impotent excuse for faith. True believers know that active compassion and silent prayer are symbiotic, mutually dependent on each other. My action for justice *is* my spirituality. My faith *is* my kindness to others, like the song from the '60s, "They'll Know We Are Christians By Our Love." There is no other way to know.

I have a friend who grimaces every time I call myself queer or gay or lesbian. "Why do you keep saying that about yourself? It's not important. It's not who you are," she says, because she lives on the safe side of a heterosexist culture. As long as so many LGBTQ teens are committing or considering suicide, as long as transgender people continue to be attacked and harassed, as long as lesbians lose custody of their children, or gays around the world are caned, tortured, or executed, I will continue to bring it up. I have nothing to lose and I will speak out for any of us who have so much to lose, including our lives. As long as the institutions of racism, sexism, heterosexism, anti-Semitism continue to persecute people, those of us who have borne that injustice must continue to rail against it.

Joseph Campbell spoke to this in his book *Myths to Live By*: "We can no longer hold our loves at home and project our aggressions elsewhere; for on this spaceship Earth there is no 'elsewhere' anymore. And no mythology that continues to speak or to teach of 'elsewheres' and 'outsiders' meets the requirement of this hour."

The level of disruption in our collective imagination is personal, political, psychological, and spiritual. The steering committee that invited Michael and me to facilitate a weeklong seminar to a body of Christian believers, pastors, and administrators gave us no instruction. They trusted us to show up and have an impact. They called the week *Beyond Dreaming*, which to me meant *Okay, roll up your sleeves, get out the Kleenex, put on your work boots. We've got five days to evolve ourselves forward.*

Michael and I brought two different perspectives to the table, in two very different packages. I was a storyteller using song, poetry, and videos that urged people to reel God in from celestial realms to cellular realms, to give divinity a change of address and localize the creative force in their own beings. I spoke about the relationship of our feelings and commitments to our faith and prioritized this over an unexamined adherence to religious beliefs.

Michael's work was less emotional, more cerebral, and theologically grounded. His hope was to bring people back to the life of Jesus the man, who reminded us we were similar in nature, one with creation, and capable of doing anything he did. What Michael chiseled away at was the abstract notion of *Christ the anointed one*, which was foisted on Jesus by Paul, who never even met the Jewish teacher and first wrote about him 20 years after the crucifixion. He encouraged us to let go of traditional religious teachings that are not helpful or believable and to let the simple teachings of Jesus infuse our lives: take care of the poor; stand for justice and peace; ground yourself in your oneness with Creation.

We had five days to dust off the debris of outdated ideas and break into hearts so the Spirit of Now could wash over us. Eighty-three evolutionary journeyers convened every day in a huge, cold Gothic church. We meditated, we prayed new prayers, sang old songs, listened hard, and questioned deeply—resisting, advancing, burrowing, burying.

So many of them were pastors with congregations to return to, with half of their members eager to evolve while the other half clung to traditional prayers and age-old songs no matter how sexist and patriarchal. How should they be with them? How does one who has grown beyond beliefs like original sin, the need for atonement, the notion of people as incorrigible sinners pastor to a people who still believe? A conversion of consciousness was in the air and in our lungs, changing everything, shattering mindsets, opening doors to new perceptions. Day by day Michael dismantled the scaffolding of religious doctrine and retold the story of Jesus the man—not as a being half-God, half human, but as a fully human person who fulfilled his potential and lived with passion. Our teachings and stories were personal invitations to leave God for GOD, to let go of concepts and enter into the Fire Itself, as Jesus did, through prayer and solitude, community, and service.

The challenge was huge as many of them were bound to the religion they knew, the stories they'd lived with all their lives. Who would they be if they let this go? How would they relate if they took this leap of faith and landed on another shore? How would they preach? How could they share this momentous change?

Near the end of our week I looked into faces and saw pain, angst, and worry on a few. I asked the group outright if we needed to grieve the losses we faced, remembering my own struggle to let go of the old. It's not that they hadn't been exposed to these ideas before. They had heard them from the prophets themselves—Borg, Spong, O'Murchu—but it was more intellectual then. And now Michael and I were asking them to live it out loud, to take a stand for a new and evolving faith.

In response to my question, a few half-raised their hands, holding them in front of their hearts, not wanting to be seen. I offered myself as a container for their sorrow, so they could direct their grief to me to hold, sanctify, and release in a sacrament of our making. I put on the music of Rafe Pearlman singing an Aramaic version of the "Lord's Prayer" and its haunting sound filled the cavernous cathedral. Next, I approached the altar, lay down on the red carpet, and rested my head on my crossed arms.

I then began to keen—weeping, sobbing as I took in their pain and felt my own grief. This went on for the length of the song. Agony and ecstasy comingled in the moment. I lost touch with everything but the sound of letting go. Boundaries fell away. My sense of self folded into a sense of All. I was a vessel, receiving energy, blessing it, pouring it out. I was a human in the act of being and there was nothing else, nothing else. As I reflect on it now, tears roll down my face, and a soft memory looms of consecrating our losses like holy loaves.

I have no way of knowing what happened to the others that day, for we have no language to speak of such mystery. There is fire on my tongue but no words. I do know that something transcendent happened. People were different before and after. There was a lightness of being. Intimacy in the air. Sighs of relief and gratitude.

We had left God for GOD. We were cells in the body of Unfolding Creation—*part* of that, *one* with it—not separate and alone, calling out for help, but intimately and infinitely connected. We looked exactly the same—crumpled corduroy pants, flannel shirts, slacks and thick sweaters, sneakers and work boots—but we were transformed in our very cells.

And when they spoke after, it was with conviction: *I will return to my church and we will evolve together. I will not say prayers I cannot believe in. I will write music to replace the hymns we must retire. I will share this with my people and we will walk a path of our own making.*

Forays into divinity are not rare for people who give up the notion of a faraway God and dwell like salt in the sea of infinity. For those who imagine God as the ongoing, unfolding miracle of creation—a verb, not a noun—it is not a stretch. There is nothing to seek when that force is the air you're breathing, the air in your lungs, the oxygen in your blood. There is no place to get to. Just walking away from that idea religion has crammed down your throat: That God is out there judging you and you will never live up. That is not true. Say it: *That is not true.* Say it as often as you need to until you are whole again, until you reimagine yourself as a spark from the original flame, stardust from the mother star, composed entirely of materials and atoms that originated 14 billion years ago.

It is possible for any one of us to know that intimacy, to feel it in our bones when we sit in our practice and open ourselves like satellite dishes to receive the "bulletins ... from Immortality" that Emily Dickinson referred to. Just as a tree is one with the air and the sun, breathes it in through countless leaves, transforming light into food with its magical ingredient chlorophyll, so do we, as beings of Nature, creatures born of Light, convert one thing into another for the sake of the whole.

With our magical ingredient—our imagination—we convert the intelligence we receive from Mind-at-Large, Supreme Intelligence, Unfolding Creation into inspiration for ourselves and each other. It's a natural process and we do it all day long with barely a thought about what we're doing. Things happen to us and we turn them into stories or whittle them down into poems or song lines. We take a hit from life and when we're done yelling and blaming, we can mine it for usefulness since there's always some gain in every loss. Rules of Nature. Most curses wind their way around to become a blessing.

You can stop seeking right this minute. You can relocate God in your own body as both are one: ongoing creation, ever-expanding. You can stop yearning and pray *thank you* and *thank you* a hundred times. The Force of Life is breathing you. You can relax now. You're in the arms of heaven and earth, your Father and Mother. You can breathe. This is it. This is the "kingdom of heaven spread out around you." Welcome home. You have nowhere else to be but here.

Leaving God for GOD

A nun of eighty-four years
sits in the circle,
her shawl draped over
the back of her chair,
her cane resting near her
on the floor.

Among the group,
she is the smallest, the quietest.

When she speaks to us, she smiles:

It was hard, as a child, to give up
Santa Claus and the Easter Bunny,
hard to let go of the Tooth Fairy,
but the hardest thing I've ever done
was to give up God.

I had to give up
what I learned about God
in order to feel the Divine
inside me.

I no longer believe in a Heavenly Father
who sits on a throne and judges our lives.

I no longer seek a faraway God
but feel one with what is
when I sit in prayer, walk in the garden,
share with my sisters.

I am in love now.
It took me eighty four years
but I am more alive
than I've ever been.

I have entered the Fire.
I am one with the Flame.

CHAPTER 29
CROCK OF AGES

I tell you this in order to rouse you from your sleep.

I am like the Zen master walking through the room with a keisaku, *an "awakening stick" for the meditators slouched over in drowsiness. One smack on the back and the blood starts racing through the system.*

I get smacked awake all day long by masters educating me in a myriad of disciplines: systemic racism, patriarchal power imbalances, criminal justice inequities, outdated theologies.

It is not simply the new I must expose myself to, but the old I must retire and renounce. This is the beginning of a new epoch and those of us who understand our role as cocreators of the future know it's our time to act. Old myths perpetuate injustice, war, intolerance. I have had enough of them and I am on the front line here.

That's why the keisaku. *I want you to wake up, get up, put on your walking shoes and take your place in the proper lineup. Follow your joy. Listen to your heart's desire.*

It will lead you to the place that's circled on a map for you. The place where you will unfold, where you will come alive and shine. This is your invitation to leave behind the old and enter into a future of your own making.

✽✽✽✽

—San Diego, California, 2021

In the first week of 2021, people around the world witnessed the fabric of America being torn asunder. While right-wing rioters stormed the Capitol looking for politicians to disrupt, hang, or shoot, a group of them paused in the House Chamber to give thanks and praise. A self-proclaimed shaman Jake Angeli removed his buffalo garb and called out in prayer:

"Thank you, Heavenly Father, for gracing us with this opportunity … to allow us to send a message that … this is *our* nation … Thank you divine, omniscient, omnipotent, and omnipresent Creator God … Thank you for filling this chamber with patriots that love you and that love Christ … In Christ's holy name we pray!"

Before resuming their deadly mission, fellow rioters raised their arms and shouted, "Amen!"

How we got to this point—where the sacred gets woven into the wicked and it makes sense to anyone—is a vexing question. I close my eyes and go back to the beginning where we first surfaced in Africa as a species with consciousness.

The ability to wonder must have brought with it some primal questions and anxieties: *Where did we come from? Why are we here? What's to become of us?* Early humans would have gone to the tribal leader seeking answers, and the leader would make up a story to calm them down, having no more clues than the tribe as to beginnings and endings.

Stories and myths gave early humans a way to relate to the powerful and invisible forces that surrounded them. In the Paleolithic Era, as agriculture developed, people thought of fertility as a sacred event and showed reverence to Great Mother, the first deity humans would create. Her image was carved into sculptures more than 40,000 years ago, and some now sit on museum shelves.

Over time, humans created a pantheon of gods and goddesses to represent the unseen forces. What they couldn't understand logically, they attributed to beings in the invisible realm. From the very beginning, we made up stories about everything.

Creation myths evolved and shape-shifted as tribes migrated in every direction. In the Middle East, the people worshipped a multitude of deities until Zoroaster and the Hebrew prophets presented the idea of a monotheistic God who sat on a heavenly throne and intervened in human affairs. Pharaohs, kings, and tribal leaders on each continent took different positions regarding the gods. Some advocated for one God, some for many; some worshipped the spirits in nature; some found the sacred in every living thing. For the most part, people believed in the stories put forth by their leaders.

Today, Christians in America live in a monotheistic culture inherited from Moses, with just one God to praise or blame. Humans made the whole thing up—*the stories, where we came from, who was in charge*—and that worked for a long time. But now, for the first time in history, science has verified a creation story that is true for everyone. The Omnipotent Father the rioters lifted their arms to may someday be upstaged by a story that is now being brought to us by science and underpinned with facts.

With the most sensitive radio telescopes, astronomers have detected cosmic background radiation that has emanated through space since the Big Bang nearly 14 billion years ago, providing evidence about the beginning of everything. The good news is we are all from the same source, all made of stardust, all evolving, expanding in consciousness as the universe itself expands in immensity. The astrophysicist Carl Sagan, one of our most revered public scholars, put it like this: "The nitrogen in our DNA, the calcium in our teeth, the iron in our blood, the carbon in our apple pies were made in the interiors of collapsing stars. We are made of starstuff."

While we know from science what is true about our beginnings— that we're children of the cosmos—some of us still cling to stories from a pre-biblical era when people thought the earth was flat. Many faithful believers think Adam and Eve were real people who communicated with a male God in the Garden of Eden. Millions today worship a God who pulls all the strings and makes everything happen, praying to an almighty being dwelling in the heavens whenever anything goes wrong. We are all on our own unique spiritual trajectories, and the only thing I know for sure is that my beliefs change just as I do. Just as the cosmos changes. Just as nature changes. Few of us hold beliefs that we held as first graders. As we expose ourselves to different teachers, we accept new possibilities, uphold new views. This is what revolutionaries do: They work on their evolution. The New Thought community is called that because we are open to new thoughts; we know how it feels to lean into our limitlessness, to recall our connectedness.

I used to sing "He's Got the Whole World in His Hands" like a Salvation Army soldier. My family belts it out around campfires all summer long like we're the Mormon Tabernacle Choir, adding verse upon verse about what God holds in His hands. I boycott that song now. I will not sing it as written and I say so publicly. We've reached a point where humans are destroying our planet, and it's unconscionable to think someone else is going to take care of it. *We've* got the whole world in *our* hands. That's what I sing now.

Religion fails us when it encourages us to abdicate our authority and trust the future to a deity in the heavens. It may be time to heed Walt Whitman's advice from the preface to *Leaves of Grass*: "Re-examine all you have been told at school or church or in any book, [and] dismiss whatever insults your own soul."

What might happen if we dismissed religious beliefs that insult our souls? What if we stopped saying "I am not worthy" and started saying "I am responsible." What if we stopped calling on God or the saints to help us find our keys or feed the poor or tend to the sick and took it upon ourselves? What if we stopped saying racism isn't so bad because it's right there in the Bible, or homosexuality is wrong because the Bible says so, or women should be subordinate because it's right there in St. Paul?

The veracity of biblical texts cannot be determined. Every word has been translated and retranslated over the centuries by human beings with agendas of their own. The Book of Genesis wasn't even compiled until 600 years after Moses was alive. The original Aramaic, which Jesus spoke, was a Semitic language lending itself to multilevel translations and interpretations.

Imagine the history of what we now call the "Lord's Prayer." Jesus speaks Aramaic to a mostly illiterate crowd around the year 30 C.E. Nobody takes notes. Fifty years later, someone writes down in Greek what has been passed along orally. From the Greek, the prayer gets translated into Latin, then Old English, Middle English, and finally into the 400-year-old version most Christians have memorized from the King James Bible. What are the chances of the original Aramaic staying intact through all those iterations?

Neil Douglas-Klotz, a scholar who has delved into the Aramaic language, has come up with an English version of the Christian scripture that may be truer to the words Jesus actually spoke. The words "Our Father which art in heaven" from the King James translation of the Aramaic *Abwoon d'bashmaya* can be rendered several different ways. Four possible interpretations offered in *The Hidden Gospel* liberate the phrase from a patriarchal, hierarchical expression to a richer, more relational prayer:

> *O Thou, the One from whom*
> *breath enters being in*
> *all radiant forms.*
>
> or
>
> *O parent of the universe, from your*
> *deep interior comes the next wave*
> *of shining life.*
>
> or
>
> *O fruitful, nurturing Life-giver!*
> *Your sound rings everywhere*
> *throughout the cosmos.*
>
> or
>
> *Father-Mother who births Unity,*
> *You vibrate life into form*
> *in each new instant.*

You can *feel* the difference in these translations. They expand the imagination. They open doors to broader perceptions and invite us into the mysteries of the unfolding cosmos. Divinity feels closer here, more accessible. There's a fluidity in the words. Windows fling open to the possibility of union. Awe winds its way around each line.

That's how important language is and that's why the words we use when we speak of *spirit, faith, religion* must be evolved by us at this time in history. The old is failing us. The notion of a personal deity who intervenes in our affairs keeps us childish, lazy, irresponsible. This is a time for clearheaded, conscious, faithful people to create a language that startles people alive, awakens us to our birthright as creators, our responsibility as stewards.

In his book *The Great Work*, visionary ecologist Thomas Berry writes:

> We must consciously will the further stages of the evolutionary process ... Our responsibility ... is to be present to the Earth in its next sequence of transformations. While we were unknowingly carried through the evolutionary process in former centuries, *the time has come when we must in some sense guide and energize the process ourselves.* (Italics mine.)

Human beings collaborate in evolutionary change. We rewire our own neural networks, retrain our brains to think originally and non-dualistically. We update our own software through our intentions, meditations, and actions. The *I* that I am is a pendulum in perpetual motion between receiving and giving, prayer and action.

When societies go awry, activists jump into action. The Inquisition stopped because of individuals' efforts to stop it. The Reformation occurred because Martin Luther reached a boiling point and went public about wrongdoings in the Vatican. Women in the United States got the vote because of people like Susan B. Anthony, Ida B. Wells, Elizabeth Cady Stanton, and Alice Paul. Black civil rights and the right to vote were advanced by Harriet Forten Purvis, Mary Ann Shadd Cary, and Frances Ellen Watkins Harper. A time of racial reckoning is upon us as a nation because of the work of Black Lives Matter and the torrent of activism that erupted after the murder of George Floyd by police in 2020.

People like us, committed citizens, stood up and spoke out, century after century, when old traditions had to be laid to rest. Ordinary people ushered out notions of a flat earth, the divine right of kings, the validity of slavery. There were no superheroes. No miracle workers or saviors. Just hardworking people who spoke the truth, took to the streets, insisted on change, created the future from a fading past.

Though the burning of witches is behind us, the execution of gays is not, the trafficking of women and children is not, institutionalized racism is not, pollution of our waters and air is not, religious bigotry is not. This is the world that's in *our* hands, waiting for our pendulum to swing from prayer to action.

Our Capitol was attacked by rioters who insist that God is on their side, just as slave owners insisted, lynch mobs insisted, the whole Jim

Crow South insisted. God-talk is part of the problem. The personalization of God is part of the problem. Claiming that God wants *this* or God wants *that* is part of the problem. The wrongs we face are invitations for us to step forward and meet the requirement of the hour. There is no being out there who is going to save us.

If we have holy work to do, it is to relocate the Divine from celestial realms to the cellular, to divinize the earth, to speak a language that lifts us above literalism and honors the sacred and mysterious complexity of our commonness.

Retired Episcopal Bishop John Shelby Spong spent his entire career trying to rescue the Bible from fundamentalism, using every teaching device possible to upgrade the consciousness of the faithful. His biblical scholarship is revelatory and disquieting to those who want to believe in the literalness of the texts. It's understandable. We *want* to believe what we were told. The summons to defend our faith gets installed right along with the tenets we inherit. It's a matter of honor. I remember slugging Billy Hogle so hard his lip bled when he said Jesus wasn't born on December 25. I was 10. *Onward, Christian soldiers.*

The stories of the New Testament are interpretive tales meant to show how fully realized Jesus was as a man. He came as a great example, not a great exception. One hundred percent human. A man who said (perhaps), *Anything you see me do, you can do, and even more.* For reasons we'll never know, the writers—Paul, Mark, Matthew, Luke, John— wrapped him in divine language and attributed miracles to him that may or may not have occurred.

Paul, a fellow Jew who once persecuted the followers of the teacher called Yeshua, had a conversion experience and became a zealot. He never met Jesus, but he called him *Christos*, meaning "anointed one" in Greek, elevating him to a status higher than mere mortal. That got us all off the hook. If we couldn't compare ourselves to Jesus anymore, we couldn't be expected to live with the same light, magnitude, capacity for love that he did—a total betrayal of what Jesus worked toward.

Jesus taught in simple words, through simple stories. The message was not complicated. *The kingdom is here now; don't hide your light under a bushel; help the poor; take care of the sick; heal people by listening, touching, loving.* He did not say we were sinners in need of atonement. He did not say people would not be saved if they didn't believe in him. He never said anything about homosexuality, abortion, prostitution. He spoke of justice, kindness, inclusion, respect. *Pray and love with all your heart.* He gave us a template for how to live, not a treatise for how to judge.

The writers of the New Testament were limited. They never saw or heard Jesus. They made up stories based on stories they'd heard, and they wrote to show how Jesus fulfilled the predictions of the Hebrew prophets. Paul never mentioned a virgin birth, nor did Mark who was the next to write, but in the ninth decade Matthew introduced the idea of a virgin birth and created a narrative that included a flight into Egypt to escape Herod's wrath. He wrote about wise men from far-off lands who bore gifts for the Messiah. Their GPS was a star in the East. According to Matthew, the holy family lived in Bethlehem.

A decade later Luke told a story that included an archangel Gabriel telling Mary she's pregnant, a journey not to Egypt but to Bethlehem, angels appearing to the shepherds, no wise men, and the family, according to Luke, hailing from Nazareth. One might think they came up with the virgin myth to fulfill the words of Isaiah, but according to Bible scholars, when Isaiah 7:14 is translated from the Hebrew, it reads: "Behold, a woman is with child." In Luke's story, there is no mention of a stable or an innkeeper. There are no camels, no wise men, no three kings from the east like the ones we've been singing about all our lives.

For any of us raised to believe in the literal veracity of the Bible, taught that the writers were actually on the scene interacting with Jesus, that everything happened exactly as it was described, it's a shock to the system to learn otherwise. Paul's letters and the four gospels were all written 20 to 50 years after Jesus was crucified.

Jesus had no intention of building a church. He was antiestablishment, moved by the Spirit, not the letter of the law. He cared about right action, not right doctrine. His messages might be relevant to the millennials and Gen Zers of today because they are timeless and limitless, but where do they go to hear it? Where do they go to experience that "religionless Christianity" that Lutheran pastor Dietrich Bonhoeffer spoke of before he was slain in a Nazi concentration camp? How are they guided to see beyond the external God of the Christian church and enter into the God at the heart of life itself—the God who did not create a universe but who is the universe, supreme intelligence, ever expanding, ever broadcasting itself to us as love and beauty and information.

A spirituality for these times is a spirituality of reverence for the ground we walk on. Its sacred texts are being written today by artists, writers, and musicians, rappers, novelists, and poets who say *this is our time, this is the call, this is our world*—priests of the imagination who rev us up for action that is joyful, useful, forward moving.

It's about *today's* prophets who are on the ground and taking their place in the lineup wherever they are—with the migrants along the border, with the Black Lives Matter movement, with the climate change activists, the healthcare workers, the childcare providers. These are the faithful of today—churchless most likely, but full of light, full of song and hope.

The patriarchal institution of Christianity in the 21st century doesn't have much of the largesse, the love for life, that the brown-skinned young Jew Yeshua had. The biblical renderings of his life are as arid as a desert compared to the exuberance and passion I imagine he embodied. Exhortations from many modern-day pulpits run from mean-spirited to intolerant, from *you're nothing but terrible sinners* to *God hates fags*. As a queer woman, I have a litany of religious abuses I've encountered along the way, all coming from well-meaning Christians of all sects.

Samaritan Center, Syracuse, New York—formerly St. John the Evangelist Church.

I'm glad the churches are emptying out, so they can be repurposed as dining halls, meeting places, childcare centers, and coffeehouses. I'm glad the young are not learning of a vengeful God who sent his son to die for their sins. I'm glad to hear people of faith admit that the theology we inherited is dysfunctional, that we can look to nature as a source of revelation, that it's time to create a religion of the earth and release our attachment to a religion of heaven.

There is not one field, one discipline, that has not changed with the times. From the sciences to the arts, from technology to teaching methods, from design to engineering, every cultural component evolves inexorably. That is the nature of life, and if religion is to be seen as a living force, it too must evolve and grow.

It is all mystery, and we are making up stories just like the early humans who did their best to conjure up a narrative about why we're here and where we're going. The mystery of it all, the abundance of power and potential, the sacredness of the waters, the birds, the mustard seeds—that fierce fire and passion that ripped through Jesus. He felt it in every cell. He knew he was one with it, came from it, would return to it. He showed us what to do with it. Heal the sick. Feed the hungry. Heaven is all around us. We're one with Creation. The light of the world, he said. *Be the light of the world.*

This earth is our altar, our most sacred dwelling place, our Holy Mother.
O come let us adore her.

CHAPTER 30
STILL ON FIRE

The God that I once related to has gone the way of the wild goose, but the time I spend in prayer and meditation only increases. I redefine prayer every morning as I light my candle and open to the Divine, which feels to me like the air in my room and the air in my lungs—both inside and all around me. I imagine everything as energy or light vacillating between two forms: particle and wave. I am the particle version (visible, finite, mortal) and the Divine is the wave version (invisible, infinite, immortal).

My relationship with this force is conscious and all-consuming. I dedicate my life to it. It is my primary work—not an arduous task but a jubilant encounter. I am in a love affair with an invisible lover. Every morning I raise my being to the condition of oneness. I begrudge nothing. I wake up eager to light my candle and announce my presence. There is no heavy lifting.

God, to me, is a moving force, a verb, creation ever unfolding—the supreme force that I come from and belong to. I am the shape it takes, the form it melts into, the mirror it sees itself in. The ground of being—consciousness itself—pervades and saturates the universe. There is nowhere I can go to escape it. It is not inaccessible. It is unavoidable. Like the Hassidic saying: "He who does not see God everywhere does not see God anywhere."

Every one of us creates our own relationship with the sacred, or not. It's really nobody's business how that connection gets created. Religion has tried to corner the market on all things spiritual, but from where I sit, there is nowhere to get to and nothing to seek. We are swimming in the sea of it. We are *made* of it. We are cells in the being of it. Nothing that exists is not it. When the apostle Philip said to Jesus, "I do see you, but I want to see God," Jesus replied: "Whoever has seen me has seen the Father," according to traditional translations of John 14:9. Catholic philosopher and scholar Beatrice Bruteau in *Radical Optimism* suggests some other words Jesus might have used: "Whoever sees anything at all is looking into the eyes of the Only One Who Is."

When Buddha said, "Make of yourself a light," and Jesus said, "Let your light shine before others," we can only imagine they were urging us toward complete self-expression. When we are most ourselves, we are most on fire, most alive, most enlightened. The Hindu mystic Ramana Maharshi said that self-realization "is the best help you can possibly render to others." "Wake up, come alive, share your light," is what the masters urge of us. We don't grow our light by study. We grow our light by union with our Source, Light itself. It is not what we learn, but what we unlearn that is useful to us now. We need to give up our sense of separation from Source and others, give up our notion that there is a heavenly father out there taking care of us, let go of the notion that we are anything but creators, cocreating the destiny now of civilizations to come.

As we evolve ourselves, we see ourselves as agents of change, creators of our lives, our families, our communities and cultures. As we deepen our awareness, let go of limiting beliefs and inherited ideas that no longer serve us, we rise above the fear that has silenced us and shine our light for those in the dark.

What does it mean to be the light of the world? To radiate love, to act in peace, to speak for justice? It means to see beyond the opposites, to enter into unity, to find the sacred wherever we look. Everything we need is in the air we breathe. Everything we long for is in the love we give.

This is the time to come out of our solitude and accept that we are saturated with divinity and instruments of its grace. This is our time to shine for ourselves and each other all the days of our lives.

Prayer from My Morning Meditation

I have no name for you
coursing through my veins, feeding me
like sun feeds the tulip and rain feeds the rose.

I can't call you Father, Mother, God
I call you mine, I call you me.
We are entwined and not a molecule
separates us.

This bond of seen and Unseen,
Infinite and finite,
this ardor—O Unnameable Mystery!
Words of gratitude fly from my mouth
like starlings.

Every nanosecond you swirl through me—
breathing me, lifting me, lighting me—
I blaze across your sky like a runaway comet.

Rain from your thundercloud
saturates my desert—
the sound of your hail
awakens my joy.

Yes! I am a star birthed
in the big bang of you,
spiraling toward the black hole of you,
all ravenous and voracious,
craving your emptiness.

Nothing exists but the breath of you
breathing us day and night.
We call ourselves seekers
though wherever we look you are there.

I proclaim you in verbs and nouns.
I wear the skin of you,
dispense your aroma with every move.

The splendor of you graces the world
when I walk by
(so casually)
radiating your Fire.

Acknowledgments

I thank Mother Earth and this Cosmos for bringing me forth and stunning us all with your intelligence, love, and beauty.

I thank Margaret Lalor (Sister Robert Joseph), who died during the writing of this but whose spirit infuses the entire book.

I thank Barbara Haber for being an exquisite thought partner and friend through these years of digging down, and June Gould for reading chapters as they entered the world, keeping some alive with her own breath.

I thank Carole Landberg; Lois Barton, CSJ; and Mary Ellen Shirtz, CSJ, for reality checking my memories about the postulate and novitiate.

I thank my friend Ruth Westreich for emotional support and retreats into the wild when I needed the comfort of trees and water.

I thank my sisters Marni and Patricia Wogan for our happy hour reading sessions and your fabulous support.

I thank the Unity community for your New Thought consciousness, your work to combat racism, and your boldness in creating a community that embraces us all.

BIBLIOGRAPHY

Baudelaire, Charles, *The Painter of Modern Life and Other Essays*, Phaidon Press, London, 1964.

"Behavior: The Homosexual: Newly Visible, Newly Understood," *Time*, October 31, 1969, < http://content.time.com/time/subscriber/article/0,33009,839116-1,00.html>, accessed on August 5, 2021.

Berry, Thomas, *The Great Work: Our Way into the Future*, Bell Tower, New York, 1999.

Bonhoeffer, Dietrich, *The Cost of Discipleship*, Macmillan, New York, 1949.

Bruteau, Beatrice, *Radical Optimism*, Crossroad, New York, 1993.

Burton, Naomi (ed.), et al., *The Asian Journal of Thomas Merton*, New Directions, New York, 1973.

Campbell, Joseph, *Myths to Live By*, Viking, New York, 1972.

Chopra, Deepak, *The Way of the Wizard*, Harmony, New York, 1995.

Congregation for the Doctrine of the Faith, "Letter to the Bishops of the Catholic Church on the Pastoral Care of Homosexual Persons," October 1, 1986.

Douglas-Klotz, Neil, *The Hidden Gospel: Decoding the Spiritual Message of the Aramaic Jesus*, Quest Books, Wheaton, Ill., 1999.

Eckhart, Meister, *The Complete Mystical Works of Meister Eckhart*, Herder & Herder, New York, 2009.

Godman, David (ed.), *Be As You Are: The Teachings of Sri Ramana Maharshi*, Arkana, London, 1985.

Hersey, John, *Hiroshima*, Knopf, New York, 1946.

"The Homosexual in America," *Time*, January 21, 1966, < http://content.time.com/time/subscriber/ article/0,33009,835069,00.html>, accessed on August 5, 2021.

Keyes, Ken, Jr., *The Hundredth Monkey*, Vision Books, Coos Bay, Oreg., 1981.

Kooser, Ted, "After Years," *Delights & Shadows*, Copper Canyon, Port Townsend, Wash., 2004.

Lessing, Doris, *Shikasta*, Granada, London, 1979.

"Margaret Lalor," *The Post-Star*, April 1, 2018, < https://poststar.com/lifestyles/announcements/obituaries/ margaret-lalor/article_e275dd99-509c-57bd-b432- bca0e78070de.html>, accessed on August 5, 2021.

Merton, Thomas, *Conjectures of a Guilty Bystander*, Image Books, New York, 1966.

———, *Mystics and Zen Masters*, Farrar, Straus and Giroux, New York, 1967.

———, *The Seven Storey Mountain*, Harcourt Brace, New York, 1948.

Millett, Kate, *Sexual Politics*, Doubleday, Garden City, N.Y., 1970.

Morwood, Michael, *Is Jesus God?*, Crossroad, New York, 2001.

———, *Tomorrow's Catholic: Understanding God and Jesus in a New Millennium*, Twenty-Third Publication, Mystic, Conn., 1997.

Newberg, Andrew, and Mark Robert Waldman, *How God Changes Your Brain*, Ballantine, New York, 2009.

Ocasio-Cortez, Alexandria, speech given at the Women's March, New York, January 19, 2019.

Phillips, Jan, *The Art of Original Thinking*, 9th Element, San Diego, 2006.

———, *Making Peace: One Woman's Journey Around the World*, Friendship, New York, 1989.

Piercy, Marge, "To be of use," *To Be of Use*, Doubleday, Garden City, N.Y., 1973.

Sagan, Carl, *Cosmos*, Random House, New York, 1996.

Spong, John Shelby, *Rescuing the Bible from Fundamentalism*, HarperSanFrancisco, San Francisco, 1991.

———, *Unbelievable*, HarperOne, New York, 2018.

Stevenson, Robert Louis, *Travels with a Donkey in the Cévennes*, Scribner, New York, 1905.

Strong, Anna Louise, *I Change Worlds: The Remaking of an American*, Holt, New York, 1935.

Teilhard de Chardin, Pierre, *The Divine Milieu*, Harper & Row, New York, 1960.

———, *The Phenomenon of Man*, Harper & Brothers, New York, 1955.

Todd, Mabel Loomis, *Letters of Emily Dickinson*, World Publishing Company, Cleveland, 1951.

Updike, John, *Rabbit Redux*, Knopf, New York, 1971.

Watson, Lyall, *Lifetide*, Simon & Schuster, New York, 1979.

Watts, Alan, *Behold the Spirit*, Pantheon, New York, 1971.

Whitman, Walt, *Leaves of Grass*, Norton, New York, 1973.

About the Author

Photo by Gilda Adler.

Jan Phillips' quest has led her into and out of a religious community, across the country on a Honda motorcycle, and around the world on a one-woman peace pilgrimage. After a trip to Nigeria, she founded the Livingkindness Foundation, cocreated the Livingkindness Centre for Learning in Ikuzeh, Nigeria, and supports creative projects addressing the problem of structural racism in the United States.

An artist in many arenas, Jan has three CDs of original music, a YouTube channel, a monthly Museletter, podcast, and videos that connect the dots among evolutionary creativity, spiritual intelligence, and social action. She facilitates workshops throughout the U.S. and Canada using her music, videos, and poetry to keep the heart and brain connected.

She has been a writer and photographer since the mid-1970s and her work has been published in the *New York Times, People, Christian Science Monitor, Ms. Magazine, Parade Magazine, Utne Reader, Sun Magazine,* and *National Catholic Reporter.*

Jan is the author of 10 books including *No Ordinary Time, Marry Your Muse, Divining the Body, There Are Burning Bushes Everywhere, Born Gay,* and *Finding the On-Ramp to Your Spiritual Path.*

Read more at *janphillips.com.*